# MORE PRAISE FOR *ON BICYCLES*

"I proclaim *On Bicycles* the *Whole Earth Catalog* of bicycle culture for the current era. I'm not usually one to preach that bicycles are the solution for all the world's problems, but the more people use bikes, it seems, the more problems do start to melt away. As a lifelong member of the bike industry, I was delighted and awed to discover this amazing collection of articulate and knowledgeable writers who are also bike lovers. Amy Walker has done a stellar job in putting this grand vision into a holistic reference of bicycle knowledge. She weaves together the style and substance of the many writers, whose subjects range from fundamental motivations to bike-shop collectives to public policy and of course the nuts and bolts — the what, where, and how of finding the right hardware and knowledge to bike smart and ride safely. I highly recommend this read to anyone who knows the thrill of pedal-powered motion."

— Stephen Bilenky, Bilenky Cycle Works, Philadelphia, PA

# On Bicycles

# On Bicycles

## 50 WAYS THE NEW BIKE CULTURE CAN CHANGE YOUR LIFE

*edited by*
*Amy Walker*

New World Library
Novato, California

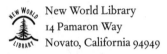

New World Library
14 Pamaron Way
Novato, California 94949

Text design by Tracy Cunningham
Illustrations by Matthew Fleming

Photo credits: Amy Walker, pages 12, 69, 299, and 332; Jason Gardner, page 16; Aaron's Bicycle Repair, page 100; Bilenky Cycle Works, page 116; Dave Bryson Photography, page 152; Missouri Bicycle & Pedestrian Federation / mobikefed.org, page 178.

Library of Congress Cataloging-in-Publication Data
On bicycles : 50 ways the new bike culture can change your life / edited by Amy Walker.
        p.    cm.
Includes bibliographical references and index.
ISBN 978-1-60868-022-1 (pbk. : alk. paper)
1. Cycling.  I. Walker, Amy.
GV1041.O6 2011
796.6—dc23                                                          2011025485

First printing, September 2011
ISBN 978-1-60868-022-1
Printed in Canada on 100% postconsumer-waste recycled paper

New World Library is a proud member of the Green Press Initiative.

10 9 8 7 6 5 4 3 2 1

*This book is dedicated to the memory of Terry Lowe,*
*my collaborator and friend who delightfully shared the joy of cycling*
*and worked steadfastly with many of us to realize*
*the vision of bike friendliness.*

# Contents

# PART THREE: COMMUNITY AND CULTURE

# Acknowledgments

***My heartfelt*** love and appreciation go out to all those who contributed to this book. First, to all the folks at New World Library and especially to senior editor Jason Gardner, who had the original vision for this book and who trusted me to bring the parts together. I am grateful to all my colleagues at *Momentum* magazine with whom I have been blessed to explore and influence the transportation-biking renaissance. Thanks also to my friends Heather Tennenhouse, for her friendship and encouragement; Amanda Bell, who helped me stay calm and get organized; and Leonard Paul, who is a great listener and role model. My deep respect goes to Tania Lo and Mia Kohout, who keep *Momentum* rolling with grace and style. Power to all the cycling advocates and activists who devote their energy to building better cycling policy and infrastructure. And to all of you who simply ride your bikes — you are my inspiration!

I also thank my dad, Tom Walker, who has the best answers and a twinkle in his eye, and my amazing mom, Kate Walker — if I end up anything like her, I will have succeeded in life.

## Chapter One

# Bicycling Is Contagious

**Amy Walker**

*Warning!* Cycling can be addictive. Before you grab onto those handlebars, before you throw a leg over the saddle and start pumping away at those pedals, be aware: once you start, you may never want to stop. And like anything that looks good, feels good, and does good, you'll want to share it. Thankfully, bicycling is easy and sociable. It feels natural to ride at a moderate pace and maintain a conversation, or just fly in a flock, drifting playfully among your companions. The act of balancing combined with gentle physical rhythm activates brain waves and creativity. The bicycle's effect has even provided a key to understanding the universe: Albert Einstein said of his theory of relativity, "I thought of that while riding my bicycle." This collection of short essays about biking may not bring you revelations of that magnitude, but it was created to inspire you, whether you are new to cycling or an expert.

Without bicycles, my life would have taken a completely different path. I have always been interested in problem solving and making sense out of the world, and when I first started commuting by bike over twenty years ago (I was 16 and riding forty-five minutes each way to my high school), a major puzzle piece of my life fell into place. Cycling clicked. It simultaneously gave me fast, accessible transportation, exercise, and a clear environmental conscience. I knew that if it worked well for me, it could work well for others, too. I noticed there was a movement growing around transportation cycling, and even though I was a bit shy, I wanted to get involved. Finally, in 2000 I met my cycling mentor, Carmen Mills (author of chapter 10, "Notes from a Bicycle Buddha"), who inspired me with her vision, humor, and collaborative spirit. Together, in 2001, we cofounded *Momentum* magazine.

Sharing what I love is a great way to learn — and I have learned so much and met so many amazing people through *Momentum*. Most of the contributors in this book were people I met through the magazine, and it has been a great honor to work with them to share our passion for cycling with you. This book does not cover all aspects of cycling. It merely scratches the surface of a rich and fascinating topic. In truth, most of what cycling can offer you cannot be described in words — it must be experienced. But that doesn't stop us from trying! I hope this book will be a starting point for many conversations and two-wheeled journeys, whether they take you to the four corners of the Earth or to the corner store.

In their everyday lives, the contributors to *On Bicycles* prove that biking is like a juicy secret: it's hard to keep it to yourself. We've decided the best way to introduce this book is by telling you a few of the different ways we've shared our passion for cycling, starting with Jeff Mapes (chapter 35, "Ciclovia," and chapter 41,

"A History of Bike Advocacy"), who reminds us that we often share without even trying: "Just striding into work on even the dankest mornings with a bounce in your step and a smile on your face is enough to persuade some people of the value of getting around town on a bike. Or to annoy the hell out of them."

Even moderately experienced cyclists have knowledge to share. We know how to relax into the ride and point our eyes where we want our bike to go. We know how to dress for the weather and which routes to avoid because of hills, potholes, or heavy car traffic. Stephen Rees (chapter 6, "The Environmental Good of Switching from Car to Bike") was a committed cyclist, but he didn't think he knew anything special until other people started treating him as though he did. So he rose to the occasion and shared bicycling stories and information on his blogs and online forums.

Perhaps the best way to share bicycling is one-on-one. When people you know want to start biking, simply accompanying them on a ride and being a sounding board for their excitement and their concerns is helpful. Things might not work out according to plan, but as Sarah Mirk (chapter 38, "Bikes Work") explains, they usually work out beautifully anyway: "I bought a $200, very heavy tandem off Craigslist.org with the hope that I could see my parents bike around on it together. They came to visit Portland on a warm June weekend, and both wound up riding around on (slightly more practical) bikes while my boyfriend and I muscled down the roads behind them on the tandem. We biked a few miles to a restaurant around sunset on Friday night. I thought the highlight of their trip would be the food or the scenery, but my mom gushed about the unexpected and familiar joy of riding a bike for the first time in a long while. She couldn't stop talking about how fun it was to pedal through the neighborhood streets, taking in the sights and the warm summer air."

Since their beginning, bicycles have inspired artists to share their visions. In 1913 Marcel Duchamp mounted a bicycle fork and wheel upside down onto a stool, spinning the wheel occasionally. "I enjoyed looking at it," he said. "Just as I enjoy looking at the flames dancing in the fireplace." Two years later, when Duchamp began making what he called readymades (arrangements of manufactured objects presented as art), he decided that *Bicycle Wheel* was the original readymade. *Bicycle Wheel* is also said to be the first kinetic sculpture. Later Duchamp said, "I'm not at all sure that the concept of the readymade isn't the most important single idea to come out of my work."[1]

Like Duchamp, many of the authors of this book have had bicycling and bicycles as their creative muse. For Ulrike Rodrigues (chapter 11, "How to Help a Bike Shop Help You," and chapter 21, "Folding Bikes"), biking has always been a solitary, freeing activity. "I've really never wanted to share that. But what I have wanted to share is my love of how the world looks from the seat of a bicycle. In 1999, I returned from a life-changing three-month journey of solo cycling the back roads of Thailand and Laos. The stories wouldn't stay inside me; I had to share them with *Momentum* readers and in my Mitey Miss blog. More than ten years later, I still have a hard time keeping them to myself."

Bicycle dance is a form of expression that reflects the young urban cyclist's sensibilities and physicality especially well. Writes Lori Kessler (chapter 45, "Designing Our Cities for Bikes"): "My sharing of bike love stepped up several notches when I joined Vancouver's B:C:Clettes, an all-women bicycle-inspired performance group! We rock streets and dance floors and create performances that celebrate bikes and inspire community engagement in DIY 'red, black, and shiny' outfits. Performing allows me to engage in the bicycle community and to spread the love to a wide range of audiences, from local farmers' markets to workshops for Brownies to rock-star street parties in Portland and Los Angeles."

Bicycle clubs are fun and the epitome of sharing. I've met a lot of friends through monthly bike club rides to visit and explore our cities together. If you don't find a club that fits what you're looking for, you can start your own. Shawn Granton (chapter 30, "Travels with a Bicycle") not only has artistic talent but also is a keen student of our environment and its history and is possessed of gentle leadership abilities. He started a roving bicycle club called the Urban Adventure League (http://urbanadventureleague.blogspot.com), with the purpose of amiably exploring civic geography — and his ride posters are outstanding!

Sometimes your mission is very straightforward. Like Bonnie Fenton (chapter 37, "Bike-Friendly Workplaces," and chapter 50, "Disappearing Car Traffic"), you may simply ascertain a need and a way to fulfill it: "Having worked on cycling advocacy in Vancouver, Canada, for several years, I'd heard lots of people say they would love to cycle but were afraid of traffic or didn't know how to get started. It was clear there was a need for education. In 2005, the stars aligned, and I wrote a funding proposal for a grant to start a commuter-cycling skills course. We gathered together a group of eight amazing instructors — who understood both cycling and teaching — and began offering classes in 2006. We trained hundreds of people to ride their bikes safely and confidently in traffic and received some incredibly gratifying feedback from our participants. The courses are still going, and getting them started is still one of my proudest achievements."

In an effort to understand others and make sense of the world, Elly Blue (chapter 31, "Women and the Benefits of Biking," and chapter 43, "Safety in Numbers") first felt compelled to share her love of bicycling after her first Critical Mass ride: "I couldn't understand the hostile way Portland police officers treated the people on bicycles. It was the first time I realized that transportation is completely intertwined with cultural assumptions. I've spent the past six years learning and writing about the concrete ways that bicycling and culture affect and change each other."

Sometimes we share because we want others to understand us. Says Dan Goldwater (chapter 36, "Bike Party"): "As Americans biking across rural Sichuan province in China, we were constantly greeted by smiles and shouts. Buses of big-city Chinese tourists would pass through this mountainous countryside every day, but a cycle tourist was hard to comprehend. Why would rich Westerners use a bike when they could afford a car or bus? Despite countless Chinese cyclists, we found ourselves often explaining the immersive joy of experiencing cities, towns, and countryside by bike."

And sometimes that initial need to be understood becomes a lifelong vocation. Todd Litman (chapter 4, "Cycling for Health, Wealth, and Freedom") recalls: "My career as a professional transportation planner and policy analyst started with my love of cycling during college, which led me to managing a bicycle shop and becoming a local bicycle activist in Olympia, Washington. Being in a capital city, I was asked to be the state legislative representative by the League of American Wheelmen [now League of American Bicyclists]. In that capacity I was often responsible for explaining why bicycling should receive the same consideration as other transport modes. I recall once, after arguing with a motorist who honked at me, creating a list of reasons why bicyclists deserve to use public roadways — that we are not freeloaders, and we provide many benefits. I produced a fact sheet that summarized these benefits. This motivated me to return to collage as a graduate student in order to better understand these issues. My master's thesis was a comprehensive analysis of the costs and benefits of different modes of transport — a generalized application of my benefits-of-bicycling fact sheet, which I've continued to update [www.vtpi.org/tca]. The rest is history."

As the bike economy grows, sharing a love of biking is becoming part of our everyday employment. As *Momentum* editor Sarah Ripplinger (chapter 24, "E-bikes Offer an Extra Push") relates: "So many amazing stories cross my desk at *Momentum* magazine that demonstrate how cycling is changing lives and making cities stronger and more people-friendly. Often, when people find out what I do, they share with me their stories about biking in their cities or ask me if I would like to go for a ride with them sometime."

And even if biking is our job, sometimes we still give a little extra, as Aaron Goss, owner of Aaron's Bicycle Repair (chapter 15, "The Case for Internally Geared Bicycle Hubs"), relates: "I feel bike love when I do something for free, whether it is tightening a kid's quick-release skewer before he boards the chairlift at Whistler or oiling a homeless person's chain. If I can keep one more person on a bike, the world is a better place!"

Sometimes it's just part of being a friend. John Greenfield (chapter 34, "Earn-a-Bike Programs") says, "Years ago I dated a very cool woman who unfortunately had to spend lots of time in her car for work and didn't get enough exercise. I tried not to be pushy about bicycling, and she took the initiative to buy a bike so we could ride together on dates. She even wound up joining me for the AIDS Ride from Minneapolis to Chicago, though I was worried she wouldn't be able to complete the 400-plus-mile journey. But she was determined, and she did great. Near Baraboo, Wisconsin, as I reached the top of a roller-coaster hill, I realized she was still less than halfway up, struggling in the afternoon heat. So I turned around, rolled back down, and cheered her to the summit. She later sent me a nice thank-you note recreating the scene with stick figures and the caption, 'You helped me reach my goal!' "

And then there are times when magic happens, as in this story from David Hay (chapter 40, "The Individuation of the Cyclist"): "My oldest daughter took to biking very well, but my youngest daughter took a lot longer. Her reticence became chronic. When she was 8 years old, I asked her to come for 'a walk.' Knowing she wouldn't go if I brought her bike, I did not mention it or bring it along. What she didn't know was that I'd stashed her bike in some bushes at the park. When we got there, I feigned surprise at seeing the bike in the bushes and speculated that it must have been stolen and ditched in the bushes. She laughed and agreed to give riding a try in response to what I characterized as an 'omen.' There was a man playing congas at the park. He was playing in short intervals and would stop and start. I convinced her to ride on her own for only as long as the drummer played. Up to that point, his bursts hadn't lasted more than a few seconds, so my daughter regarded the challenge as reasonable. She got on the bike, I push-started her, and for the first time the drummer continued playing long enough for her to cross the entire park! I ran after her, and when she and the drummer finally stopped, we fell to the grass laughing with excitement at her triumphant first ride."

Biking can hold magic moments like these for anybody who rides. We hope you will enjoy this book and that it will inspire you to ride your bike more. We believe that bikes can help make the world a better place, and we're grateful for the opportunity to share our love of biking with you!

1 Calvin Tomkins, *Duchamp: A Biography* (New York: Henry Holt and Company, 1996), 158.

**PART ONE**

*All the*
*Right Reasons*

## Chapter Two

# Because It's Fun!

Terry Lowe

*Ahead* of me is a long, swooping downhill with no stop sign at the bottom. I climbed this ridge to enjoy the view overlooking the city, with the harbor bridge below and the North Shore mountains looming nearby. This is my city — Vancouver, Canada — and, as the sticker on my bike says, I ride everywhere. And every day.

There is nothing like riding a bike. It's not all sweat, strain, and endurance, as some riders would have you believe. It's more the happy awareness of a small, lightweight machine carrying you easily through the streets, the movement of your body, the air on your face, and the world in all its shapes, colors, and flavors.

A light push of the foot sets me off. As my speed increases, I feel like I'm flying. A big, happy grin lights up my face. For adults, riding a bike is one way to recover the sense of play that little children enjoy. That's the reason we cyclists smile at each other when passing on the bike routes.

Some people guiltily reason that they "should" ride a bike because: (1) it's green, and they will therefore reduce their carbon footprint; (2) it's good for them, and they will thus improve their overall health and fitness; and (3) by doing so, they will enjoy the substantial financial savings associated with not owning a car. Those things are all true, of course, but to me they're side effects. The best reason to ride a bike around town is that it's fun.

I zoom down the hill. This pavement's in good shape, so potholes won't be a problem. No cars in sight. Let's roll and generate some adrenaline!

Now I'm going too fast. If I exceed 32 mph, little windstorms erupt behind my glasses and cause my eyes to tear up. I can't see very well, so it's time to stop and catch my breath. The endorphin glow will linger through the long ride home.

Speeding down hills is only one way to enjoy your bike. Summer group rides, with a potluck picnic, are convivial, relaxed, and delightful. We meet somewhere central, everyone brings some food or drink, and we ride somewhere nice and share it all. Bikes can stop and park anywhere, and I know of three here with attached barbecues (the owners of these are always invited). I raid the local bakery and bring along bags of pastries, and I've never had to take any back home.

Group rides that start at midnight are a great source of discovery and surprise. Many cities have an informal group that meets at a park somewhere just before midnight and takes off for a ride around town. The city looks different late at night, silent and glowing, and the absence of car traffic means you have it much more to yourselves. Your band of merry cyclists owns the streets it rides on. Someone will surely show you a hidden corner of the city that you've never seen before.

Bikes are inherently sociable for those who are not in a hurry. Rare is the day when I do not unexpectedly meet someone I know and stop for a friendly chat. We catch up on news, vow to keep in touch better in the future, and ride away. Even cyclists you don't know will nod and say hi; if you ask, they'll stop and offer advice on the best route to ride. We're friendly, and we often carry maps.

Inclement weather is (usually) not a big problem. Like most cycling accessories, raingear is cheap, and much of it can be improvised. It doesn't take much to stay dry, and pedaling keeps you warm automatically. Downpours are short and can be waited out, and gentle rain on a quiet evening street is lovely, reflecting the lights in millions of raindrops.

## On Bicycles

In winter, a set of studded tires provokes a sense of ridiculous exhilaration at being able to do something that should be impossible: riding on sheer ice. Bike hockey, anyone? Snowflakes bouncing off my nose are amusing, too.

My bike feels like an extension of my body. It's cheap and easy to fix and gives me independence. I know its idiosyncrasies, how well it rewards my efforts, and how far and fast it will take me. I know the secret, quiet routes through my city and the areas to avoid. I know the slow, easy back routes up the hills and the fast, heart-pounding routes back down. I know the streets of my own neighborhood block by block and pothole by puddle. And I know how long it will take me to ride somewhere and back, once weather and wind have been considered. I can go anywhere, anytime on my bike.

Some days are better than others, of course, and some are close to perfection. On a warm autumn afternoon, I'm heading downtown with a pannier full of newsletters to deliver. The sky is bright blue, and most of the leaves on the trees are still green, while others are turning a fiery yellow-orange. I spot a bald eagle perched on a church steeple. I stop briefly to return a ball to some kids who've kicked it over their schoolyard fence. They yell happily and wave at me as I leave.

Much to my surprise, the downtown traffic is accommodating today. Every time I need a gap between cars to change lanes, one opens up for me. A clear lane for a short block to make a turn? Done. Somewhere to lock up right in front of every building I need to go into? Right here. Women on their way back to the office smile at me and mimic my right-turn signal as they wait for me to turn. I smile back and race off.

Days like this are treasured, and they happen often enough to remind me why I love riding my bike around town: it's just so much fun!

A talented writer, editor, and visual artist, **TERRY LOWE** was a creative and supportive influence to his many friends and colleagues. Terry was also an editor of *Momentum* magazine and an enthusiastic supporter of cycling. He passed away in January 2011, and his smiling face will be missed on Vancouver's rainy bikeways.

*Chapter Three*

---

# Cycling Is Faster
## Lars Goeller

*When* I claim that cycling is faster, the first thing you'll ask is, faster than what? Well, everything else, I'll say, and mostly cars.... Then you'll expect me to toss out that old tortoise-and-hare routine and say that slow and steady wins the race. Yes, compared with cars, bicycles are both slow and steady. (Steady because cyclists are notorious for ignoring stop signs.) Unfortunately that particular moral is a load of bull. People never describe Usain Bolt as "slow and steady," and he wins lots of races. The real moral of that fable is "Don't be cocky, and don't take things for granted." Heeding this moral will help you get where you're going faster than if you were driving a car.

If you're traveling less than six miles (ten kilometers), there's a good chance that riding a bike will be faster than driving a car or even taking the bus. This isn't because you're a fast cyclist; it's because God invented traffic signs. They do several things that favor the cyclist: they limit the speeds that cars travel, the directions they can travel, and where they can park. They also often provide free parking for cyclists right outside their destination. So if you're traveling a shorter distance, take your bike and get there faster.

In major urban centers, motorists can get held up for hours in traffic jams with little to do but try and out-idle the person next to them. But what happens when you drop a big rock into a river? A river of cyclists doesn't smash against the rock; it goes around. Really, it's best to avoid driving a car regardless of the circumstances surrounding you, whether it's the traffic or climate change. Besides, being fast on a bike doesn't have to mean risking your life dodging between lanes of traffic. More and more cities in North America are creating congestion-free bike lanes that make riding a bike faster and safer than driving a car. Of course, if you live in a rural area where there's no traffic and no traffic jams...well this is why people in those areas drive large pickup trucks, and people who live in New York City don't.

Parking is one of the great time wasters of driving. Not only do you have to find a parking spot, but then you have to walk from your parking spot to your final destination and back again. Great if you're on a date, but then if you're on a date, speed isn't really important, and we all know that arriving too fast can be a big problem. Bicycles face very few parking restrictions, so unless you've locked your bike to a fire hydrant, no one is going to care what you've done with it. I rarely have to lock my bike more than a thirty-second walk from my  destination. So before you decide to drive, ask yourself how far from your destination you're going to have to park.

Be careful not to let those club riders in their team colors make you think you've got to wrap yourself in Spandex and train to be fast on a bike. You're faster when you just wear your regular clothes and take it easy on the hills. You'll save time on your commute by not changing clothes and taking a shower when you don't get carried away and turn yourself into a sweaty, stinky mess; that will shave fifteen minutes off your trip. But if the Tour de France is on TV and you get a little carried away in the peloton on the way to work, it never hurts to have a change of clothes tucked away. Some people keep a week's worth of clothes at their workplace and bring them home and wash them on the weekend. That way they can have their shower and their clean clothes at work and still commute without bulky luggage.

Some bikes are obviously faster than others: nobody competes in the Tour de France on a mountain bike. Even the average rider needs the right tool for the job. If the job is efficient urban transportation, you need relatively narrow, well-inflated tires with minimal tread that roll quickly on the roadway. You also need to maintain your bike properly, because breakdowns are slowdowns. Finally, your bike shouldn't be too flashy. Bicycle theft is a reality in most cities, and having to walk home will really slow you down.

Still a doubting Thomas? Check out Streetfilms.org for their excellent feature on the Great New York City Commuter Race of 2007. In a race from Fort Greene in Brooklyn to Union Square in Manhattan (4.3 miles, or 7 kilometers), the cyclist easily beat the driver and the public-transit rider. She won by six minutes in street clothes and didn't even break a sweat. When you look closely at where you're going and what you're doing, the fastest way is often on two wheels.

Age and experience have changed **LARS GOELLER** from a car-dodging Torontonian to a mellow Vancouverite who's happiest when he's just riding along.

# Chapter Four

# Cycling for Health, Wealth, and Freedom

## Todd Litman

*For* honesty's sake, car advertisements should show motorists who look overweight, impoverished, and stressed, since that is the real outcome of a lifestyle dependent on the automobile. A lifestyle that includes plenty of cycling can make you truly healthy, wealthy, and free.

If irony could kill, driving to a health club to exercise on a treadmill or stationary bike would be deadly. Yet many people see this as normal: exercise is considered a commodity they must purchase with time, money, and effort. This approach is also a prescription for failure. Health clubs sell about five times the number of memberships their facilities can actually accommodate because they know most people quickly drop out.

A much better approach is to integrate exercise into your daily transportation routine by walking and cycling. Even if such trips are slower than driving, they provide savings overall by eliminating the need to devote time and money to exercise at a health club.

With a little planning, many trips, even long ones, can be made efficiently by a combination of walking, cycling, and public transport. Social, recreational, and shopping trips, errands, and journeys to school — trips that account for a major portion of personal travel in the United States — are particularly well suited to nonmotorized travel. Automobile transportation is costly. In the United States, owning and operating even a basic car costs $3,000–$5,000 annually in depreciation, fuel costs, insurance, registration, maintenance and repairs, and parking expenses. For many middle- and lower-income households, owning and operating a car for each adult can impose significant financial burdens that prevent people from fulfilling their aspirations. For example, data from the U.S. Bureau of Labor Statistics' 2008 Consumer Expenditure Survey for the lowest income quintile (households with the lowest 20 percent of incomes) show that costs associated with a motor vehicle accounted for 30 percent of total household income: the average household income was $10,608, and households spent an average of $3,310 on each vehicle they owned, as illustrated in table 1.

Automobile ownership is a trap. Cars are expensive to own but seem cheap to drive because most user costs are fixed (that is, they are not directly affected by how much a vehicle is used: these include vehicle financing, insurance, and registration fees) or external (that is, they are not charged directly to users: they include subsidized parking, and congestion and accident costs imposed on other road users). These are market distortions that encourage motorists to maximize their driving in order to get their money's worth from their purchase, resulting in economically excessive motor vehicle travel.

| Income quintile | Percentage of household income spent on transportation |
|:---:|:---:|
| 1 (lowest) | 30.26 |
| 2 | 13.00 |
| 3 | 8.03 |
| 4 | 5.73 |
| 5 (highest) | 3.38 |

**TABLE 1.** Vehicle costs relative to household income. Calculated from U.S. Bureau of Labor Statistics, Consumer Expenditure Survey, 2008, www.bls.gov /cex/#tables.

In an economy in which driving seems cheap because costs are externalized, other things are made more expensive, including housing, health, and environmental quality. For example, a major portion of roadway and parking-facility costs are financed through local property and sales taxes and incorporated into building development costs. This practice increases the costs of housing and retail goods. Artificially low fuel prices increase the economic and environmental costs of producing, importing, and burning fossil fuels.

Driving may seem to provide freedom, but it is an illusory freedom, like that of a child rebelling against household rules. True freedom is not simply selfish indulgence: it often involves complicated trade-offs. Automobile travel increases freedom in some ways but reduces it in others. It imposes hidden costs on drivers: because driving is expensive, motorists must work more hours or spend less on other goods, at a cost of time and fiscal freedom. (See table 2 on page 28.) And because automobile-oriented land-use development increases sprawl, the faster speeds and directness of automobile travel are often offset by increased travel distances and congestion.

Driving also imposes costs on others. People who do not drive face degraded walking and cycling conditions, reduced public transportation and taxi services, and the same challenges and costs of sprawling development. Fear of injury from crashes reduces people's walking and cycling mobility (particularly among children, the less affluent, older people, and people with disabilities). When crashes do happen, injuries and deaths cause severe losses of freedom as well as economic costs.

Automobile travel depends on public resources and subsidies and imposes nonmarket externalities, such as environmental degradation. It deprives people of freedoms. For example, consumers are often forced to pay for roads and parking facilities regardless of how much they use them: they lack the freedom to say no to such costs or to choose alternative investments and travel options. Similarly, the freedom to drive a noisy motorcycle conflicts with residents' freedom to enjoy quiet.

The recipe for health, wealth, and freedom is to lead a multimodal lifestyle, using each transportation mode for what it does best: walking and cycling for local trips, public transit when appropriate, and automobile transport when necessary. This approach can save thousands of dollars annually. For some people, this means more money to spend on things like education, housing, and entertainment. For others, it means the freedom to work less and devote more time to travel, family, or personal interests.

## On Bicycles

Cycling is much more affordable than owning a motor vehicle. A reliable bicycle and accessories cost less than a thousand dollars new, and even less if they are purchased used. Assuming the bike has a ten-year life span (a conservative estimate), costs average out to about $250 annually for depreciation and maintenance. Of course, cycling does require fuel, in the form of food, but most of us consume too much already and benefit from burning off excess calories, so this consumption generally does not represent an additional cost.

| Internal fixed | Internal variable | External |
|---|---|---|
| Depreciation | Fuel | Congestion imposed on other road users |
| Most maintenance | Some maintenance and repairs | Accident risk imposed on other road users |
| Insurance | Road tolls | About half of roadway costs |
| Registration fees | Short-term parking charges | Subsidized parking |
| Residential parking | | Air pollution |
| | | Fuel externalities and subsidies |

**TABLE 2.** Internal and external costs of motor vehicle ownership

Multimodal transportation can vastly expand the distance you can travel comfortably with a bike. An average cyclist rides about ten miles (sixteen kilometers) an hour. This speed provides access to about thirty square miles of territory within twenty minutes of riding time, the area of a typical small city. In large cities, a traveler can often reach urban destinations as fast as a motorist by combining cycling and travel on public transit.

If you can't imagine doing without a car entirely, rental cars and car-sharing programs (now available in many cities) offer a solution. These options not only free you from the costs of owning a car but also give you access to a wider range of vehicles: you can choose a truck for moving, a van for carrying friends, and a snazzy sports car for a Saturday-night date.

Multimodal travel requires a combination of personal preparation and community planning. Here are some steps you can take toward this lifestyle:

- Walk as much as possible in your neighborhood and get to know your neighbors.
- Keep appropriate clothing — shoes, hat, raingear, and an umbrella — ready at your front door.
- Have a bicycle ready for errands, equipped with rack, panniers, lights, and lock.
- Avoid owning an automobile.
- Use car sharing or share a vehicle among several drivers. Rent a vehicle when necessary.
- Promote walking, cycling, and public-transit improvements in your community.

→ Promote smart-growth land-use policies, including more compact and mixed development, more connected and multimodal roadway design, and more efficient parking management.

→ If you can, choose to live in a walkable and bikeable community, with sidewalks and bike lanes, traffic calming and speed controls, and numerous services (shops, schools, and parks) within your neighborhood.

→ If possible, choose to live near high-quality public transit, with efficient bus or train service.

**TODD LITMAN** is founder and executive director of the Victoria Transport Policy Institute, an independent research organization dedicated to developing innovative solutions to transport problems. His work helps expand the range of impacts and options considered in transportation decision making, improve evaluation methods, and make specialized technical concepts accessible to a larger audience. His research is used worldwide in transport planning and policy analysis.

## RESOURCES

Center for Neighborhood Technology, *Housing and Transportation Affordability Index* (Chicago: Center for Neighborhood Technology, 2008), http://htaindex.cnt.org.

Todd Litman, *Evaluating Non-motorized Transport Benefits and Costs* (Victoria, BC: Victoria Transport Policy Institute, 2011), www.vtpi.org/nmt-tdm.pdf.

National Center for Bicycling and Walking, *Increasing Physical Activity through Community Design: A Guide for Public Health Practitioners* (Washington, DC: National Center for Bicycling and Walking, 2010), www.bikewalk.org/pdfs/2010/IPA_full.pdf.

*Chapter Five*

# Youth, Sex, and Cake
*The Physical Gifts of a Bicycling Lifestyle*

## Kristen Steele

*I know* of something that can turn back the clock on aging, make you more attractive, let you eat chocolate cake without gaining weight, make your penis look bigger, and give you more orgasms. And I'm not hawking the next miracle pill.

While millions of well-intentioned folks are popping pills and pharmaceutical executives are getting rich, there is a much simpler, cheaper, and less risky remedy waiting in your garage. It's called a bicycle.

Saying cycling is good for you is like saying the sky is blue: it's fairly obvious that riding a bike is healthy exercise. However, many would-be cyclists are letting their bikes collect dust because cycling seems dangerous. Of course cycling has risks (though far fewer than many prescription remedies). Unlike those pharmaceutical commercials that list all the "possible side effects" in triple speed at the end, I'll deal with those first.

Cyclists risk injury or death if involved in a serious accident.

But risks while cycling are actually relatively low. For example, cycling results in 0.005 injuries per hour, compared with 0.06 injuries per hour for playing soccer or 0.19 injuries per hour for football. Urban cyclists also risk effects from increased exposure to smog.[1] But a 2010 study by the Dutch researcher Jeroen Johan de Hartog and his colleagues quantified the risks and benefits of cycling, measuring them in life years lost and gained, and concluded that the gains are about nine times greater than the losses.[2]

As it turns out, a lifestyle devoid of physical activity is the most dangerous. Too little activity paired with too many calories is a recipe for disaster. In 2010, obesity became the single greatest cause of preventable death in the United States.[3] Obesity is a leading cause of various diseases, particularly heart disease, type 2 diabetes, sleep apnea, certain types of cancer, and osteoarthritis. A 2003 study found that on average, adults who were obese at age 40 lived six to seven years less than their normal-weight counterparts.[4] A 2010 report by the Alliance for Biking and Walking found that states with the highest levels of cycling and walking had the lowest levels of obesity, diabetes, and high blood pressure.[5]

# I DON'T EXERCISE, I BIKE

My friend Dave once explained to me that he commuted by bike so he didn't have to exercise. One of the greatest things about bicycling is that it doesn't (have to) feel like exercise, but it still brings the benefits. I rarely bike just for the sake of biking, but I do ride to go to the grocery store, meet up with friends, and attend events.

An investigation by four Australian researchers recommends

that exercise be "moderate, *habitual*, and not seasonal." According to the researchers, the activities that best meet these requirements are cycling, walking, and gardening. These activities trump other sports and "packaged" forms of exercise, such as aerobics classes, because the latter often involve greater risks and exclude large segments of the population (such as the elderly or unfit), and people are more likely to quit.[6]

Utilitarian bicycling requires almost no willpower once the habit is formed. The exercise is merely a positive by-product of going somewhere. Because bicycling is often a lifestyle choice, someone who bikes regularly is less likely to quit than someone who plays volleyball or basketball for exercise.

## CYCLISTS CAN EAT!

When I got my start in bicycle advocacy, organizing a multi-day cycling event, I met Charles Fox, event director and bicyclist extraordinaire. He gave me an important tip for planning bicycle events. "Most people bike so they can eat," he said. So Charles made sure his events had food: shrimp and grits, chocolate obsession gardens, and pimento cheese were his trademarks. He was right. The aging boomers who dominated his rides could burn thousands of calories on a hundred-mile ride, and they rewarded themselves by indulging in food that would otherwise go straight to their butts.

Cycling burns more calories per hour than most other activities. Even while biking to and from work at under ten miles per hour, a 180-pound man burns about 327 calories in two casual thirty-minute rides.[7] That more than covers the croissant and latte he splurged on at the café.[8] Although the number of calories burned varies with the duration and intensity of exercise and the weight of the individual, it's clear that cycling is an easy way to cancel out some indulgent treats.

## BEATING THE WINTER BLUES

Cycling is also a great way to beat the winter blues (or any blues, for that matter). Seasonal affective disorder (SAD), the mood disorder responsible for much wintertime depression, affects between 10 and 25 million Americans.[9] Exercise is widely recognized as an effective treatment for SAD: it releases endorphins that dull pain and give us a sense of well-being. Repetitive movements, such as turning the pedals, also increases levels of serotonin, another good-mood inducer. Cycling trumps many other forms of exercise for beating winter depression because it also gets us outside in the sun. Lack of sunlight is theorized to be the major contributor to SAD, and light therapy is an effective treatment. But why undergo an expensive medical therapy if hopping on a bike will fight your blues?

## BETTER IN BED

So cycling makes you trimmer and happier, sure, but better in bed? A number of factors make cyclists sexier, more sexual, and better performers. For starters, cycling can make you more attractive. Getting somewhere with pedal power brings a sense of accomplishment. Whether you're biking cross-country or out to dinner, getting there on two wheels can boost confidence. And enhanced self-esteem makes people feel sexier — and look that way, too. Cycling also happens to be an excellent way to tone the legs and rear end, the two sexiest parts of a man (according to a *Men's Health* survey).[10] And for people who believe that size does matter, cycling can also help make a man's penis appear larger. As men age and deposit fat in the belly, the area around the base of the penis also thickens and gradually swallows a portion of the penis — roughly a quarter inch for every nine pounds gained. Because cycling helps prevent fat build-up, it keeps the penis looking as large as possible.[11]

Cycling can also boost sex drive. According to researchers at the University of California, San Diego, men who got regular exercise reported a 30 percent increase in frequency of sex with their partners and experienced 30 percent more orgasms.[12] A University of Texas at Austin study found similar benefits for women. Researchers measured sexual arousal in thirty-six women ages 18–45 on two occasions, using a device that measures blood flow in genital tissue. Before the first measurement, they cycled vigorously for twenty minutes. The second time, they did not exercise beforehand. The study found that vaginal responses were 69 percent higher after cycling than after inactivity.[13]

You might have heard that spending too much time on a bike can damage the genitals. It is true that bike seats should be chosen and positioned with care. Many bike seats are not wide enough to support the sit bones properly, and this causes riders to sit on the perineum, applying too much pressure to our most delicate organs. Luckily, researchers and manufacturers have teamed up to make ergonomic seats, such as those with dual platforms or cutouts, that eliminate damaging and painful pressure on the perineum, prostate, tailbone, and genitalia.

With a proper bike seat, cycling can actually help keep the parts greased and working smoothly. A Harvard School of Public Health study found that inactive men were about 30 percent more likely to have erectile problems than men who ran for an average of twenty-five minutes daily. The same study concluded that erectile dysfunction is more common as men gain weight.[14] The magic moments can't happen without good blood flow to the sex organs. Cycling stimulates the cardiovascular system, improving blood flow throughout the body (including the genitals).[15] And with all that cardiovascular conditioning, cyclists don't tire as quickly in the sack, or elsewhere.

## FOUNTAIN OF YOUTH

People with active lifestyles don't just appear to age more slowly: they actually do. Recent research shows that people who exercise regularly have cells that look much younger under a microscope. The study measured the length of telomeres, the portions of DNA at each end of the chromosomes, and found that athletes who ran regularly had longer telomeres than healthy adults who did not exercise regularly. Salynn Boyles of WebMD explains: "Just as the plastic tips on the ends of shoelaces keep the laces from fraying, telomeres protect the chromosomes that carry genes during cell division. When telomeres get too short, cells can no longer divide, and they die."[16] Research suggests that telomeres affect health and aging. If they get shorter than a critical length, it is believed, people become more susceptible to maladies such as cancer, diabetes, and heart disease.[17]

## CYCLING REPLACES PHARMACEUTICALS FOR WEIGHT LOSS, DEPRESSION, AND MORE

While a bicycling lifestyle promises to remedy many ailments and contribute to a happy life, just how much cycling can change your life is still a secret from many. Those hawking miracle pills would just as soon keep it that way. But imagine how different streets would look if the advertising budgets of bike companies rivaled those of pharmaceutical companies. I can picture the millions canning their Prozac, Viagra, and weight-loss pills and greasing up the old bikes.

**KRISTEN STEELE** works for the Alliance for Biking and Walking and is a freelance writer, collage artist, and gardener living in Northern California with her husband and two children.

1 Jonathan Leake, "Toxic Cities Mock 'Healthy' Cycle Riding," *Sunday Times* (London), May 30, 2010, www.timesonline.co.uk/tol/news/environment /article7140213.ece.

2 Jeroen Johan de Hartog, Hanna Boogaard, Hans Nijland, and Gerard Hoek, "Do the Health Benefits of Cycling Outweigh the Risks?" *Environmental Health Perspectives* 118, no. 8 (August 2010), http://ehp03.niehs.nih.gov/article/info: doi/10.1289/ehp.0901747.

3  Haomiao Jia and Erica I. Lubetkin, "Trends in Quality-Adjusted Life-Years Lost Contributed by Smoking and Obesity," *American Journal of Preventive Medicine* 38, no. 2 (February 2010): 138–44.

4  A. Peeters, J. J. Barendregt, F. Willekens, J. P. Mackenbach, A. A. L. Mamun, and L. Bonneux, "Obesity in Adulthood and Its Consequences for Life Expectancy: A Life-Table Analysis," *Annals of Internal Medicine* 138, no. 1 (January 2003): 24–32.

5  Kristen Steele, *Bicycling and Walking in the U.S.: 2010 Benchmarking Report* (Washington, DC: Alliance for Biking and Walking, January 2010).

6  Ian Roberts, Harry Owen, Peter Lumb, and Colin MacDougall, *Pedalling Health: Health Benefits of a Modal Transport Shift*, 1996, http://safety.fhwa.dot .gov/ped_bike/docs/cyhealth.pdf.

7  NutriStrategy, "Calories Burned Bike Riding or Cycling," www.nutristrategy .com/fitness/cycling.htm, accessed November 2010.

8  Calorie Count, "Calories in Croissant," http://caloriecount.about.com/calories -croissant-i73416, accessed May 2011; Calorie Count, "Calories in Latte Small," http://caloriecount.about.com/calories-dunkin-donuts-latte-small-i1 40873, accessed May 2011.

9  Marian Brown, "Walk Away the Blues: Seasonal Affective Disorder Helped by Walking," *Holistic Health News*, www.hhnews.com/sad.htm, accessed May 2011.

10  Timothy McSweeney, "Cyclists Make Better Lovers, Says *Bicycling* Magazine," July 21, 1999, www.mcsweeneys.net/links/press99/cyclists.html.

11  Joe Kita, "Why Cyclists Make Better Lovers," *Mountain Bike South Africa*, www.mtbsa.co.za/Health/lovers.htm, accessed November 2010.

12  J. R. White, D. A. Case, D. McWhirter, and A. M. Mattison, "Enhanced Sexual Behavior in Exercising Men," *Archives of Sexual Behavior* 19, no. 3 (June 1990), www.springerlink.com/content/j83234218p25kl72/.

13  Cindy M. Meston, "Sympathetic Nervous System Activity and Female Sexual Arousal," *American Journal of Cardiology* 86, no. 2A (July 2000).

14 C.G. Bacon, M.A. Mittleman, M. Ichiro Kawachi, E. Giovannucci, D.B. Glasser, and E.B. Rimm, "Sexual Function in Men Older Than 50 Years of Age: Results from the Health Professionals Follow-Up Study," *Annals of Internal Medicine* 139, no. 3 (August 2003): 161–68.

15 American Council on Exercise, "Studies Show Exercise Can Improve Your Sex Life," www.acefitness.org/fitfacts/fitfacts_display.aspx?itemid=159, accessed November 2010.

16 Salynn Boyles, "Molecular Proof: Exercise Keeps You Young," *WebMD Health News*, December 1, 2009, www.webmd.com/fitness-exercise/news/20091201/molecular-proof-exercise-keeps-you-young.

17 Lynn F. Cherkas, Janice L. Hunkin, Bernet S. Kato, J. Brent Richards, Jeffrey P. Gardner, Gabriela L. Surdulescu, Masayuki Kimura, Xiaobin Lu, Tim D. Spector, and Abraham Aviv, "The Association between Physical Activity in Leisure Time and Leukocyte Telomere Length," *Archives of Internal Medicine* 168, no. 2 (January 2008): 154–58.

## Chapter Six

# The Environmental Good of Switching from Car to Bike

Stephen Rees

*Reducing* the impact of the automobile on the environment was important even before we realized, in the late twentieth century, how much the oil we burned in our cars was contributing to climate change. There were already programs and regulations to cut the tailpipe emissions of pollutants like carbon monoxide, nitrous oxides, and airborne particulates, which created the unhealthy air of most North American cities. New technologies improved the way gasoline was burned, but instead of becoming more fuel efficient, cars became heavier and more powerful. Because the U.S. Corporate Average Fuel Efficiency standards were much less stringent for light trucks than for cars, automobile makers promoted the sales of heavier vehicles.

Motor vehicle emissions account for 31 percent of total carbon dioxide, 81 percent of carbon monoxide, and 49 percent of nitrogen oxides released in the United States. Car emissions also contribute to smog, acid rain, and ozone depletion. Now the challenge is to cut greenhouse gases, and there is more competition to build efficient cars and look for alternative ways to power them. Unfortunately, these efforts will hardly dent the production of greenhouse gases. Many of the other problems we face as a result of car dependency will persist and probably get worse. Fortunately, there are other choices we can make about where we live and work and how we get between these places. The use of a bicycle instead of a car (or light truck) creates immediate benefits — for ourselves and the environment.

## THE ENVIRONMENTAL COSTS OF CARS

What's so bad about cars? According to the U.S. Environmental Protection Agency, "Driving a private car is probably a typical citizen's most 'polluting' daily activity."[1] The environmental impact of a car in use is only part of the problem. Making cars consumes huge amounts of resources and produces large quantities of waste and pollutants. So does scrapping the car at the end of its life. The following list is based on European data; North American figures are probably greater, as vehicles tend to be larger.

### Life-Cycle Pollution from a Single Car

→ Extracting raw materials: 26.5 metric tons of waste, 922 million cubic meters of polluted air

→ Transporting raw materzals: 12 liters of crude oil in ocean, 425 million cubic meters of polluted air

→ Producing the car: 1.5 metric tons of solid waste, 74 million cubic meters of polluted air

→ Driving the car: 18.4 kg of abrasive waste, 1,016 million cubic meters of polluted air

→ Disposing of the car: 102 million cubic meters of polluted air

These figures are for a medium-sized car with a three-way catalytic converter, driven 130,000 km (about 80,000 miles) over ten years, and averaging 100 kilometers per 10 liters of unleaded fuel (approximately 23.5 miles per gallon).[2]

# CAR DEPENDENCE PROMOTES URBAN SPRAWL

People who get around under their own power use much less space than those who drive. Most cars on the road are single-occupancy vehicles (SOVs), which represent a very inefficient use of fuel, materials, and space. One lane of urban road can, theoretically, move about 750 vehicles per hour; in reality, turning and parking movements cut that by a quarter. The same lane can easily move ten times that number of people (and it's people that should be counted, not vehicles) if the space is devoted to either public transit or human power. And the space used to park one car in a paved lot could accommodate ten to fifteen bicycles.

The saving of land now used by roads and parking lots will be very important in the future. As the world's population grows and oil becomes scarce, we will need more land close to where people live just to grow food. And that is actually the least of the benefits we will achieve by "depaving." If people drive everywhere, they need much more space — or rather, their cars do. The environmental benefits of compact urban areas include the ability to protect land needed for food cultivation as well as green space for recreation and biodiversity.

## THE DANGERS OF PAVING THE PLANET

Paved areas (roads and parking lots) create all kinds of local environmental problems. The most obvious is the polluted water that drains from these surfaces in wet weather. Oil, grease, antifreeze, and heavy metals combine to make a toxic soup that drips from the underside of cars. Anywhere cars are parked, you can see oil on the pavement and the drips from leaky antifreeze and transmission hoses. When it rains, these substances accumulate in puddles and runoff.

In many cities, stormwater drains are designed to catch this water and direct it to treatment facilities. In heavy rains, however, the excess flows directly into nearby open water (streams, lakes, and oceans), where it harms aquatic life and contaminates our water sources. According to the Sightline Institute, polluted runoff long ago surpassed industry as the number one source of petroleum and other toxic chemicals that end up in the waters of the Pacific Northwest.[3]

## REDUCING THE ENVIRONMENTAL HARMS OF CARS

While there is a great deal of interest in producing cars that do not run on gasoline, the alternatives have their own problems. They are still cars, so they occupy no less space, and they take as many — or more — resources to build. Hybrid cars use less energy to operate but need special batteries. These batteries require rare earth elements that must be mined at considerable environmental cost. Battery production is already creating significant local pollution problems in China. Moreover, many so-called alternative fuels come from the same sources as gasoline: natural gas and propane are just different types of fossil-fuel hydrocarbons. Electric cars would require a huge investment in charging infrastructure as well as more generating capacity. Hydrogen is similarly problematic: processing it into automotive fuel requires huge amounts of electricity, and it is extremely difficult to store and transport. How electricity is produced is going to be critical — coal and nuclear power are more likely sources than renewable sources such as wind, solar, or tidal generation — but the time and resources used in any alternative-fuel strategy will only delay the inevitable need to reduce car production, use, and dependence.

## THE ENVIRONMENTAL BENEFITS OF BIKES

Many trips in cars (and trucks used instead of cars) in urban areas are quite short and could easily be made on a bicycle. According to the U.S. National Personal Transportation Survey, 25 percent of all trips are made within a mile of the home, 40 percent of all trips are within two miles of the home, and 50 percent of the working population commutes five miles or less to work.[4] Yet more than 82 percent of trips of five miles or less are made by personal motor vehicle. Short car trips (over distances that could easily be bicycled) are much more polluting than longer trips on a per-mile basis because 60 percent of the pollution resulting from auto emissions is released during the first few minutes of operation of a vehicle. Bikes, by contrast, use no fossil fuels, emit zero carbon in use, and deposit very little polluting material on the paved surfaces they travel.

Making bikes uses a lot fewer resources than building cars, and environmentally conscious bike builders are producing even more efficient bike designs. There are even bamboo bikes, like those found at www.bamboosero.com, that, in many places, would allow the use of a locally grown, renewable material as well as reducing shipping and manufacturing costs. And an old bamboo bike can be composted and returned to the soil!

Designing communities for human-powered travel has many benefits. People in compact, well-serviced neighborhoods are less likely to drive. People who live in such areas are also healthier. Denser development leaves more space for growing food locally and protects green space from future development.

The capacity of any transport system to carry people is more important than its vehicle capacity. We ought to be measuring mobility in terms of how easily people can get around, not how easily we can drive. But we also need to keep in mind that transport is not really a benefit in and of itself: it is mostly a way of achieving other objectives. By building more compact urban areas, we increase accessibility, which is much more important.

If more of us start making our daily trips by bike, foot, and public transit, we can dramatically reduce environmental harms and begin building the kinds of compact, bike-friendly communities where we can work, live, and play without killing the planet.

**STEPHEN REES** was born in England over sixty years ago, moved to Canada in 1988, and worked for Vancouver's transit authority from 1997 to 2004. They gave him a free bus pass, but he found it was quicker to ride his bike home.

1 U.S. Environmental Protection Agency, "On the Road: Resources; Protecting the Environment," www.epa.gov/epahome/trans.htm, accessed April 20, 2011.

2 *Cradle to the Grave Study*, Umwelt- und Prognose-Institut Heidelberg, 1993.

3 Lisa Stiffler, *Curbing Stormwater Pollution*, Sightline Institute report, http://www.sightline.org/research/environment/stormwater/curbing-stormwater-pollution/, accessed June 2011.

4 NPTS uses US Census data, for example, www.allcountries.org/uscensus/1033_national_personal_transportation_survey_npts_summary.html, accessed June 6, 2011.

# Chapter Seven

# Less Is More
Amy Walker

*Perhaps* you know the feeling you get when you go camping and leave your house and most of your possessions behind. You have magical moments making dinner on the seashore, washing your dishes with sand, or looking at the stars that you can never see in the city because of all the lights, and you realize that this is the way nature intended you to be.

Well, biking is a lot like that. Ask people who bike what they love about it, and at least half will say, "Freedom." Biking is so simple. It gives a big boost to our locomotion and a modest one to our capacity for cargo, without the excessive layers of metal, glass, rubber, upholstery, paperwork, and oil that come with cars.

Offered unlimited power, humans are easily seduced. We overshop, overeat, and overdrive, and then wonder how we got to be overdrawn, overweight, and overtired. We need limits: the internal limits set by our bodies and our intuition, and external limits that we create as a society. Riding a bike to get from A to B — and restricting our ability to impulsively drag stuff back to our dens — is a positive kind of limit.

Cyclists know intimately how much time and energy a trip across town will take. And we're not all athletes! We schedule trips to include multiple stops or errands rather than expending more energy by taking several separate trips. Modest consumption habits and voluntary simplicity are an inherent part of the cycling lifestyle. Bike riders carefully consider decisions to buy large objects and bring them home. If we had big trucks we could easily collect more stuff, which feels powerful and attractive, but, as we all know, it takes energy and effort to store and maintain all our stuff. Riding a bike as your main means of transport makes you more careful about what you bring into your life.

The cost of our consumption is more than monetary. Because of the greedy practice of planned obsolescence, by which manufacturers deliberately design products to be cheap to produce, to break quickly, and not to be repairable, most consumer goods have a tragically short life span. Most likely hit the landfill only a few years after they leave the factory, and their owners go shopping for replacements that will meet exactly the same fate.

Too much of our precious energy is devoted to acquiring and caring for our possessions rather than our relationships. Like overgrown children, we have spoiled ourselves by creating a world where we seem to be free to exploit nature and each other. The costs are often hidden, but they are real. It's time for us to wake up, grow up, and reorient our priorities. The good news is that by doing so, we escape the nightmares, the fears, and the worries that being part of a nation of overgrown spoiled children can provoke.

Less stuff means less stress. Fewer expenses means more money saved — or the ability to work fewer hours, reducing stress and creating more time for leisure, education, community, family, and friends. Since the 1950s, typical Americans have had more things, yet they have fewer close friends and report being less happy. Many people are studying happiness (and unhappiness) these days. One of them is Charles Montgomery, whose book *Happy City* describes how modern feelings of stress and isolation are created by the design of our cities, neighborhoods, and transportation systems.

Living simply does not mean suffering or lacking in enjoyment. Living in gratitude and taking the time to simply enjoy what we have is a gift in itself. Living lightly is elegant and beautiful. Sometimes people make things more complicated to make it seem that they are smarter or better. In fact, sometimes they are just more confused and no more satisfied.

Followers of practices such as asceticism, Jainism, and Buddhism believe that living simply clears the way for a more spiritual existence. Many of the founders and earliest practitioners of these and other religions (including Christianity) lived extremely austere lifestyles, refraining from excessive sensual pleasures and the accumulation of material wealth. This is to be understood not as an eschewal of the enjoyment of life but as a recognition that spiritual insight is impeded by indulgence.

Living simply also connects us with other people. When consumers in the privileged, industrialized world make a choice to buy less stuff and use less energy, we're offering tangible support to people in countries whose economies serve our own through labor and resource exports. By purchasing fewer goods, and refusing to buy those manufactured with sweatshop labor, we help take the pressure off people in poorer countries. Those of us with more possessions can offer some solidarity to the world's poor by giving up some of our stuff.

In our environmental education, most of us have learned the three Rs: reduce, reuse, and recycle. Notice that the first of these three Rs is *reduce*. It is popular to tout wise or conscientious purchasing decisions, but it is also essential to simply buy less stuff and reduce the cycle of production and waste.

Sometimes to spend less in the long run, it is necessary to spend more up front. Conscientious consumers invest in high-quality goods that last a long time, are repairable, and are made of sustainably and ethically sourced materials. Another beautiful thing about bikes is that they are easy to maintain and repair, and replacement parts are relatively easy to find. Keeping your bike in good shape doesn't have to cost a lot of money, and most people can learn to do their own basic repairs.

Bikes are beacons of simplicity and elegance in this overly complicated world. I think that's why they have become such a popular symbol on T-shirts and in advertisements: they express our latent desire to return to a simpler way of life.

To start you just need one simple bike that you love to ride. Get into the habit of riding it to work, to school, and on errands. Notice your new-found freedom, and how fulfilling it can be to travel lightly. Nirvana is a few pedal strokes away.

# Chapter Eight

# The Curious Cyclist

## Deb Greco

*Biking* is my favorite way to get to know a new neighborhood. I don't own a car, so driving is out as a means of exploration. I enjoy the easy pace of walking, but it's a little too slow when I'm not sure what the payoff might be. I'm not likely to trudge up a big San Francisco hill just to see what's at the top, because walking down is no more fun than walking up. But on my bike, the ride up is worth it for the downhill alone.

So I wasn't deterred by the BFH (big f — — ing hill) I had to tackle when I moved to the Richmond district of San Francisco. My new neighborhood is perched on the edge of the Presidio, a former military base turned urban park, with great views of the Golden Gate Bridge and the San Francisco Bay.

I used to ride to work downtown along the well-wheeled bike lanes of the Panhandle, the Wiggle, and Market Street. These are popular bike-commuter routes because they skirt the larger hills. I always see someone I know on this route. Once I ran into a friend I hadn't seen in a decade and rode away with his old surfboard. This could only happen in the bike lane.

My new commute through the Presidio meant sacrificing some of this camaraderie and easy pedaling, but it brought other, unan-

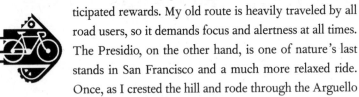

ticipated rewards. My old route is heavily traveled by all road users, so it demands focus and alertness at all times. The Presidio, on the other hand, is one of nature's last stands in San Francisco and a much more relaxed ride.

Once, as I crested the hill and rode through the Arguello Gate, breathing hard, I entered another world. Fog clung to the cypress, pine, and eucalyptus trees. Hawks and falcons spiraled overhead. The road was lined with late summer blackberries, so I stopped to gather and eat a handful. Breakfast doesn't get much better than that.

My morning ride continues past views of the Golden Gate Bridge and the bay. Then I get to enjoy one heck of a downhill, the BFH in reverse. The best part of all is that there's a speed meter on this stretch to warn cars to slow down. It has quite the opposite effect on me, and each morning I strive to break my record of thirty-four miles per hour.

Evenings are a different story. First I fight serious headwinds along Crissy Field. Once I reach the cover of the Presidio forest, it's all uphill. That marvelous morning descent becomes the slow grind up to the top of the seemingly endless hill. I drop into my granny gear and huff and puff and sweat my way to the top. When I first took up this route, joggers used to pass me. The most humiliating were the cute girls who called out, "You can do it!" I could only curse them silently, because I didn't have enough lung capacity to curse them aloud.

It soon got easier. Now the BFH is just another hill, and I keep discovering things I wasn't looking for. Recently, on a two-wheeled meander along Presidio trails I hadn't yet ridden, I discovered two outdoor sculptures, *Spire* and *Wood Line*, by the nature artist Andy Goldsworthy. If my commute gets any more interesting, I may stop showing up at work altogether.

Oddly enough, one of my favorite bike experiences in my new neighborhood was a funeral. I was on my way to the library when I was held at a light by a motorcycle cop who was waving through the last cars in a long funeral procession. In the distance I could make out the joyous sounds of a brass band. It struck me as curious, and I wanted to hear more.

On foot, I never would have been able to catch up with the band, nor would I have tried. In a car, I imagine, I would have merely been annoyed at the traffic delay. But my bike is perfectly made for following where my curiosity leads me. I turned around and outflanked the procession to take up a position at a promising corner a few blocks ahead of it. I could hear the band getting louder and louder, and then I could see them coming toward me.

A full-on brass band walked slowly down the busy street. Everyone was decked out in white, spinning and lifting their instruments or white umbrellas in time with the music. My heart lifted right along with them. My local shopping district, Clement Street, home to Asian markets and noodle houses, had transformed in a heartbeat into jazzy New Orleans.

## On Bicycles

Hundreds of my neighbors likewise stopped their Sunday errands to watch, listen, tap along, and smile. Behind the band came a convertible bearing a poster-sized portrait of the deceased in a gilded frame. This is how some of San Francisco's Asian communities do funerals; the larger-than-life likeness of the deceased sits upright in the backseat as if to enjoy one last, triumphant ride through the city. Chinatown meets Jazz Fest: what a way to go out.

I headed toward the library as planned, but I was too full of music and joy to go in. Besides, a funeral is nothing if not a reminder to seize the day. I kept on riding right past the library, following my curiosity. Eventually, I found myself at Ocean Beach, watching the sun slip into the sea. I turned on my blinky lights and pointed my front wheel toward home. I rode slowly, savoring every sight and scent of my new 'hood along the way.

**DEB GRECO** is a book geek who thinks writing is the most fun you can have after reading. She loves composting, gardening, and riding her bike around San Francisco.

## Chapter Nine

# Cycles and Relocalizing
### Amy Walker

*Think* globally, bike locally" reads the sticker from my local bike shop, a two-wheeled twist on a familiar environmental mantra. Today, it seems, "think globally, act locally" simply describes our lives. Roughly a third of the world's seven billion people are online. As wired — and wireless — Earthlings, we understand other cultures from the inside out and make "friends" with strangers we may never meet face-to-face. We can fly across the world in a day. Our iPods play flamenco, bhangra, and desert blues. Northerners gobble acai and goji berries, quinoa and coconut water while sushi is served in the desert. The Earth seems small.

The "global village" is amazing and full of wonders — yet the globalization of business has increased the divide between rich and poor. An elite few possess obscene wealth while the vast majority live in poverty. The richest 20 percent of people consume over 76 percent of the world's goods. As far as I can tell, that's you and me.

## On Bicycles

The huge profits of the few are built on inequality and cheap oil. Cheap oil makes it possible to produce food in large-scale factory farms with petroleum-based fertilizers and ship it to markets halfway across the world. Cheap oil makes it possible to manufacture cheap plastic products and distribute them to big-box and dollar stores, where they make their way into our lives and the environment like glittering shrapnel — lodging where they land, promising not to degrade for thousands of years. Cheap oil allows people to unthinkingly drive single-occupancy vehicles (SOVs) on marathon daily commutes between cities and suburbs while polluting the air and water as well as the spatial and cultural landscape. Yet the era of cheap oil is coming to an end.

As an effort to address this type of unsustainable development, Transition Towns are a network of local groups working toward creating resilient local communities. Rob Hopkins is a cofounder of Transition Town Totnes (UK) and of the Transition Network (http://transitionnetwork.org). He is also the author of *The Transition Handbook: From Oil Dependency to Local Resilience*. The goal of Transition Towns is to create alternative community structures to defend against the three major threats of peak oil, climate change, and economic instability. As Hopkins writes: "Something very powerful is stirring and is taking root the world over. People are starting to see peak oil as the Great Opportunity, the chance to build the world they always dreamt of."

Sophy Banks is a trainer with the Transition Network in England. She leads visualization workshops where she asks people to "close your eyes and imagine what your community would look like if you had the future you really wanted for your children. What would that look like, what would it feel like, what does it taste and smell like. What are you eating? What do you wear? What do the buildings look like? What are people doing in their day? What do they look like when you look into their eyes?" In the film *In Transition 1.0*, Banks said, "These sorts of questions are really important to bring people out of the despair and have a sense that there could be another future. If we don't do that visioning and imagining the world we want and then take steps toward it, we're going to get a world that someone else wants."

Waking up to our circumstances may at first seem challenging, but with each step taken toward sustainability, the journey gets easier. You might start by taking an inventory of your personal activities, such as commuting, work, and leisure, and your spending. Does your expenditure of time, energy, and money match up with your values? Next, examine all the things you own and use. Do you know where they came from and what materials they are made out of? Do you know anything about the conditions under which they were made? Though these questions may not be new to you, many of us become complacent over time, and we simply enjoy all the cheap products and foods available to us, without asking, "What is the true cost?" Although it seems impossible sometimes when we actually look at where our goods come from, voting with our wallets, by choosing to keep our money circulating locally, is still the average person's most powerful tool for change.

Where globalization capitalizes on cheap fuel and cheap labor to manufacture cheap goods, localization encourages self-sustaining and secure systems of trade and fulfillment. Localization is a systemic economic strategy to create resilience by removing dependence on fossil fuels and imported goods. Though there are good reasons to encourage diverse, globalized media and communication technologies, in the case of food and most consumer goods, relocalization seems to benefit individuals and communities better than globalization by recirculating energy and resources within their own ecosystem.

Bicycling has a role to play in the transition to sustainable, local communities. According to the American Automobile Association, Americans spend on average $9,641 each year on their cars (based on a person driving a medium-sized sedan fifteen thousand miles a year, excluding loan payments).[1] Most of that money leaves the local economy. By shifting our transportation away from private automobiles and toward cycling, walking, and public transit, we retain more of that money in local economies. If just one hundred people in a city or town switch from cars to bikes, that's $964,100 — almost a million dollars — that they can instead spend locally. When cities create spaces for bicycles (bike lanes, bike boulevards, bike parking), they enable people to shift to bikes for transportation. When we bicycle, we are more aware of our local environment, and since our travel requires effort and is not at the touch of a button, we make more careful choices about our consumption and shopping. Creating a bicycle-friendly economy and transportation system allows people to shift to this efficient, self-sufficient form of economic activity.

Since food is our fuel, we cyclists also pay a lot of attention to what we put into our bodies. Eating locally grown food gives you a lower carbon footprint, and it's better for you. During the

Second World War, urban dwellers were encouraged to plant victory gardens to increase their resiliency to food shortages. Civic and state governments supported these efforts. Photos from 1943 even show a food garden planted in front of city hall in San Francisco, one of the most successful cities in urban wartime food production, with sevety thousand victory gardens. Food garden-  ing is seeing another massive surge in popularity today. Organizations like Growing Power, a year-round, two-acre urban farm in Milwaukee, Wisconsin, and the six thousand-square-foot Eagle Street Rooftop Farm in Brooklyn, New York, demonstrate that agriculture can thrive in the urban environment. Urban community gardens are re-introducing traditional practices and educating younger generations about where food comes from and how to grow it.

North American cities and towns have seen a proliferation of multinational big-box stores (Walmart, Target, etc.) that undercut locally owned stores and force them out of business. These big-box retailers resist unionizing, increase sprawl and the need for car traffic, and leave many neighborhoods without local services. Money spent in the big-box stores does not circulate locally. It flows away from the communities and the people who shop in the stores and toward head offices to create returns for shareholders. When the local businesses shut down, the root system of the local economy dies. When local self-sufficiency is damaged, many towns suffer economic depression and social ills like emotional stress, isolation, and addictions.

As an antidote to this damaging business model, relocalization often works from principles of permaculture — a way of designing our land use and communities as whole systems. Rather than ignoring parts of our communities that do not serve profit-driven development, the needs of all the parts are seen as important and vital to the success of the whole. A Portland, Oregon, organization founded on permaculture principles, City Repair (http://city repair.org), holds an annual event called the Village Building Convergence. The gathering attracts locals as well as people from around North America to help community development in Portland and learn skills to bring back home. A fundamental idea behind City Repair is that people who live in a community know, better than any centralized planners, where benches and traffic calming and bike lanes should naturally be placed, because they live there and they observe what happens on a daily basis. It's a different model of planning, and it cannot be delivered from the top down. It is something people have to create in their own communities. And they are doing it!

Randy Chatterjee, a founder of Village Vancouver (www.village vancouver.ca), a transition network in Vancouver, Canada, said, "The transition movement is about communities around the world responding to peak oil and climate change with creativity, imagination, and humor. It is positive, solutions focused, viral, and fun."

As Chatterjee explains, there are efficiency gains as well as very positive social gains from having good connections with your neighbors: "Two summers ago, I had kale and lettuces coming out of my ears, but my tomatoes just didn't make it." He and others in the neighborhood developed a practice of trading their vegetable surpluses. "I had friends with greenhouses and tons of tomatoes, and without knowing people, we would not have been able to engage in that local trading."

Village Vancouver changes people's lives by introducing neighbors to one another and fostering those relationships through events like local potlucks, discussions, and bicycle repair and gardening classes. "One of the things we are doing is building seed libraries in each neighborhood, and we use bicycles to transport the libraries and trade seeds between neighborhoods." This type of positive vision and direct local involvement is necessary to create cities and towns we can truly love to live in. This is as true for bicycling as it is for any other area of our lives. In the words of the anthropologist Margaret Mead, "Never doubt that a small group of concerned tvcitizens can change the world. Indeed, it is the only thing that ever has."

1 American Automobile Association, "2011: Your Driving Costs," www.aaa exchange.com/Main, accessed June 10, 2011.

## Chapter Ten

# Notes from a Bicycle Bodhisattva

*May All Beings Be Liberated!*

## Carmen Mills

*May all beings everywhere, with whom we are inseparably interconnected, be fulfilled, awakened, and free. May there be peace in this world and throughout the entire universe, and may we all together complete the spiritual journey.*

**— BUDDHIST PRAYER**

*Once* upon a time I went for a ride on Cortes Island, with a sore knee, a rusty chain, and a battered heart. I had no destination in mind, and I chugged over hill after hill until finally the gears seized. I leaned the heavy old bike against a sign in the shape of a wheel and started to walk. An odd warm wind was pulling me forward, playing gently through the fine hairs on my forearms. I heard the distant chime of wind bells and kept following the dusty path, arriving finally at Dorje Ling Dharma Centre — an ersatz Tibetan fantasy of cedar and film set castoffs, rusted metal and sky. I walked into the meditation hall and knew I was home. Years of cycling in city traffic make a person brave, and in that moment I called up all I the courage I could gather. I walked under the prayer flags and stayed for six months, while my dharmic path and my bicycle path merged into a single lane.

At Dorje Ling I investigated one particular 2,500-year-old road map, but there are so many ways to awakening. The bicycle path is another bumpy road to liberation, which every 6-year-old recognizes the first time the parent lets go of the seat and she flies free. The experience of self-propelled flight is a taste of freedom from parental control and, later, from governmental and social restriction. It offers freedom from the repressive craving for vehicular status: that perfect car as promised on TV. Freedom from the global matrix of fossil-fuel addiction. Freedom from suffering through boredom, ill health, and lethargy. Freedom from the sodden weight of empty consumption. Freedom from slavery to financial debt. Freedom from the sucking maw of bad credit and bad karma, where we sell off our world's future for today's speedy commute. Freedom, yah man, freedom, I say, *freedom!*

Freedom lives in the notion of Zen — of simple elegance of function and form. Zen lives in the bike's spare geometry, a simple tool kit and a drop of oil. My life on the bike path has trained me to appreciate the minimal. With the bicycle as my primary mode of transportation and recreation, it is clear how little I really need in order to be content, how much is superfluous, how most of my needs can be so well satisfied with so little. Bike-tour adventuring especially has turned me into a minimalist — 'cuz who the hell wants to cart all that junk up a hill? To this day, whenever I pack a bag for a trip I agonize over whether I really need three tank tops, or whether two are enough. I don't need a house or a storage locker, and I certainly don't need a garage. My needs are few and my debts are none, and thus I am rich beyond words.

Cycling can be good meditation. Meditation expands the mind, makes it calmer and stronger. I think of the scene in the movie *Deux secondes* where newbie Montreal bike courier (hottie Charlotte Laurier) zones out on her run and spins off into reverie, jolted back at last by the squawk of her radio to find herself far away, in the Quebec farmland. Every cyclist can identify with the experience of getting into the zone, leaving the self behind as boundaries dissolve into the rhythm of the ride. The circular forward motion, the merging of self into air — merging into everything, and into nothing. Becoming One with the big picture.

Riding a bike breaks down the physical and conceptual barriers between our selves and the world. When it comes to eradicating the deadly illusion of separation, surely there's nothing like biking for getting all up close and personal with the Universe. The air, the concrete, the bugs and roadkill and trees — there they are, right in your face. When humans are liberated from metal cages, we smell the smells and hear the sounds — all of them, from the toxic to the divine. We're all in the soup together. We see the horror and mad beauty of the city that drivers will never slow down enough to apprehend. And we get to see our sleek and beautiful selves, mirrored in the eyes of our cycling *sangha* — our community of practitioners — as they flash by in smiling conspiracy.

The freedom of cycling gets into our blood, and we stop being self-conscious, we lose our consciousness of Self. We start to know in our physical bones that if we treat ourselves well, then we treat our planet well. And if we are doing no harm and defending our planet, then we are healthier people; we have more fun, and we have more energy to give back to the world. Everything we do for the good of "others" rebounds right back at us. There is no separation. Bicycles are karma-generating machines, relieving suffering for self and for others. Bicycles provide the strength, spirit, and courage that warriors need. Courage to follow the path. What goes around comes around, and around and around and around. Like a wheel, spinning true.

*May all beings be happy — may all beings be free.*

**CARMEN MILLS** is a Vancouver-based Director of Free Will. Her eccentric résumé includes cofounding *Momentum* magazine and Car-Free Vancouver Day and managing Dorje Ling Dharma Centre on Cortes Island. To read Carmen's blog, visit http://bicycle buddha.org.

# PART TWO

## Gearing Up

## Chapter Eleven

# How to Help a Bike Shop Help You

**Ulrike Rodrigues**

*I'm* a lifelong bike rider and sometime bike-shop staffer, and I know the hardest part of getting into biking can be getting into a bike store. Sure, enthusiasts think of the local bike shop as a lively meeting place stocked with cool parts and cool people, but many average folks (and bike forum commentators) say they feel intimidated by bike shops' unfamiliar gear, jargon, and particular style of customer service.

But according to a Shimano-sponsored study, today's bike shops are changing. Because they're surviving on slim profit margins in an extremely competitive industry, they *need you* to like them. Sure, they want you to buy lots of stuff, but they also want to see you riding your bike. It's good for them and it's good for you. But they can't help you with that if you're too nervous to walk through the door.

My advice? Remember that — as the customer — you hold

the power. Armed with some basic information and a few insider tips, you can help a bike shop help you.

# KNOW YOUR BIKE SHOP

A bike shop is just a retail environment that sells products and services. One tip to finding the right bike shop for your needs is to understand that there are different kinds of bike shops with different products and services.

## *Boutique*

Small shops with highly specialized products, such as vintage cruisers, fixed-gear bikes, or hand-built frames.

## *Community*

Hands-on, usually nonprofit cooperatives staffed by volunteers: ideal for locating obscure parts and catching up with left-leaning friends.

## *Neighborhood*

Family or enthusiast-run businesses that have been around a long time, sponsor local bike events, and support the community's cycling culture.

## *Station*

Bustling pit stop/coffee shops near public-transit hubs for four-season cyclists who ride for environmental, economic, or cultural reasons.

## On Bicycles

### General

Chain stores with a variety of bike styles in different price ranges.

### Sport

Stores with high-end bikes for competition and training in specific types of cycling, such as road, triathlon, cyclocross, and trail riding.

### All-sport

Sports stores that carry bikes in addition to other sporting equipment.

### Big-box

Large, warehouse-style retailers that carry bikes in addition to appliances, food, and other products.

### Consignment/used/pawn

Owner-operated outlets that sell secondhand bikes, sometimes of questionable origin and mechanical integrity.

## TAKE AN INVENTORY OF YOUR NEEDS

Before you visit a bike store, ask yourself what you actually want.

Do you want to buy a bike or just look? Buy a complete bike or install some accessories? Pay an expert for a repair or learn how to do it yourself? Fondle new technology or dig for bargains? Fix a flat or sip a latte? Bankroll a multinational corporation or support a passionate small entrepreneur? Watch the Tour or plan a trip? Spec components or compare piercings?

Match your needs to the shop's services. Rather than wheel your bungee-and-milk-crate ride into a high-end boutique, consider a community cooperative instead. You'll be happier for it because you'll receive the level (and price) of service you seek.

## IDENTIFY YOUR BIKE STYLE

What kind of riding will you do? How often, how far, how fast, with whom? Be realistic. What will you wear, what will you carry, where will you go? What are your limitations and expectations? Past injuries? Fears? Goals? How much are you willing to spend? Have you budgeted for additional accessories that will enhance your safety, security, and comfort?

If you feel challenged by unfamiliarity, budget, age, weight, injuries, or your level of fitness or hipness, share your concerns with the staff so that they can set you up right. Many know a lot about bikes, but not a lot about you. The more you tell them, the better they can help you.

## STUDY SOME BIKE ANATOMY

Equipped with some basic product knowledge, you'll feel more confident and less intimidated by staff when shopping for bikes and gear.

What do you know about bikes? If you're shopping for a new bike, can you identify brands of bikes? Models? Styles? Do you know the difference between a wheel and a tire? Can you describe where a creak is coming from and when it happens?

Rather than rely on just bike-store staff for all your information, ask your friends, neighbors, and coworkers. Browse the web for products, reviews, user forums, and how-tos. *It's okay if you don't know* — so long as you *know* that you don't know!

## COMPARE AND SHORT-LIST SHOPS

If you can, visit a few recommended shops and compare — the businesses, not the products. Note how you feel when you enter the shop, how quickly someone greets you, and how your conversation goes. Be like a mystery shopper and ask the same question at multiple stores to compare their response. You'll discover that excellent bike-store staff know how to patiently listen and ask questions.

Once you have a short list of stores, research the strengths of each — location, price, selection, repair facilities, hours. Isn't it reassuring to know that if you have an unsatisfying experience at one, you can take yourself, your bike, and your wallet to another?

## KEEP GLITCHES IN PERSPECTIVE

A bicycle is a simple device. Most repairs go fairly smoothly, but there are times when even the most experienced bike shop needs to take a few passes at fixing a troublesome bike. What may seem like a small job to you — like installing a fender, calibrating a computer, or loosening a stuck chain — may actually be a time-consuming task. And not only are there many ways to fix an item, but mechanics can disagree among themselves about the best way to do it.

Relax. Trust the informed choice you made in selecting the shop in the first place. Time is money to a bike shop, so you can bet they want to locate that chronic creak as quickly and efficiently as you do.

## EXPECT BIASED OPINIONS

People who are passionate about bikes can also be very opinionated. That applies to bike staff *and* bike riders. Your well-meaning friends can offer long-winded accolades or tirades that don't necessarily address your needs. Likewise, staffers in a bike shop may be personally biased toward what they ride or what wowed them at the last Alley Cat ride. And you have biases that shape your judgments, too. What influences your perception of a bike shop? What attitude are you bringing in the door with you? Do you expect to be helped or intimidated? What are you assuming about the expertise of the staff?

## EXPECT VARYING LEVELS OF SERVICE

A bike shop isn't McDonald's — you'll likely receive different service from different staff on different days. It's not personal, it's timing. People who work in bike shops are generally smart, passionate, underpaid, and underappreciated. They work in bike shops because they love being around bikes. Some like working with machines, some like working with people, and some like both. Accordingly, you have about a one in three chance that you'll talk to the right person at the right time. If you have a memorable experience — bad or good — get the staffer's name, and let the manager know.

# BIKE SHOP DO'S AND DON'TS

## Do

→ Remember that you always have a choice: different parts, different staff, different store.

→ Troubleshoot your bike at home before you bring it to the bike shop. Run some tests, listen to the sounds, try to locate the problem, and think about how to describe it.

→ Schedule regular tune-ups and inspections: they'll keep your bike running smoothly and help you develop a relationship with bike-shop staff.

→ Understand that some installations and repairs can be challenging and take longer than you think.

→ Bring all the broken bits from a part that needs to be replaced: it helps the staff find a replacement.

→ Test-ride new bikes when you have lots of time and you're wearing comfortable clothes. Keep in mind that bike shops are less busy during the week.

## Don't

→ Be intimidated. Think about what you want ahead of time, but be open to advice.

→ Be embarrassed about your old bicycle. Bike shops are just glad that you're riding.

→ Tell the sales staff that you can get it cheaper online.

→ Underestimate how a few small and inexpensive adjustments can increase your riding enjoyment.

Bike shops may have an intimidating image, but as the number of cycling consumers increases, shops are changing their ways. Going in prepared can have a huge effect on your bike-shop experience because you'll have a clearer idea of what you want, and you'll be able to articulate it.

And knowing how to talk to the people at your local bike shop is a great way to help them help you. Not only will you learn more about yourself, but you'll connect with the hub of your community's bike culture.

**ULRIKE RODRIGUES** is a lifelong, car-free cyclist who shares her female-flavored tales of travel, sex, and magic in print, web, and wine bars (Pinot Grigio, if you're buying).

# Chapter Twelve

# A Rough Guide to the City Bike

## Wendell Challenger

*In* North America, bikes sold as ready to ride in the city are often anything but. While the geometry and handling of "hybrid" or "comfort" bikes have been designed with urban riding in mind, these bikes often lack important transportation-oriented features such as a chain guard, fenders, lights, and racks. This sends a message that these bikes should not be ridden with regular clothing, in the rain, at night, or with a load. In other words, they are for recreational purposes only. By comparison, in Europe, where cycling is a well-accepted form of urban transportation, city bikes come standard with all these features.

In North America, the onus has been on the urban cyclist to do a three-step city-bike shuffle: buy a bike; buy everything else you need; mount these extra purchases on said bike; and (optional) curse profusely when purchased add-ons don't fit the bike, requiring exchange or modifications. While all this may be great fun for DIY types, it is an unnecessary barrier for most others. The message is clear: either cycling is not for daily transportation, or bike commuting is only for some type of cycling elite.

Thankfully, the times, they are a-changin'. North American bike manufacturers have been listening to their customers, and we have been seeing the emergence of more transportation-focused bikes. While every urban cyclist's needs are slightly different, what follows is advice that has been gleaned from nearly two decades of daily city cycling.

## YOU HAVE TO BE ABLE TO USE IT — ALL THE TIME

If a bike is to be used as a primary form of transportation, neither rain, nor sleet, nor snazzy party dress should keep you from riding to your destination. Look for full-wrap fenders (which should cover a large proportion of the wheel) to keep road grime and water off your clothes. Look for a chain guard to prevent loose clothing from tangling in the chain. Ideally, the bike should also come with a lighting system to get you home when the sun goes down.

## MODERN PACKHORSES?

For better or worse, we will always need to carry stuff with us, and a true city bike should make that easy. Look for bikes that come with either pannier racks or baskets to carry your goodies to and fro. Check to see how the bike handles with a load: a good city bike should keep its manners while working.

NORTH AMERICAN CITY BIKE

headlamp

frame pump

rear rack

front rack

panniers

water bottle cages

fenders

chain guard

## SIMPLE AND RELIABLE

City bikes need to be ready to ride year-round without much intervention. Smart design considerations can facilitate this. To prevent shifter and brake cables from rusting and getting gummed up in inclement weather, cables can be routed along the top tube or through full-length cable housings. A flat tire is the last thing you need when you have somewhere to go, so look for puncture-resistant tires.

The drivetrain is also a key consideration when commuting year-round. External gearing (i.e., derailleur systems) gets gummed up over time, leading to less efficiency. Internally geared hubs do not suffer in the same way, as all the gears are sealed and protected from the elements, providing many more miles of riding before requiring maintenance (see chapter 15). That said, the external derailleur system is much more common and can be a good choice if kept reasonably clean. It is one of the most efficient multispeed drivetrains available if it is well maintained. For those with an aversion to all types of maintenance, derailleur systems with fewer gears are generally more robust and require fewer adjustments.

Recently, some city bikes have been coming equipped with a belt drive (usually a carbon or Kevlar belt) instead of a metal chain. The technology promises to be cleaner and require less maintenance (it requires no lubrication), and it has a longer lifetime than metal chains, but it is still relatively new and unproven. Early adopters may face unique issues not present in more mature technology.

Finally, a universal task for city cyclists is parking your bike. Bolted-on (rather than quick-release) wheels and saddles offer more security, because quick-release parts can be easily stolen. That said, long-distance riders might still prefer quick-release wheels in order to make repairing flats easier.

## SAFETY BY DESIGN

City bikes should have a relatively upright riding position to provide good sightlines, to reduce strain on the wrists and neck, and to increase the rider's visibility in traffic. The bike's handling must be stable, so that if you hit a pothole unexpectedly you will not be thrown into traffic. This is especially important when you're carrying a load. Stability may mean opting for a bike that does not feel as fast or responsive as a more performance-oriented model.

You must be able to stop your bike rapidly in all conditions.

Rim brakes, which are standard on most bikes, work fine except that they lose efficacy when the wheel rims are wet. Avoid rim brakes on steel-rimmed wheels, as wet-weather braking will be nonexistent. Steel rims are easily detected with a magnet. Modern alloy rims provide better wet-weather braking and are not magnetic.

Disc brakes are rapidly becoming more commonplace and typically provide the strongest and best-modulated braking action while performing equally well in dry or wet weather. These brakes are also reliable and long-lasting once set up properly, which a good bike shop can do for you. Drum and roller brakes are enclosed brake systems that are some of the most reliable and low maintenance available. They perform equally well in wet or dry weather but do not have as much braking power as disc brakes.

## SEEING AND BEING SEEN

Even though most city bikes are ridden at night at least occasionally, most bikes in North America are sold without lights. The problem of lighting is left to the buyer to solve. Here's where the industry is still letting urban cyclists down. Although most riders have good intentions, many either don't outfit their bikes with adequate lighting or, all too often, buy battery-operated lights and forget to change or charge the batteries.

A true city bike should come with lights that are bright day or night and are powered by a dynamo or generator on the wheel instead of by unreliable batteries. They should continue to work for a short period of time even when the wheel is not moving (a feature termed a "stand light").

The newer generation of dynamo-powered LED lights meets all three of these criteria, but these lights are rarely available as standard equipment. Aftermarket dynamo-lighting systems can be expensive and challenging to set up. But the expense and effort are worthwhile: reliable lights can literally be lifesavers for daily commuters. And no matter what the manufacturer promises about run time, with battery-powered lights there will always come a time when you forget to replace or charge the battery and are left in the dark.

For dynamo lights, hub dynamos (built right into the front-wheel hub) are preferable to sidewall dynamos for cyclists who ride year-round, as they are more efficient and will not slip in wet conditions.

## COMFORT *AND* EFFICIENCY

City bikes need to be both comfortable and efficient. You don't want to show up at your destination with a sore back and covered in sweat. Larger-diameter wheels combined with slick or semislick tires reduce rolling resistance and make the bike easier to pedal. Bikes that have a reasonably large selection of gears make it easier to tackle hills.

Body positioning and contact points are often overlooked. These include the saddle, handlebar position, and handgrips. If you plan to ride for long periods, look for a high-quality saddle (firm and supportive), supportive handgrips, and handlebars with multiple hand positions. Each person's body is different, so take your time to find out what works for you. Here again, the staff at a good bike shop should help you.

Long-distance riders should book an appointment for a proper bike-fitting session before any bike purchase. A properly fitting bike is always more comfortable and will prevent a number of common injuries associated with an incorrectly fitting bike.

## STYLE IS AS STYLE DOES

Who doesn't want to look smoking hot as they get around town? If cycling is a lifestyle choice for you, a bike can be an extension of yourself. Don't hesitate to style it up; the more attractive you feel, the more you'll want to ride!

**WENDELL CHALLENGER** is an ecological statistician by day and has been a passionate cyclist since he was a teenager. He believes the simple act of cycling can be transformative and will be one of the many important steps toward a more sustainable future. http://twitter.com/wchallenger

# Chapter Thirteen

# Bike Style
## What to Wear When Riding a Bike

## Amy Walker

*When* Novella Carpenter, urban farmer, forager, and author of *Farm City*, invited Hamish Bowles, the editor at large for *Vogue*, to visit Oakland for a taste of gourmet urban scavenging, one of their only non-food-related stops was a visit to the artisan tailor Nan Eastep. As passionate about natural fibers as she is about cycling, Eastep creates some of the most comfortable and attractive wool cycling attire on the continent under the moniker B Spoke Tailor (bspoketailor.com). So on questions of what to wear on a bike, Eastep's opinion carries some weight.

The Minnesota-born Eastep favors clothing with old-world styling and an active edge. Her designs have room in the shoulders and knees and anywhere else the body moves: "Before the car, tailored clothing was made for hunting and fishing and sport. Once we had cars, . . . the typical suit-wearer was not doing anything active — they took the action out of suits. So I'm putting the action back into suits."

For Bowles, Eastep fashioned a vest of grape- and moss-colored Lumatwill, a reflective-threaded tweed fabric. Along with gusseted wool knickers, the vest is a garment particularly suitable for cycling: "A vest protects the front of your body from the wind, and it protects the whole heart area and the stomach area. For women, I'm tucking them in tighter so they're supportive, almost like a sports bra. There are no sleeves, so you have full mobility of your arms, and I create a collar so you can close it up through the neck. I think about warmth and mobility — you can take off your jacket, and you still have that wind buffer."

When asked what effect clothing and style have on the bicycle rider's experience, Eastep said, "I feel like we've been in cars for so many decades, designing what the exterior of the car looks like, with people buying cars for the fashion of it, and meanwhile people are less and less interested in their clothing. So a great thing about the bike is that we get to see each other again."

Seeing each other on bikes is what Patrick Barber's *Velocouture* blog is all about. What began as a Flickr group in 2006, inspired by street style, cycling, and photo sharing, turned into a harbinger of the trend of bike-style blogging and has transformed the way Barber himself regards cycling and clothes.

Before starting *Velocouture*, Barber found an outlet for his interest in fashion through a Flickr group called Wardrobe Remix. Group members shared photos of their outfits, commented, and made style recommendations to one another. Barber noticed that his style decisions were a mixture of what worked visually and what worked for riding a bike, as that was his main mode of transport. "At the time, I was still wearing clippy shoes and riding a fixed-gear, and I was still using some special equipment." Barber quickly made the connection that he was thinking about something the others were not, so he started the Velocouture group on Flickr as a sort of Wardrobe Remix for people on bikes.

To find the group on Flickr.com, just search for "Velocouture." You'll find a wealth of fun, creative, and bike-friendly clothing — and a fabulous array of stylish bikes to boot. Velocouture is a great resource and a way to feast your eyes on people sharing their everyday bike style with ingenuity, whimsy, and joy. "It's a thriving pool of inspiration and ideas from a fashion standpoint, a bike standpoint, and a photography standpoint."

After several years of swapping images and style tips, Barber noticed that his views on bike style had shifted: "For me it's been a trajectory from thinking, well, you need some special stuff to ride your bike and still look good, to realizing what you need is a bike that can accommodate your regular, everyday clothes so you don't have to worry about that, you can just worry about looking good, and you can just ride your bike."

After viewing thousands of submitted photos, Barber observed that the best bike style was coming from places in Europe and Asia where cycling was part of mainstream culture and people were just hopping on bikes in their everyday clothes.

In North America, too, the most interesting bike fashion is coming out of cities where cycling is becoming more mainstream, as well as places with colder climates, like Portland, San Francisco, Chicago, and Boston. Though he sees plenty of photos from people riding their bikes in warmer places like Santa Monica and Santa Barbara, he says, "There's just not much fashion involved in a tank top and shorts."

When asked what trends he sees in the images, Barber said, "I see a lot of boots. It was a revelation to me. They keep the wet off your ankles, and you stay drier and warmer. On men I see a resurgence of nice pants-and-shirt combinations. Now you see men wearing shirts with a collar, a tie, and suspenders — or an interesting combination that may not be business wear, but it looks really sharp. For women, I see them wearing opaque tights — and a lot of color."

When asked about his favorite piece of bicycle clothing, Barber responds, "You know, the most amazing thing that's happened to me since I started this blog is that I put a chain guard on my bike.

It's been revolutionary because one of the things that's happened to me is that I've bought regular pants, and I don't have to worry about them because both my bikes now have chain guards." And that should be a clear message to the bike makers of North America: it's the key to bringing cycling to the mainstream and the reason why Europeans and Asians and people in other countries where biking is more popular have better bike style. People don't spend much time thinking about their bike clothes, because they buy city bikes that have chain guards. They just wear what they would normally wear  off the bike, and it's no big deal. You can read Barber's extensive review of his chain guard (the SKS Chainboard) as well as his other stylish observations at www.velocouture.wordpress.com.

Style is a visual conversation. What we wear communicates something about us to everyone we pass or meet. Whether they mean to or not, stylish and interesting-looking cyclists are performing a subtle and powerful form of advocacy and lifestyle marketing by attracting attention to themselves and their bikes.

But let's face it, no one looks worse for riding a bicycle — and there are as many ways to dress on a bike as there are cyclists. Whatever you're wearing right now will probably work just fine. The key is to ride and observe and experiment, and enjoy the process. As the fashion world catches on to the biking trend, they'll try to sell cycling back to us at a higher price. But true style — on or off the bike — is more than being a carbon copy of what is trendy or cool: it's about enjoying being yourself and wearing what feels right for you.

## Chapter Fourteen

# Five Stages in Le Tour de Parent

## Chris Keam

*Propelling* our special snowflakes by bike in the earliest stages of their lives also means shepherding them through some distinct phases. At each stage, the right gear makes life simpler. Here are some of the things to keep in mind when you're choosing the equipment to pedal-power your family's everyday travels.

### BIKE BABIES

They say you shouldn't take a kid in a trailer before the age of one. "They" say a lot of things, but a lot of people are finding out that even small babies can be safely transported by bike. When your baby is an infant, you have essentially two options: a Dutch-style bakfiets, with the baby carried in a cargo compartment in the front, or a regular bike with a trailer. Either way, if you use an appropriate baby car seat and secure it to the bike, barring a serious accident, your child is just as safe as in a car. When my daughter was an infant, I used a double kids' trailer and suspended her car seat with bungee cords from the top of the trailer's aluminum frame. It was secure and relatively isolated from road shock. The bakfiets is the more elegant solution but requires buying a large, expensive bike and finding a place to store it. The upside is the convenience of being able to toss kids, groceries, and even small, well-behaved pets into a big wooden box right where you can see them, making riding with kids less like flying blind.

Although I don't like children's bike seats (the sight of young kids' heads flopping around when they fall asleep in a bike seat makes me cringe), many parents prefer this option to towing a bulky trailer. A front-mounted bike seat (between rider and handlebars) is a lot of fun for the kid, but it is only recommended for children ages 1–3. Carrying bigger children puts too much weight up high on the bike, and the bike is prone to fall over when stationary, even if leaned on a kickstand. The same caveat applies to rear-mounted bike seats. A better option is the Xtracycle cargo bike (which is rated to carry 200 pounds) along with their PeaPod child seat. Since the Xtracycle can be fitted with a sturdy double kickstand, it is much less likely to fall over (www.xtracycle.com).

## TOTING TOTS IN TRAILERS

The most important question when buying a trailer is, double or single? Even parents with only one kid may find a double useful for the added space it offers to carry groceries and outdoor gear or for securely mounting a car seat. However, parents who enjoy the occasional off-road ride may appreciate a single trailer's narrower design. Look for trailers that hitch onto the bike at the rear axle, with a ball-and-socket or cotter-pin hitch.

## YOUNG RIDERS

Long before your children grow out of a bike trailer, you can start them on the path to two-wheeled freedom. Tricycles and training wheels were once common stages in a cyclist's evolution. Now both are rapidly becoming obsolete: a twenty-first-century child cyclist starts on two wheels. Run bikes are two-wheelers without pedals; resembling the velocipedes of the 1800s, which were forerunners of the modern bicycle, they offer a very easy way to learn how to ride a pedal-powered bike. Kids learn balance by scooting themselves along without pedaling and quickly become able to glide longer and longer distances. Because they have no chain or pedals, these bikes are tidy and easy to store and transport.

## THE PRIMARY YEARS

As your child grows, the world expands. The baby that once spent much of its time at home or in the neighborhood starts to have a life of its own. The need to get to school, music and dance classes, sports, and social events such as weekend birthday parties means you need to decide whether you are going to continue to cycle together or settle for the car or bus. If you want to keep biking, your choices include the trail-a-bike, trail-gator, and tandem bike. The first two attach to the seatpost of your bike. A trail-a-bike is a bike frame with one wheel, without a front wheel or fork; the child sits on it behind you and can pedal or coast. The trail-gator is essentially a tow bar that lets you attach your kid's bike to your own with the front wheel suspended. This arrangement is more versatile than a trail-a-bike, but some users find connecting the two bikes correctly much harder than attaching a single-wheeled trail-a-bike.

*Children riding behind on a trail-a-bike can pedal or coast.*

If you want to tow your kid somewhere and then separate the bikes so you can both ride on your own, a trail-gator is worth a try. If you are trying to get a grade-schooler to and from school and other activities on relatively safe streets, the trail-a-bike is a workable solution. The chief concerns are route selection and visibility, which can be addressed by affixing so many blinky lights to yourself, bike, and child that you look like a low-flying UFO. A tandem, whether a specific adult-child model or an adult tandem with aftermarket adapters to fit a child, is the fastest, best-handling option for families planning to commute regularly; but as always with cycling, they are out of reach for those whose budget or storage space is limited.

## TWO-WHEELED PRETEENS

Eventually you'll be faced with deciding whether your kid is a skilled enough cyclist to venture out alone. This is actually a pretty good problem to have. It means your kids are still riding and haven't abandoned their bikes to fit in with a noncycling peer group. The best bike is almost always the lightest, most durable model in your price range — unless it won't get ridden because it's the wrong style, color, or brand.

"I know that some kids make better choices after hearing about a variety of bike types and their benefits...and some just want that new or cool thing that their friends have," says Paul Bogaert of the Bike Doctor, a bike store in Vancouver, Canada. "Just don't get the cheapest one of that type available. That is the biggest mistake. Hopefully the family can negotiate a good decision and avoid an unnecessarily heavy or otherwise inappropriate bike, which may slow down their kids and make a family ride much slower and harder than need be."

## PEDAL PARTICIPATION

Lots of children need little or no encouragement to become daily cyclists. Others might benefit from organized activities. A skills course such as those offered by many local cycling advocacy groups can whet the appetite of beginning cyclists while delivering essential street smarts. For children who already know how to ride, the camaraderie of the local BMX track, a junior triathlon or road race, or the cadet division at an area mountain bike race can provide motivation.

BMX racing is especially popular with young people and recently became an Olympic sport. In fact, there are BMX classes for all ages, from kids as young as 5 years to the over-40 crowd, so the whole family can participate. The various cycling events in the X Games and other competitions are also getting kids of both sexes out on bikes to practice gravity-defying tricks. Many places now have bike parks where custom-designed ramps and jumps give young people a chance to build their bike-handling skills, whether for BMX riding, dirt jumping, or downhill/freeride mountain biking.

For budding triathletes, the North American Ironkids events provide organized competition for kids ages 6–15. Mountain bike racing also offers young riders the opportunity to train and compete. NORBA (the National Off-Road Bicycle Association) has a comprehensive juniors' program starting with an under-10 division, as well as a collegiate series, and high schools in many areas with thriving mountain bike scenes typically have clubs. Sanctioned road-racing events start at age 10 in North America.

If your kid has a competitive streak but doesn't enjoy the typical organized sports such as basketball, soccer, or baseball, bike racing offers a multitude of opportunities to excel. For kids who are already athletes, cycling is a great way to build strength and endurance without the bone and joint stress of running or weightlifting.

## CHOOSING A BIKE

Kids' bikes come in five main sizes: 12, 16, 18, 20, and 24. The numbers refer to wheel size (in inches) rather than frame size. Because kids grow at different rates, inseam length is a better guide to bike sizing than the child's age. Here's a rough guide.

| Child's age (years) | Inseam (inches) | Bike tire size (inches) |
|---|---|---|
| 2–4 | 14–17 | 12 |
| 4–6 | 16–20 | 14 |
| 5–8 | 18–22 | 16 |
| 6–9 | 20–24 | 18 |
| 7–10 | 22–25 | 20 |
| 9–12 | 24–28 | 24 |
| 12+ | 28+ | 26 (regular mountain bike size) |

After size, the next factors to consider in choosing your child's bike are brakes and gears. First-time riders of any age are probably going to be better off with a single-speed, coaster-brake bicycle so that they can concentrate on balancing, pedaling, and recognizing potential hazards. Fiddling with gears, or with hand brakes that are too big for small hands, is frustrating for kids and parents. For older children capable of using gears, the additional range and speed they provide often make the upgrade worth the investment.

Biking always involves challenges, and incorporating kids into your biking routine adds to them. But as the growing number of kids' bike trailers, baby-toting bakfiets, and pint-size pedalers attests, lots of families are finding a way and having a blast doing it.

**CHRIS KEAM** has been delivering words by bike since his days as a rural paperboy. He began combining cycling and writing again in the mid-1990s, covering racing, travel, and industry news. With public interest in active transportation reborn, much of Chris's cycling coverage now chronicles the cultural and personal effects of the shift to cycling-friendly cities.

# Chapter Fifteen

# The Case for Internally Geared Bicycle Hubs

**Aaron Goss**

*Take* a look at the next bike you see. Chances are it will have a derailleur drivetrain, with a cluster of different-sized gears at the center of the rear wheel. I like to call them external gears. The modern bicycle's derailleur-based drivetrain has evolved with one purpose in mind: racing. There is a more sensible alternative for everyday bikes: the internally geared planetary hub (IGH). Along with fixed-gear or coaster (back-pedal) brake bikes, those with internal gears have a simple drivetrain that is more durable and easier to maintain. Belt- and shaft-drive bikes are also included in this category. Instead of being externally mounted on the rear hub, an internal gearing mechanism is contained within the rear hub. Like a derailleur system, it is controlled by a shifter mounted on or near the handlebars. The number of gears varies among models, from as few as two to as many as fourteen. The range of gears can be varied to suit your riding terrain.

Internal hubs offer several key advantages over derailleur systems.

## SIMPLICITY

Many folks do not like the look or complexity of a derailleur system. A bike just looks cool with a single front chainring and rear sprocket. The chain can't fall off, and there is nothing sticking out to get bent if you crash (or if the bike falls over).

## DURABILITY AND EASE OF MAINTENANCE

Internally geared hubs are easily ten times more durable than external gear (derailleur) systems. I have seen IGHs with tens of thousands of miles on them that show very little wear inside, even when they are used in all conditions. A wider ⅛-inch chain can be used to make your drivetrain even more durable than a derailleur system's ³⁄₃₂-inch wide chain.

The number one adjustment or repair we do at my shop — second to fixing flats, of course — is to rear derailleurs With an IGH the only maintenance required, besides cleaning the chain, is a yearly internal cleaning or oil change. Some hubs (such as the Rohloff Speedhub and Shimano Nexus) are sealed well enough to use an oil bath exactly like a manual transmission in a car. Less tightly sealed hubs, like a Sturmey-Archer 3-speed, require periodic oiling, as they seep oil slightly (which is normal).

IGHs are a better choice for wet, snowy, and dirty conditions. On bikes ridden for commuting in rainy cities like Seattle, road grime will quickly wear out a modern external-gear system, often in just one winter. On cold winter rides, it is common for derailleurs and rear cogs to freeze or become packed with snow, making shifting impossible.

## CHAIN-CASE COMPATIBILITY

Many bikes come with chain guards that do not completely enclose the chain. A chain case is a cover completely encasing the drivetrain. It can be made of metal, fabric, or plastic, and it covers the front chainring, chain, and rear cog. With a chain case, there is no need to roll up your right pant leg or use an ankle strap to keep your clothes clean and away from the chain. You can ride in your nicest clothes! Most simple-drivetrain bikes are chain-case compatible. Another benefit is that if your chain is protected by a case, it stays cleaner, and you only need to oil it once or twice a year.

## STATIONARY SHIFTING

With an IGH, you can shift gears just as you do with a stick-shift car, either stopped or moving. This is particularly useful if you have to stop suddenly or while riding uphill, which can make it difficult to get rolling again. With an IGH you simply shift down before starting off again. The only requirement, and one that is different from riding with derailleur gears, is that you shift when *not* pedaling: think of it like pushing in the clutch of a manual-transmission car. With an IGH, the rider usually has to ease up the pressure on the pedals while shifting. Many new hubs (such as the SRAM i-Motion 9) are designed to mimic the feel of derailleur shifting, and the manufacturers claim that you can shift while pedaling, but too much pressure on the pedals could still damage the internal mechanism.

Most IGH shifters are the twist-grip type, but other types are starting to be offered in response to demand. North Americans seem to prefer lever-type shifters, while Europeans don't mind twist grips. Several companies are even making after-market shifters that are IGH-compatible, like bar-con (handlebar-end) shifters and integrated brake and shift levers suitable for road bikes with drop handlebars.

## LOW OPERATING COST

Internally geared hubs, especially the high-end models, seem expensive at first, but when you compare the life span of an internally geared hub to that of a derailleur system, the cost of ownership goes way down. Most external gears will need replacing yearly on a bike that is ridden daily. Modern, race-inspired bicycle drivetrains are categorized by the number of cogs in the rear wheel's gear cluster, now between five and eleven. For example, a typical road or touring bike now has twenty or thirty gear combinations instead of the classic ten. To fit this many cogs into the available space, the teeth are made very narrow. Consequently, they wear out fast — and they can get very expensive to replace! If you compare IGH and derailleur systems of the same quality, internal gears are always less expensive in the long run.

## VARIATIONS

Although belt-drive bikes are being promoted as convenient alternatives to the conventional chain and derailleur drivetrain, they have disadvantages. Belt-drive bikes require a custom frame with an opening to pass the belt through, as belts cannot be connected like chains. Belt drives are brand specific and expensive to replace. They are not maintenance-free as advertised, and the gears can wear out, the way chain sprockets do. And your pant leg can still get caught in the belt.

Internal gears can also be driven by a shaft instead of a chain. Several companies currently make shaft-drive bicycles, but they are

*Internally geared hubs are a better choice for wet, snowy, and dirty conditions since all the gears are protected by a metal casing.*

either very expensive or of low quality. They often require modifications to the hub or shifting mechanism.

Some hubs combine an IGH with external derailleur gears. A common example is a 3-speed internal hub with a 9-speed rear cluster. This combination eliminates the need for a front derailleur and is particularly well suited for specialty bikes like folding, recumbent, and hand cycles.

Hubs are not the only place on the bicycle where you may find internal planetary gears. A Swiss company named Schlumpf makes an internal-geared 2-speed crankset that can be used on almost any bike, including fixed-gear, mountain, and road bikes — and unicycles. It is also popular on folding and recumbent bikes.

If internal gears are so great, then why are they not on every bike? Despite the advantages, many folks still cannot be persuaded to switch to an IGH, even when facing hundreds of dollars in repair costs for a derailleur system. The most common objections cited are lower efficiency, limited gear range, and weight.

IGH maker Rohloff has a very interesting article on efficiency for the techies out there (see below), but let's just say that in the real world, riding your bike in normal clothes to work, you won't really notice any power loss or extra weight. If you did, you would be sweating profusely, which of course you don't want to do on the way to work. When most people ride a bike downhill, there's a speed at which they choose to stop pedaling and start to coast and enjoy the ride. An IGH can be customized to suit your needs by changing the size of the front chainring and rear sprocket.

The hubs themselves may seem heavy, but when you add up all the parts that an internally geared hub replaces, you might even save weight! A typical IGH replaces one or two chainrings, all the rear cogs but one, a length of chain, the rear hub, both front and rear derailleurs, and the front shifter and cable. Some models even replace the brakes.

Some bikes when retrofitted with a simple drivetrain require a chain tensioner if they don't have a built-in way to tension the chain, like slotted horizontal rear dropouts or an eccentric (horizontally adjustable) bottom bracket.

Given that most objections can be overcome, it would seem that the main reason we don't see more internally geared bikes is unfamiliarity. Product managers (the folks who design bikes) perpetuate this, in part because they themselves are not familiar with internal gears. They may be afraid to take a risk on designing bikes with internal gears because they think bike shops (their customers) won't buy them.

Many people in the bike industry have disdained bikes with internal gears. They have been seen as cheap and old-fashioned, something only a college professor would ride. "If it doesn't have a Shimano rear derailleur, it will not sell" was the mantra all through the 1990s. Ironically, Shimano has recently helped promote the use of internal gears with their Nexus and Alfine IGHs. They are seeing some competition: SRAM made a big splash with their amazing i-Motion 9 hub, and Sturmey-Archer offers many hubs with lots of different options.

Bike shops traditionally have been afraid to stock anything unfamiliar or out of the ordinary. Because bicycle mechanics is seen as a temporary college job for many folks, shops find it hard to train and retain experienced, career-minded staff. Being enthusiasts themselves, bike-shop employees often get caught up in promoting the latest cool and trendy technology, even if it is unproven. Ironically, a common test of skill for bike mechanics is to overhaul a Sturmey-Archer 3-speed hub!

Derailleur systems do have their advantages. Replacement parts are often inexpensive (though upgrading can be very expensive). They *seem* easy for cyclists to work on themselves. The whole system is lightweight and offers a wide gear range. For these reasons, external gears are well suited for long-distance touring and racing bikes. However, many world-touring cyclists still choose the Rohloff Speedhub. It is an internally geared 14-speed hub, arguably the world's best. It offers the same range as a typical mountain bike. Loyal customers praise the low maintenance and extreme durability of the hub. We have seen several that have traveled more than fifty thousand miles with no wear! Try that with a derailleur system.

The disadvantages of derailleur gears are well known to your local bike mechanic or any first-time rider. They're complicated to learn to shift, especially on hills. Many folks just give up and ride in a high gear all the time. External gears require constant maintenance, cleaning, and fine-tuning. Modern indexed derailleurs and shifters are finicky and cannot tolerate exposure to much real-world dirt and grime before needing adjustment or cleaning, or just wearing out.

As internally geared hubs gain in popularity (see the bike list at the end of this article), replacement parts will become more widely available. Retrofitting will become easier and more common, especially for city riding. In any case, since internally geared hubs are so durable, replacement parts are rarely needed, and when they are, they are often inexpensive, small internal parts. The internal gears themselves rarely wear out!

IGHs are perfect for many applications, including cargo bikes capable of hauling hundreds of pounds. Currently, warranties typically do not cover use on cargo bikes, but companies are starting to make cargo-specific versions. SRAM makes a cargo version of their Pentasport 5-speed hub. Shimano offers the red-stripe Nexus 8-speed, and both the Rohloff and NuVinci hubs are suitable for cargo-bike use.

I think the low maintenance, durability, and reliability of an IGH outweigh any drawbacks. Internally geared bikes are as reliable as an automobile and just as tolerant of everyday use. Not many folks want to clean their bike and oil the chain when they get home after a party, working late, or riding home in the rain. They want the bike to just be ready to go the next day. People want a bike that can be ridden hard and put away wet. Internal gears deliver that!

Here's a selection of 2011 production bikes with internal gears:

> Bianchi Milano
> Cannondale Hooligan 3 and Adventure 2
> Civia Hyland & Loring
> Elektra Amsterdam
> Moots Comooter
> Novara Transfer
> Raleigh Superbe Roadster
> Torker Graduate

Technical links:

hubstripping.wordpress.com
www.karstilo.net/hpv/technik/index.php
www.rideyourbike.com/internalgears.shtml
www.rohloff.de/en/technology/speedhub/efficiency
_measurement/index.html

Current makers:
NuVinci
Rohloff
Schlumpf
Shimano
SRAM
Sturmey-Archer

Former makers whose hubs you may find at the used-bike shop:
Bendix
F&S
Sachs

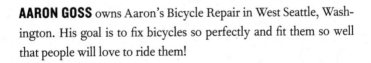

**AARON GOSS** owns Aaron's Bicycle Repair in West Seattle, Washington. His goal is to fix bicycles so perfectly and fit them so well that people will love to ride them!

## Chapter Sixteen

# Light Up Your Life

**Lars Goeller**

*The* electric light, wrote Marshall McLuhan, is pure information; it is a medium without a message. The light creates an experience that wouldn't otherwise exist: on a bike it is a medium that the rider fills with black asphalt, dirt paths, and overhanging branches. It doesn't matter if a light is used for brain surgery or bike riding at night; some things can only be done safely with an electric light.

Cyclists out at night adopt a few different styles to deal with the danger of being fast, quiet, and only lightly armored while mingling with car traffic. On the deadlier end of the spectrum, there are the ninjas. Dressed in black and gliding silently through the darkened streets, they trust in their catlike agility to save them from disaster. Without so much as a single reflector on their bikes, nothing else will. Then there are the moving stop signs. These are riders who wear highly reflective clothing in the hope that a combination of street lamps and car headlights will keep them visible.

## On Bicycles

These people may well be a thousand times brighter than the ninjas, but that isn't really saying a lot. A driver making a sharp left turn will probably lose sight of them somewhere as the car's headlights swing around, and then just barely catch a flash of reflected light as the "stop sign" disappears underneath the car.

Thrifty folks buy tiny LED lights from Planet Bike or Cateye that strap onto every part of their bike, on the assumption that on smooth, well-lit city streets they don't need to see: they just need to be seen. This works to a certain degree, but rocks, sewer grates, and streetcar tracks still lie in the shadows beyond the dim little circles of illumination, ready to trap wheels and pop tires. Besides, drivers

aren't watching for tiny LEDs: they're looking for light shining on things from a hundred feet away and reflecting off all those fancy street signs.

Admittedly, these tiny LEDs are the lights I use. First, they're cheap (a trait I share); and if you ride carefully and slow down at intersections, they're perfectly safe most of the time. But if most of the time isn't often enough for you, then buy the brightest lights available. Maybe you've got money, or maybe you've got sense, or maybe you just don't want to end up being a lesson to others. But with a set of super-bright lights, you create a bubble of daylight that can be seen for blocks.

Anyone can buy a high-powered light that will fry a driver's retinas at fifty paces, or throw down fifteen bucks at the local bike shop to buy enough LED lights to transform a bike into a lively Christmas celebration. But finding lights that express your style and that of your bike takes a bit more effort.

Environmentally conscious people who want to avoid disposable or even rechargeable batteries can take advantage of their own pedal power to create light. What's great about these systems is that the light you use to see is no longer a medium without content, but a message about how you feel about the Earth and your relationship with it. There are three main options. There are traditional friction dynamo systems: these run on electricity generated by a small wheel rubbing against the bike's tire as it rotates. There are also hub dynamo systems, made by the German company Schmidt and Son and by Shimano, among others. These are also powered by the wheel's rotation but are mounted inside the wheel hub. Both of these types of systems are now far more efficient and require less pedaling effort than the old tire burners some of us remember. A third creative solution involves attaching magnets to the bike's spokes to generate electricity in a way similar to that of electric motors. You can find instructions online to build them yourself or buy them from Reelight or Magtenlight.

All of these systems can easily generate enough electricity to power LED lights without batteries. The only thing riders have to remember is that power is effort dependent: the generator only works while you're pedaling. Though Magtenlight claims that its lights stay on for four minutes after you've stopped moving, this might not be true of your setup, so be careful at stoplights, and don't forget your reflectors. There are also solar-powered lighting options, but these require that either the lights or the entire bike be placed outside for several hours in direct sun to charge — not a practical option for most riders.

Light isn't the only message; the object that creates light can be a message as well. There are a lot of unimaginatively designed lights on the market, and it can be hard to see the difference between one array of LEDs and another. So if you've built your bike around a theme, choose lights to match. If you ride a retro bike, your lights might be modeled after the old-style bullet lights, which have a great retro look (check out www.chubbyscruisers .com for an example). Despite the classic design, these now use LEDs and are really energy efficient. If your bike is all about flash and bang, a California company called MonkeyLectric can light up your bike's spokes with any kind of image or video you want. Of course, at $2,000 the system is not for the faint of wallet, but the company also offers a spoke-lighting system that features LEDs in customizable designs and colors and costs only $65 per wheel. If you're into bicycle activism, the LightLane uses a laser to create the image of a bike lane around the rider, complete with the symbol of a cyclist often seen on bike lanes and signs. It makes a strong statement about safety and the status of cyclists on city streets and does it with style.

If you can't find a ready-made light that truly expresses your own style, a few minutes of online research will lead you to a trove of ideas and instructional videos for making your own lights — everything from strips of LEDs that turn your bike into a Lightcycle to people machining their own aluminum casings to accommodate lights bright enough to go mountain biking at night. With a little effort and imagination, you can add your own ideas to the mix.

So get out there and show people that light is a message *and* a medium, and then create your own lights and your own style. Just remember there are laws about the color of the lights you can point in front of and behind your bike; consult your local regulations before going crazy with the style.

Age and experience have changed **LARS GOELLER** from a car-dodging Torontonian to a mellow Vancouverite who's happiest when he's just riding along.

## Chapter Seventeen

# The Art and Craft of Handmade Bicycles

**Amy Walker**

*The* most influential people in bike culture today are those making and riding handmade bicycles. The intimate relationship between builder and rider is based on fine-tuning all aspects of the bicycle's fit, function, and aesthetics. An explosion of interest via the Internet and consumer exhibitions has put handmade frame builders in the spotlight. Each one-of-a-kind design is created to suit an individual's needs and tastes, but when these designs are shared online, the appreciation of bicycle art and science spreads far beyond the individual rider to become public knowledge, increasing the demand for better bicycles. With a strong and growing community of artisan bicycle builders and interested buyers for their work, bicycle craftsmanship and education are flourishing.

Assuming that you have access to a wide enough selection of bike brands, an off-the-shelf bike works well for most people. Scheduling a professional fitting and buying the best bike you can afford will usually be satisfactory. But for people who are very tall, very short, or unusually proportioned, finding a comfortable bike can be next to impossible. Consequently, until very recently, the demand for hand-built bicycles came from high-performance athletes, wealthy aficionados, or cyclists with unusual physiques.

The artisan bicycle builder takes into account the riders' body measurements as well as their strength, weight, and speed and style of riding. A bicycle has relatively few parts, but those parts have rather complex relationships. To make a functioning bicycle may not be hard, but to craft a great bicycle that meets an individual's needs perfectly requires talent, knowledge, skill, and a significant collection of jigs and machinery. Building a bike from scratch takes time, and the most sought-after builders have wait lists several years long. Because of the materials and hours required, prices for handmade frames start at around $2,000. Depending on the details and components, complete bikes generally range from about $4,000 to $10,000.

You can find handmade builders making bikes from all the usual materials, and some unusual ones: steel, titanium, aluminum, carbon fiber, and even bamboo. However, steel is favored among hand builders for its strength, versatility, and ease of repair, which also makes it a better environmental choice.

Though fit and functionality are often cited as the most important aspects of bicycle design, in the current market, according to builder Joseph Ahearne, people are very interested in aesthetics: "In the end, what people want is something totally unique and made just for them."

A multitude of national and regional events now celebrate

handmade bicycles and their makers. The largest and best known is the North American Handmade Bicycle Show (NAHBS), first held in 2005, which has grown steadily from 23 exhibitors and 700 attendees in its first year to 174 exhibitors and 7,300 attendees in 2011 (www.handmadebicycleshow.com). The show, which is held in a different city every year, features utilitarian city and cargo bikes as well as sleek sports and racing machines. In 2009, to set a standard of quality for the show, NAHBS restricted entry to builders who had completed at least fifty frames or been in business for a minimum of two years. According to Don Walker, the show's founder and a frame builder himself, "That's about as long as it takes to start knowing your stuff."

Because of the exposure these builders have received through consumer shows and the Internet, hundreds of people are now signing up for frame-building classes at schools like the United Bicycle Institute in Ashland, Oregon (www.bikeschool.com), which is celebrating its thirtieth anniversary this year. The handmade bicycle revival is part of a larger trend of appreciating craftsmanship and supporting local small industry. UBI president Ron Sutphin also sees a personal need among his students: "I think that some of the younger people don't have a lot of the craft and art and shop classes that we had when we were going through school, and I think there's a certain amount of pent-up creativity, and if there's just something accessible for them to express themselves, it just starts coming out."

UBI has been offering frame-building classes for twenty years now, and the classes have always been full. In the early days, most students expressed the intention to pursue frame building as a career, but now, when students are asked about their goals, that emphasis has shifted. Sutphin continues: "I think part of it is that there is so much free information, and people have been communicating about how hard it is to make a go of it as a business, and in the average class now, when we go around the room, people tend to say, 'Well, I just want to see what it's all about, maybe check it out as a hobby, build a frame or two and see where it goes.'" When asked how many UBI graduates go on to become successful frame builders, Sutphin offers this estimate: "If we defined it as their sole source of income, and you've got a recognizable brand and you've been sustaining that for five years or more, it's fewer than 1 percent."

Despite the often-solitary nature of their work, the loosely knit community of builders has a somewhat tribal feeling, with a healthy mixture of competition and camaraderie. Among those who've succeeded in the business, there are many dynamic characters whose brands have evolved around their creative vision, commitment to technical excellence, and personality. Though there is no guild system for the bicycle craft (like the traditional progression from apprentice to journeyman and master), there are distinguishable generations of builders working in the field. Among them are veteran builders like Bruce Gordon, Stephen Bilenky, and Richard Sachs. Newer to the craft but no less dedicated are builders like Joseph Ahearne, Sascha White of Vanilla Workshop, the Sycip brothers, Natalie Ramsland of Sweetpea Bicycles, Marty Walsh of Geekhouse, Mitch Pryor of MAP Bicycles, and Jordan Huffnagel. There is a long list of builders, and it is challenging to choose only a few names to mention.

The heart and soul of the modern bicycle builder are personified by Joseph Ahearne (www.ahearnecycles.com), whose bikes are inscribed with the words "Hand built with love and fury in Portland, Oregon." If these sound like the words of a poet or a philosopher, it is because Ahearne cares and thinks deeply about all aspects of his craft and pursues the dream with devotion. As he says: "We've been reminding people that beautiful one-of-a-kind bikes can really be made by building them with our hands, adding to them our quirks and flairs and design conceptions and creativity. Our business model is based on building bikes that people are going to have and to love and to ride for the rest of their lives.... It is assurance (or near enough to it, we hope) in the highest quality. It's supporting local economy, the crafts, and the craftsperson — a real honest-to-goodness human instead of some vague brand image imported from overseas. And this doesn't even start into the positive environmental aspects."

If all this starry-eyed enthusiasm seems too good to be true, occasionally it is. Some words of caution: when choosing a frame builder, make sure he or she has experience and a good reputation for delivering on promises. Your relationship will require careful communication, important decisions, and a lot of money. Make sure that the type of bike you want is one that the builder already knows how to make. Otherwise you might end up "eating the first pancake," an uncomfortable position in which Nancy Williams, of

Portland, Oregon, found herself a few years ago. Nancy waited two years for the bike of her dreams, only to find that because it was a style of bike that the builder had not made before, it didn't fit properly and was uncomfortable to ride. So she sold it on consignment and bought a Rivendell. "The guy who sold it for me insinuated that there are a lot of people who have had difficult experiences with handmade bike builders who have a lot to learn about the industry and about working with people." So buyer beware!

Oregon Manifest is a biennial bicycle design-and-build competition based in Portland that is centered on the craft as well as the message that bikes are transportation (http://oregonmanifest.com). The 2011 event includes thirty-four professional builders and six student teams who are challenged with creating "the ultimate utility bicycle." The show's director, Jocelyn Sycip, stresses that the show is all about driving innovation in the field: "Small builders are more at the forefront of the commuter, utility, and cargo-bike movement. They really have been paying close attention to that category in a way that the larger industry has not. It's been exciting to see their influence carry over to the larger manufacturers." Oregon Manifest is unique among the handmade shows for featuring a rigorous road test for all entries on a course that includes hills and off-road sections, with checkpoints to evaluate several mandatory bike features.

Sycip (who is married to the builder Jay Sycip) recalls that until recently, the world of custom frame makers was pretty obscure: "In 2004 we came out with a calendar called Top Tube, and all of the builders got naked. There were pictures of them in their shops basically just making fun of themselves. It came from this conversation about how ridiculous it was, in the Bay Area in particular, to promote hand-built bikes. People who knew about it were pretty excited about it, but the movement wasn't there yet. It was very underground. Then NAHBS came along and shed a lot more light on it, and has built and been really positive for bicycles as a cultural movement."

In 2009 United Bicycle Institute opened a second workshop in Portland, Oregon. Even Ron Sutphin, who has spent twenty-five years of his life educating people about how to fix and build bikes, says he's been surprised by the way people there are embracing and supporting the craft: "Oregon has always been very sustainability minded, and Portland even more so. Some people just talk about it, but a lot of people live it — and there are people here that want a nice bike, they know it's sustainable, and it fits into their lifestyle. They're not going to go buy a $400 or $500 Trek or Specialized or Giant. With a handmade bike, they know where it's made, and they'd rather support a craftsperson: Tony Pereira or Joseph Ahearne or Natalie Ramsland or whomever....I think almost everybody knows now that you can go to a local craftsperson and get a handmade bike. The word is out."

*Chapter Eighteen*

# Cargo Bikes
## Finley Fagan

*Hauling* stuff by pedal power is nothing new. In 1898, when Morris Worksman established Worksman Cycles in New York City, he believed that a well-designed cargo bike could replace the horse and wagon. Henry Ford begged to differ, and so King Car all but killed the fledgling cargo bike. The towns, cities, and suburbs of North America grew to rely on and reinforce the convenience of the automobile, bicycles were largely relegated to the role of toys, and cargo cycling didn't evolve much beyond the factory floor. But in the late 1990s, almost a century after Worksman Cycles built its first heavy-duty trike, cargo biking started making a comeback on the streets of North America, with hot spots in Portland, Seattle, the Bay Area, New York, and Colorado.

So what do we know about cargo cyclists, this curious breed who set themselves up for hauling heavy or cumbersome loads? Sales figures indicate that the buyers of cargo bikes are just as likely to be male as they are female, and that the new cargo is not strictly business. While some entrepreneurs and couriers are zipping around laden with mail, organic fruit and vegetables, baked goods, coffee, and Christmas trees, for others cargo cycling is all about the everyday A to B — getting the kids to school, the pets to the park, the groceries into the fridge, the fridge into the new apartment.

Vik Banerjee, the self-confessed bike geek behind the *Lazy Randonneur* blog, has noticed two major groups leading the renewed interest in cargo bikes: "Bike geeks that want to ride bikes more" and "families and individuals who are trying to be green and not drive...not necessarily bike people in general, but they see cargo bikes as a way to replace car trips." The wheel has turned full circle. Ironically, King Car has been responsible for both the collapse and the renaissance of cargo biking in North America.

Nicole and Anthony Stout are parents who have taken cargo cycling one step further, having now celebrated three years without a car. I was interested to find out how car-free living is going for them and their two young children in suburban Colorado.

"Living car-free in suburban America requires a pretty significant mind-set change," says Anthony. "Your world becomes smaller and bigger at the same time. You may not stray as far and wide as you do with a car, but because you see so much more and experience the world in a different way, your local world seems bigger.... At first we thought we'd have to save up and buy a Prius or something, then we discovered [cargo] bikes do the job nicely. Living car-free is very healthy for our kids. They see so much more, smell so much more, notice so much more than when they go someplace via car."

Anthony acknowledges that living car-free in the suburban United States has not always been easy. "As with most things, there is a point of diminishing returns. Living 80 percent car-free is very doable; going the next 20 percent, up to totally car-free, requires at least as much effort as, if not more than, the first 80 percent." But Anthony is quick to add, "There are few experiences that we don't enjoy more by bike than we did by car."

For those wanting to get a taste of cargo cycling, a cheap and easy way to start is to make a regular bike more cargo-friendly with any combination of racks, bags, child seats, and baskets. Play around and see what your bike is capable of carrying and what errands it can conquer. People in the developing world have been mastering this skill for decades.

If you feel the desire to increase your cargo capacity with a heavy-duty cargo bike or trike, the good news is that handling becomes second nature after a brief adjustment period. The extra weight makes for slower starts and slower stops, but riding is not difficult on flat terrain once you have built up momentum. For hillier terrain, consider stronger brakes and lower gearing, and choose between an electric assist and an extra-buff pair of legs. On your wheels, fatter tires, beefier rims, and more spokes will help cushion loads. Keeping your load low and balancing it on both sides will enhance stability.

Nowadays there is a cargo-hauling option for almost every kind of terrain, use, and budget. So, what's your cargo beast of choice? Here are some of the options.

## LONG JOHN STYLE

Perhaps the most iconic image of cargo cycling is a parent riding a two-wheeled bakfiets laden with children (*bakfiets* is a generic term for any "box bike," whereas Bakfiets is a popular Dutch bike company). With its plywood box in front, fitted out with child seats, harnesses, and canopy, and a low step-through frame and stable parking stand, these heavy-duty, ultrapractical cargo bikes have become a huge hit with families across the pancake flats of the Netherlands. The two-wheeled Bakfiets was one of the many updates on the 1930s Danish Long John, a long-wheelbase bike defined by its sturdy load-carrying area directly in front of the rider, low center of gravity, and a front wheel steered via a rod linkage below the load carrier.

European models from Bakfiets, WorkCycles, Monark, and Bullitt are available in North America, along with a growing range of locally designed bakfiets that address the demand for lower price tags, lower bike weight, or lower gearing for hilly terrain. These include a nimble cargo bike from Bilenky, the Cetma Cargo bike, Joe Bike's Shuttlebug, CAT's Long Haul, the super-stylish Metrofiets, and Tom's Cargo Bikes, with their DIY hillbilly charm.

## LONGTAILS

Longtail bikes (with one exception, the Madsen) have no single box for hauling loads. Instead the rear part of the frame is extended so that the rear wheel is about fifteen inches farther behind the seat than on a conventional bike, allowing bulky items to be strapped on either side of or above the rear wheel. Smaller items can be tucked away in large rear bags. Optional seats for children and adults can be fastened to a platform above the rear wheel.

Longtails have been around in the Netherlands since the 1970s, but North American interest spiked with the introduction of Xtracycle in the late nineties. Xtracycle's bolt-on FreeRadical is a frame extension that can be retrofitted onto almost any regular bicycle, lengthening the wheelbase and turning it into a longtail cargo bike.

Other North American designers followed, offering a range of sturdy one-piece longtail bikes capable of carrying loads of more than four hundred pounds. These include the versatile Surly Big Dummy (capable of epic off-road adventures); the rock-solid,

no-frills Yuba Mundo; the big-name Kona Ute; and the stylish Xtracycle Radish.

## TRICYCLES

Trikes, the often-forgotten siblings of bikes, found widespread popularity in Christiania, an eccentric quarter of Copenhagen, in the 1980s. Christiania Bikes developed a small, front-loading trike with a large plywood box capable of carrying up to 220 pounds of kids and freight. It became a Copenhagen icon and spurred more three-wheeled designs from the Danish company Nihola and the Dutch companies Bakfiets and WorkCycles (all imported into the United States).

Homegrown cargo trikes include Portland's TerraCycle Cargo Monster (a recumbent trike with an Xtracycle frame extension), Montana's Lightfoot Trike, and offerings from the venerable Worksman Cycles of New York City, which has been selling industrial trikes for more than a century. There is some risk of tipping a trike, especially at high speed around corners, so the word on the street is to go slow and keep the rubber side down.

**FINLEY FAGAN** likes bikes, and he likes them fat. His ride of choice is a trusty longtail cargo bike that he abuses with ridiculous loads, often topped with a doggy copilot.

Thanks to Henry Cutler, owner and director of WorkCycles, for information on the history of cargo biking.

## Chapter Nineteen

# Freakbikes
Megulon-5

## WHAT IS A FREAKBIKE?

A freakbike is a bicycle that has been cut up and put back together in a way that might not make obvious sense. Freakbikes appear wherever piles of cheap bikes can be found. Their forms may evolve from a common starting point, like the chopper, the tallbike, or the swingbike, and there are standard ways to construct one, but there is no right way to design or build one.

I made my first chopper by sawing off a few extra fork blades and hammering them onto another bike's fork. It was the obvious method for someone who only had a hacksaw and a wrench handy (the wrench was used to hammer the blades on). I got tired of jamming the forks back together every time they loosened up and dumped me on the pavement, so I learned how to weld them. Soon enough, I needed to know how a longer fork would ride, and to do this I had to change the head-tube angle and lengthen the frame to keep my weight in front of the rear hub. This adaptive process is how freakbikes are made, whether they are shiny and built by skilled fabricators or jagged and built by backyard hackers.

At this very moment, somebody with a hacksaw, a welder, and a pile of bikes is cutting them up and putting them back together, learning what works and what doesn't, often the hard way. If you make one, you will wonder what it would be like if you remade it differently. If a part breaks, you will saw it off and weld on a new one. If you see a particular piece of metal on the ground, you will wonder how to incorporate it into your ride. It doesn't have to end until it gets thrown into the river.

The only things that a bike needs to qualify as a freakbike are

to have been individually made and to be ridden in the real world. Show bikes, low-rider garage queens, and mass-produced bikes are different species. With each bike boom, bike manufacturers have noticed how their products are being abused and have started producing similar but safer versions. Those aren't quite the same, although freakbike builders love it when the wrecked ones find their way into their bike piles.

There isn't much point in trying to rigorously define what a freakbike is, however. Many tallbikes were built in the late 1800s for lamplighters to ride as they turned streetlights on and off. Factories made and sold them in Chicago. The beginning of the bicycle era saw an explosion of designs, including geared rear-steering high-wheelers, five-wheeled tallbikes, and dog-assisted dicycles. Were these freakbikes? Who cares?

## WHY WOULD ANYBODY MAKE AND RIDE A FREAKBIKE?

Well, have you ever taped a stick to your pencil to try to write faster? Put bricks in your basket for better traction in the snow? Worn a suit to the bar to see if it made you gayer? Are you tired of the confines of dignity? Do you want to prepare for an unknown future with variable gravity?

I started making freakbikes to see if I could: to see what kind of bike I could make and ride. Bikes were something I rode and tinkered with every day. I was already putting together rides from scrounged parts; why not try and put them together differently? Riding a bike was automatic; why not ride something that would take some physical and mental effort? It was a practical joke that

I played on myself. Sure, I can get to work on this thing. No, it's normal to see my legs doing that. Once I started, I had to continue challenging myself to make more. Freakbikes changed the way I thought. It became a compulsion, and others should probably be warned about it. Is this making any sense? If it isn't, go saw your bike in half and weld it back together, and you may understand.

## WHAT HAPPENS TO THE FREAKBIKE RIDER?

Freakbike riders interact with the road, and the world, differently when they're on their bikes. The rider will see the same places in different ways, and must work to do what was once easy. The familiar becomes unfamiliar. Things make sense that didn't make sense before.

This, combined with the unavoidable stupidity and pointlessness of most freakbikes, brings about a change in behavior. I've never met someone who rode a freakbike for any length of time and wasn't affected by it. The rider will visit different streets and encounter different people. New vistas open up. This may sound like the same hippie, life-changing bullshit that everyone has heard too much of, but it's the truth. It's a kind of freedom similar to wandering a city where the signs are written in a different language. Nobody will hassle you if you stop wearing pants, because you might be an ambassador from a rich and exotic country. Nobody can tell you you're doing it wrong.

## WHY FREAKBIKES?

Why not just dump washers in your underwear, or vow to think in pig Latin, or become a vegan? There's something about bikes that is fundamental to humanity. They're a very recent invention, yet they're obvious now, a part of us. The human race will never forget how to make bicycles. It may be hard to see these days, now that bikes are fashion accessories for so many, but for bike people, our bikes are part of us. They are us. They define how we flow through the city and meet other people. They change us, but they stay out of the way, and they don't come between us. Besides, anyone can learn to make and ride them.

I probably haven't convinced you that this isn't an incredibly moronic activity to undertake — I haven't convinced myself, either. But I have no regrets. Freakbike riding has made me able to do things I wasn't able to before. I've jousted, derbyed, and set my bike on fire. I've ridden a brakeless tallbike in traffic and floated an amphibious pedal-jet boat over an underwater toxic-waste dump. I've watched my  bike come unexpectedly apart while I rode it. I've been hassled and cheered by strangers. Now I am able to do difficult things because I can remind myself that I've been knocked off my bike and got right back on it, again and again. I can smuggle contraband while singing at the top of my lungs. I can ask girls out on dates after crashing in front of them.

Flippin' superpowers. Is that enough of a reason?

**MEGULON-5** is a founder of C.H.U.N.K. 666, a mutant bicycle club and civic betterment society in Portland, Oregon. He has left a record of his accomplishments at http://dclxvi.org/chunk.

## Chapter Twenty

# Fixed-Gear Bikes on the Street
*A Dangerous Fad?*

## Martin Neale

*Fixed-gear* refers to a bicycle drivetrain that has no free-wheel (the ratcheting mechanism that allows you to coast, or to backpedal without going backward). If the wheels are turning, then so are the pedals, and vice versa.

In recent years you've probably become aware of the "fixed-gear trend" or "fixie culture." Mainstream media stories about this trend usually involve fashionable twenty-somethings careening (and skidding) around the world's cities on brakeless track bikes, crappy old 10-speeds, or, sometimes, nice old road bikes converted to fixed-gear.

The current spike in popularity of urban fixed-gear riding, particularly on track bikes, can be traced back to New York City messenger style and international messenger/courier culture in general. It is said that New York city's messengers were influenced by Jamaican immigrants delivering goods on bikes either brought from home or styled after them.

More recently, this culture has been influenced by Japanese *keirin* (track) racing. It's de rigueur to have parts stamped "NJS," denoting authorization by the Japanese Bicycling Association, keirin racing's governing body. Though NJS approval is hardly necessary for riding on North American streets, the parts are bound to be beautifully designed and made, and the fact that keirin racers are infamous for hard living just adds to the street cred.

Bike messengers have always enjoyed a certain mystique, so it made sense that identifiable messenger accoutrements — clothes, bags, track bikes, and U-lock holsters — would eventually become fashion statements. With all the turnover and seasonal employment in the trade, there are also a lot of ex-messengers riding around in their old gear, perpetuating the trend.

In the interest of full disclosure, I have more than six years of courier experience, and I feel that the fashion and gear refinements developed by the messenger (and "posenger") bike industry are generally damn good-looking. Of course, any trend that is so identifiable invites ridicule, stereotyping, and ignorant assumptions from the media and general public. Providing fodder is a small but highly visible percentage of participants who barely know how to ride a regular bicycle, let alone a brakeless track bike. Others are finely honed athlete-performers, inspiring to watch.

Somewhere in the middle are those who just want to get around quietly, efficiently, affordably, and, may I say, elegantly.

The point is, there is no reason to dismiss fixed-gear as merely a fashion trend.

The fact that all bicycles were fixed-gear (or fixed-wheel, in some countries) before the introduction of the freewheel around 1900 does not, as some have asserted, make contemporary use of fixed-gear merely nostalgic. True track-racing bikes have always been fixed, and racing rules stipulate that they be ridden without brakes (paradoxical as it sounds, this increases safety for velo-drome racers in a tight pack). And all along, fixed-gear bicycles with frames designed for stability and comfort, equipped with brakes and various accessories, have been used for fitness and transportation.

## WHY FIXED-GEAR?

Before their marriage and move to Canada from England in the 1950s, my mother and father rode fixed-gear bikes together. Were these young people trendsetters? No, they were simply riding for transportation, pleasure, and, in my father's case, occasional time-trial racing or training. In fact, those forms of riding and fixed-gear use are still fairly common in England, especially in cycling clubs.

One of the factors contributing to the choice of fixed-gear in postwar Europe, among other places, was the cost and availability of bicycle parts. The setup was, and remains, simpler and more durable, and therefore cheaper.

Another factor, aside from style, is the closer mechanical connection between the rider and the road. Often described (sometimes derisively) as an almost mystical connection between rider, machine, and road, a fixed-gear drivetrain does in fact provide unparalleled feedback and control. Because the pedals and wheels drive each other, a subtle slowing of the legs also gently slows the bike. More forceful back-pressure on the pedals has a corresponding effect. With experience, the rider can adjust speed continuously, and often subconsciously, in response to conditions. This kind of control has additional advantages on wet, slippery roads, because the rider doesn't have to rely as much on the reduced stopping power of wet brake pads and can feel immediately when the drive wheel is losing traction.

Fixed-gear bikes are usually single-speed, but single-speed bikes are not necessarily fixed-gear. In the late 1940s, Sturmey-Archer offered the ASC, a 3-speed, fixed-gear hub that was recently reintroduced as the S3X model. For fixed-gear veterans as well as initiates, the S3X is ideal for recreation or transportation. There are also commonly available rear hubs that are double-sided, known as "flip-flop" hubs: these can have different-sized cogs on the two sides, or a combination of a fixed cog and a freewheel. To switch between the two, the rider removes the rear wheel and flips it around. This kind of setup increases the versatility of the bike and the terrain the rider can tackle. However, a hub for fixed-gear use should include a smaller-diameter, reverse-threaded portion outside the cog thread, to allow installation of a lock ring to prevent the fixed cog from spinning off when the rider applies back-pressure to the pedals.

Fixed-gear bikes are not necessarily track bikes, but track bikes are always fixed-gear. Track-specific bikes, designed exclusively for power and speed, have very steep frame angles and short wheelbases, very little clearance between their narrow tires

and the frame, and no facility for attachment of racks, fenders, or water bottles, and they may not be built to accept hand brakes at all.

## SAFETY AND GETTING STARTED

My choice and recommendation of a frameset or bike for urban and transportation fixed-gear riding would allow for at least a front, hand-operated brake for emergencies, somewhat more relaxed frame angles, and a longer wheelbase for handling comfort and more clearance between the rider's feet and the wheels. The frameset should also accept wider tires, with sufficient clearance and attachment points for fenders, and mounts for additional accessories like water bottles and racks.

Some people believe that a fixed-gear bike is somehow less safe than one with another style of drivetrain. A look at various factors indicates otherwise.

Let me plainly state that fixed-gear street riding without at least a front hand brake cannot be considered safe. A properly working front brake provides about 70 percent of a bike's braking capability. Speed modulation is beautifully simple with a fixed-gear, but slowing or stopping the rear wheel is ineffectual for emergency stops because the rear wheel trails behind your weight and will quickly begin to skid, especially as weight is transferred to the front wheel. But a properly equipped and maintained fixed-gear bike is no more dangerous than any other style.

Derailleur-equipped bikes are vulnerable to at least three common potential dangers. The first is caused by a worn-out or mismatched chain and rear cogs, or a dirty or maladjusted rear derailleur cable. Pushing hard on the pedals can result in the chain skipping over the teeth of the rear cog, giving the rider the feeling of having stepped into a big hole, which can result in a bad fall. Fixed-gear cogs, with their large-profile teeth, rarely get worn down to this point.

The second hazard is caused by a very common maladjustment of the rear derailleur inner-limit "L" screw. This allows the chain to disengage from the largest cog and get jammed in the rear-wheel spokes, stopping the wheel dead and potentially causing a great deal of damage to both bike and rider. Obviously, this failure is impossible with a fixed-gear drivetrain.

The third problem is caused by a failure of the freewheel mechanism, which can wear out or seize up because of contaminants, particularly in harsh winter climates. The end result can be either an unexpected (and unreliable) fixed-gear effect, so that coasting is no longer possible, or the exact opposite: forward freewheeling or slippage. Either possibility can lead to loss of control.

What *is* possible with a poorly maintained fixed-gear, with similarly disastrous results, is to have a too-loose chain jump off the chainring or rear cog and jam your rear wheel. There should only be a quarter to half an inch of movement in the middle of the bottom run of chain when it's pushed up or down. This should be tested carefully, throughout the full rotation of the cranks. A chain that's set too tight can also cause premature wear or even break dangerously while in use.

A valid but exaggerated concern with fixed drivetrains is pedal strike on the pavement while cornering. A fixed-gear rider can't coast around a corner with the inside pedal up. On the inside of the turn, a moving pedal can hit the ground at the lowest point of its rotation. To avoid this problem, shorter cranks and narrower pedals are preferred, and the rider must be attentive to curbs and other obstacles. But, for the record, the only time I've gone "over the high side" from a pedal strike was with a freewheel!

Knee injury from fixed-gear riding is sometimes cited as a risk, but it is unlikely if the bicycle is properly fitted and suitably geared (in fact, there's anecdotal evidence, at least, that gentle fixed-gear riding can strengthen damaged knees). Incorrect saddle height and use of too high a gear are common mistakes with any style of bike, and either can contribute to long-term injury. Riding fixed and brakeless on the street, relying on hard backpedaling or locking the legs for stopping, will probably inflict knee damage, especially for older people.

The rider should always have a secure connection to the pedals yet be able to release from them if necessary. Without some form of foot retention at high cadences it can be difficult to keep contact with the pedals, and trying to regain it once lost may mean slowing considerably (another reason to have a hand brake!). Toe clips and straps have made a big comeback in recent years for their simple effectiveness, affordability — and style! With some practice, and pedals equipped with a flip tab, they are easy to engage. The strap needn't be so tight as to make exit difficult. With practice and proper installation, tightening and loosening the straps on the fly is a quick and simple matter. Clipless pedal systems are another option that requires special shoes.

Some people are afraid that they will forget they can't coast and will get bucked off the bike by the rotating pedal. Although it's not uncommon for a new fixed-gear rider to forget once or twice and experience a brief moment of panic, it rarely causes a fall.

Pant legs and shoelaces must be secured so that they won't get caught in an unstoppable drivetrain. Also, when cleaning or working on a fixed-gear, it's vital to prevent rags or fingers from getting caught in moving parts: the wheel and chain won't stop. Digits have been lost!

Really, the point is that all bicycles need to be properly equipped, maintained, and ridden with care.

Fixed-gear bicycles' disadvantages are also their advantages: namely, you have only one gear, which can make hill climbs very challenging, and you can't coast down hills. However, the continuous, even pedaling that is necessary, especially downhill, promotes efficiency, strength, muscle suppleness, and fluid motion. The direct feedback from the rear wheel gives you more control, especially in slippery conditions. The system is also simple, quiet, lightweight, low maintenance, and relatively inexpensive.

The huge popularity of off-track fixed-gear use (and increasingly of track racing) is relatively new to most North American cities. Though that popularity may wane, I believe fixed-gear is here to stay — in fact, it never went away. And although it'll never be for everyone, it is an enjoyable, safe, and practical choice for the experienced cyclist.

**MARTIN NEALE** has been riding fixed-gear year-round for over a decade. His fascination with bicycles developed while he was a bike courier in Vancouver. Community and events organizing, writing, teaching, board membership, and jobs with nonprofit and commercial bike shops followed. In April 2009, Martin opened Hoopdriver Bicycles in his hometown of Toronto. www.hoopdriver.ca

## Chapter Twenty-One

# Folding Bikes

### Ulrike Rodrigues

*I live* car-free at home, so it makes sense to bring my bicycle with me when I travel. With my bike, I can pedal the Golden Triangle banks of the Mekong River or survey freshwater *cenotes* in the Mayan jungle. When I get tired, I can toss my bike onto a dusty bus, train, or oxcart, and no one thinks much of it. After all, it's just a bicycle.

But in North America, it's a different story. Here my bicycle is precious cargo. It must be disassembled, padded, boxed, labeled, weighed, and signed for before I can load it on a Greyhound bus. And, as I recently discovered an hour before boarding, my bike's ticket to ride might cost more than my own.

But we cyclists are a sneaky and crafty people, and we have ways of bucking the system. As early as 1893 (only twenty years after the first bicycle was invented), fellow rebel Michael B. Ryan invented a collapsible bicycle that could be "easily folded and thus take up less space in length when not in use or when transported or stored."

I — and growing numbers of freedom-loving citizens like me — have taken a cue from Ryan and added a folding bike to my arsenal of vehicles for the revolution. With their small wheels and big chainrings, folding bikes (and their riders) are peddling change.

I define a folding bike as a bicycle that gets smaller. Special hardware on the bike — hinges, clamps, springs, quick-release mechanisms, or couplers — makes this possible. Not all these styles of bikes literally fold or collapse: they become smaller in different ways, and they vary wildly in design.

The Folding Cyclist (foldingcyclist.com) lists more than 140 folding-bike manufacturers. Some bikes (like my 1970s-era Raleigh Twenty and my 2008 Dahon Speed TR) have hinges in the middle of the frame, while others (like those made by Birdy, Brompton, and Bike Friday) fold at the wheel, seatpost, and handlebars. Some (like Strida) use hinges and clamps to collapse like a stroller; others (such as Rodriguez) use couplings made by the S&S Machine Company and come apart into separate pieces.

According to a National Bicycle Dealers Association (NBDA) report, although recreational cycling still dominates total sales (which were $5.6 billion in 2009), the folding-bike "niche market" promises great future potential with the growing awareness of "the green movement, environmental sustainability, the need to address health problems related to inactivity, and higher gas prices."[1]

Janko Veselinovic has noticed the shift. When he opened JV Bike in Vancouver, Canada, in 2003, he wanted to specialize in folding bikes. Today, he carries more than forty different styles. "Before," says Veselinovic of the store's early years, "we sold bikes to travelers and people with RVs and yachts. Now we sell them for everyday living — riding in the city, bringing onto transit, and fitting into apartment buildings."

Up the coast in Juneau, Alaska, Matt Carpenter represents both types of riders. Matt, 39, is an engineer based in Tacoma, Washington. When he isn't testing underwater motion dynamics, he's traveling by land or by sea with his folding bikes. "I was first attracted to folding bikes because I live on a small sailboat and I don't own a car," says Matt, who owns a Brompton T6, a Bike Friday SatRDay (a folding recumbent bike), and a Rodriguez UTB. "With a bike like the Brompton, it is easy to store, and I can easily use multimodal transportation options. It's easy to take on buses, trains, passenger ferries, planes, cars, and taxis."

Carpenter has logged multiple trips in Japan, Canada, and the United States with the 6-speed, 16-inch-wheeled Brompton folder. But for longer, more rugged adventures, Matt counts on his break-apart Rodriguez. "I was looking for a touring bike with 26-inch wheels and the ability to pack down for storage and air travel without oversized baggage fees. The Brompton is great for around town or even some touring on pavement, but I wanted something more comfortable for long trips and on rougher, unpaved roads and trails."

Matt explains that with the Rodriguez, he can easily break his bike down into an airline-friendly, suitcase-sized package in less than thirty minutes. And the freedom of choice that comes in useful in Belize, Ecuador, Costa Rica, and Romania works back home,

too. "I've found that a folding bike is great if you are trying to reduce your dependence on a car. Folding bicycles and public transportation complement each other very well, both at home and while
traveling. You can use public transportation when it is convenient,
but having the bicycle with you gives you more options and more
freedom. Having a folding bicycle definitely makes the car-free
lifestyle easier."

The freedom, choice, and sustainability benefits that Carpenter lists are only part of the folding bike's appeal. Folding bikes also have style. I've found that many creative thinkers like Carpenter own at least one folding bike because they love its ingenious design and svelte styling. The smaller wheels, comfortable frame, and city-ready accessories on many folding bikes also allow their riders to replace their dowdy cycle clothing with ready-to-ride urban attire.

Folding bikes also let riders express their individuality. The bikes' design and features identify foldie riders as different — even among cyclists. Foldie riders find unlikely connections outside the bike community: a condo-dwelling urbanite discovers something in common with an RV-driving retiree, an island-hopping yachter, a ride-sharing commuter, and a World War II paratrooper.

In their historic, humble way, folding bikes have revolutionized how we transport ourselves. While fixie, mixte, and mash-up bicycles fight for a piece of the hipster pie, folders stealthily mingle with the mainstream in elevators and everyday life. Folding bikes open doors and cross thresholds. At home, they blur the lines that separate drivers, cyclists, pedestrians, and transit users. On the road, they sneak onto buses, trains, planes, boats, and oxcarts.

Folding bikes thrive in the small, dark trunk of a sedan and the sunny expanse of a piazza. They add artfulness and elegance to the urban landscape and remove barriers and boredom from the daily grind. They stop traffic, start conversations, and steer around tired transportation policies. I like to think of the folding bike as a gateway drug to modern, multimodal living. It's a unisex, unisize bicycle for the future.

**ULRIKE RODRIGUES** is a lifelong, car-free cyclist who shares her female-flavored tales of travel, sex, and magic in print, web, and wine bars (Pinot Grigio, if you're buying).

---

1 National Bicycle Dealers Association, "Industry Overview 2009," http:// nbda.com/articles/industry-overview-2009-pg34.htm, accessed May 2011.

# Chapter Twenty-Two

# Ergonomic Evolution
## The Advantages of Riding Reclined

## Vincent de Tourdonnet

*Children* laugh out loud when I ride by on my recumbent bike. Teens pause: "Is that person cool, or a total freak?" Adults blink earnestly: "What is that thing, a clown bike?" I try to respond with calm reason: "Recumbents are all about comfort: I would never switch back to an upright bike, and neither would most people who've owned a 'bent." "Oh! That does look…comfortable. But isn't it…awkward to ride? Are they slow?"

Are they? No. In 1934, recumbents were banned from bicycle racing for providing an unfair advantage. In 2010, Barbara Buatois set the women's solo record for the Race Across America on a recumbent. Long stigmatized for looking different, are recliners finally rising on the horizon?

The initial attraction of a recumbent bike for the average cyclist is not speed but comfort. Recumbents come in a variety of configurations: what they all have in common is a seat with a full backrest, supporting the rider's body weight across several square feet rather than concentrating it on the ischial tuberosities (or sit bones) and wrists as on a conventional, diamond-frame upright bike. What this means in practical terms is that on a recumbent there are no pressure points: the hands rest weightlessly on the grips, the head faces naturally forward to take in the view with no neck strain, and the feet are elevated, just as in a reclining chair.

Comfort has a bad rap in some quarters. To many athletes, it's for wimps: no pain, no gain. But some are starting to ask, comfort aside, whether the relaxed body position of the recumbent may actually be more ergonomic. If so, could it keep us on our bikes longer, riding more both on a given day and over the years? Some middle-aged or heavier people abandon riding upright bikes altogether because it simply no longer feels right. And even the young and the fit might achieve greater performance — and have more fun — if we could eliminate stress on the butt, wrists, neck, back, and perineum.

To explore a real-world performance example, I asked for the perspective of the "fastest woman in the world," Barbara Buatois. The three-thousand-mile Race Across America (RAAM), which she won in 2010, is billed as the toughest cycling event in the world. In a race where whisper-light diamond-frame bikes are the norm, Barbara rode an off-the-shelf Taiwanese recumbent. And in a race where some teams have huge sponsorship enterprises for backup, Team Buatois relied on family, friends, and a rented Ford Econoline van. Buatois simply took the lead at the start and crossed America in under twelve days. I asked Barbara, from her home in France,

*Short-wheelbase recumbents are practical for urban commuting.*

how riding recumbent made her achievement possible. Recumbents offer an aerodynamic advantage, but are there other gains?

Barbara replied: "On a recumbent, the greater the distance, the more the bodily advantage comes into play. For the RAAM, I could see how some of the upright bike riders were suffering; I could see it in how they moved as they got on and off their bikes. One woman had to quit because her seat caused a pinched nerve, and she lost control of her leg. These types of challenges are simply nonexistent on a recumbent. So at the end of the day, it goes beyond comfort. Riding recumbent has actually allowed me to go farther, to go faster."

Today we pay increasing attention to our bodies. And many cyclists are faced with some real physical challenges: distance riding on upright bikes can cause genital numbness and sexual dysfunction. If the ergonomic and other advantages of recumbents are so clear, why do they remain uncommon today? The answer lies in the history of bicycle racing. Although the average cyclist doesn't race, competitive cycling has an immense influence on the design and marketing of bikes, and thus on sales.

In the late 1920s, the Velocar recumbent was invented by Charles Mochet. People loved riding it because it felt fun. Mochet believed his design was fast but was unable to convince a top athlete to ride his oddball machine, so he settled for a second-tier rider. That rider won a number of races and then broke the world bicycle speed record.

The response of the Union Cycliste Internationale (UCI) was to ban the recumbent from competition because of its aerodynamic advantage. A recumbent rider has an aerodynamic profile about 30 percent smaller than that of an upright rider, mostly because the legs are in front of the body. The UCI felt (and maintains today) that the race should be a competition among riders, not machines. The result of this ruling was that for decades, large bicycle manufacturers have been disinclined to make and market recumbents because all the money and prestige has been in the UCI-approved diamond-frame bicycle. Thus the development of this innovative design was delayed because it was too fast.

The legendary bike mechanic Sheldon Brown once claimed that because of this historic setback, recumbent evolution has not paralleled that of the upright; but this trend may be changing, and Barbara Buatois is in the vanguard of that change. In addition to winning the 2010 RAAM, she smashed the record for human-powered speed for a woman, hitting over 75 mph or (120 kph) in a "bullet bike" recumbent, with complete fairing, designed by Varna in British Columbia. She has also set the record for distance ridden in one hour (52 miles, or 84 kilometers). Barbara has employed both the aerodynamic and the ergonomic advantages of recumbents to establish these and other records.

Recumbents have a couple of disadvantages. Some recumbents are slightly slower up hills: because riders cannot stand on the pedals, they must learn to spin uphill in a low gear. Once over the top, however, they more than compensate because the bike's aerodynamics allow them to gain significant speed on the downhills and flats. Some models are longer and thus require more room to store, and certain other models place the rider quite low to the ground, which may cause visibility concerns. And recumbents are more expensive than uprights.

Still, you may ask, what would it take to get started? Is it hard to learn to ride one? There is a large range of designs. Two good entry-level recumbent types are the compact long-wheelbase and the short-wheelbase bike. Both of these designs can have a small front wheel, which places the feet close to the ground. Anyone who rides a regular bike can learn to ride this type of recumbent almost immediately. At the other end of the spectrum is the increasingly popular high racer, with two full-sized wheels. The high racer's laid-back riding position, with the legs elevated, and its height above the ground may make it more challenging initially for some riders, but it's also a lot faster and more comfortable. Recumbent trikes are also increasingly popular, being very easy and fun to ride, although the rider is placed very low to the ground to assure stability on corners.

Although no substantial studies have been done on safety, most recumbent riders come to feel quite secure: the feet-first riding position makes one less feel vulnerable than the head-first position on an upright. Recumbent designs are continually evolving.

In the future, will the recumbent bicycle become common? Possibly. Meanwhile, for those who want to explore them, in the information age it is increasingly easy to find out more, including where to try or buy one.

And if you do embrace the recumbent position, until these bikes become more common on our streets, you may have to simply be prepared for the stares, and enjoy the laughter of the children.

**VINCENT DE TOURDONNET** is a writer of musical drama. His work ranges from large, full-scale historical musicals to smaller cabaret shows and has been critically acclaimed since 1985. An avid commuter cyclist, he's active with the Toronto Cyclists Union and serves on the board of directors of Transportation Options.

*Chapter Twenty-Three*

# Cycling for All Abilities and Needs

Ron Richings

*Martha* Simmons just got her wheels back. Several decades after she last rode a bike, Martha is pedaling and smiling again. Not perhaps so remarkable, except that she is 82 years old and never imagined she would be riding again. But a program in Portland, Oregon, that puts seniors on trikes gave her new dreams and opportunities. Although she had to be persuaded to try it out, she has now signed up for their program, which has her riding every week. At an age when many seniors face a loss of freedom and mobility, she has found a whole new world opening up for her.

Dovid Kaplan had a serious stroke several years ago that left him with little use of the left side of his body. For Dovid, previously a cyclist and photographer, his physical limitations meant that exercise and a creative hobby were denied to him. With some special adaptations made to a recumbent tricycle, including controls and a stable monopod mount for his camera, Dovid can again enjoy both of his former hobbies. There is one other crucial element in Dovid's newfound freedom: the Orange Heritage Trail in New York State, a flat, car-free rail trail that provides him with a place to ride in safety, enjoy nature, and take photographs, nurturing his physical and creative needs. While he could not ride on any road with cars, he can handle the trail and is a frequent visitor to it. That trail is crucial to his well being.

Norma Wilson is a 25-year-old mother with no conventional "disabilities." She does, however, have two small children whom she shuttles to and from school in a bicycle trailer, or occasionally on a bakfiets, or box bike. While reasonably fit, she finds that the combined weight of kids, plus their necessary stuff, plus trailer or cargo bike means that she is moving twice the weight that she would riding solo. Even with good low gears, when carrying a load she must avoid the sometimes-steep cycle routes she might use by herself when unencumbered. When she reaches the children's school, she has to negotiate a flock of cars delivering other kids. This can be a major challenge, aggravated by drivers apparently stunned to see this non-car with the temerity to pass their line-up.

## REALITY INTRUDES

Well, isn't this cheery — a feel-good piece about how disabled folks and others benefit from cycling. Well, no, it isn't. The examples cited above illustrate potential, rather than common reality. Sadly, such experiences are the exception rather than the rule. Of course there isn't a singular divide between abled and disabled. Instead there is a continuum that all of us fit on, ranging from the young, energetic, fully able at one extreme, to the older or minimally abled at the other. Age, weight, limited sight, injured limbs, and a host of other conditions contribute, and the difference is not just that of our own physical capacity. The mother with two kids in the bike trailer is differently abled from the average cyclist and needs certain conditions to make cycling possible. Low bike gears and routes placed across reasonably flat terrain address the challenges of moving a heavy cargo, but other needs have to be accommodated, too. Cyclists who ferry kids around need places to stop and care for them, likely with running water and a flat surface to change diapers. An older person (or a pregnant woman) may well be able to pedal at a modest pace along a separated path but, with a sensitive

*This recumbent hand cycle is just one of a wide variety of options available to differently abled cyclists.*

bladder, may need restrooms spaced at closer intervals than the assumed "average" rider does.

For those with balance problems or for whom a fall could be devastating, trikes can make cycling possible for many years after a two-wheeled cycle is no longer viable. But access points to bike paths are frequently blocked by bollards. Designed to exclude motor vehicles, these are often so close together that they also exclude trikes. In addition, many bike paths, built to a standard width of 1 to 1.5 meters, are too narrow for two trikes (or bikes with trailers) to pass each other, or for a trike to pass other users without generating friction.

A bike route may be well designed and follow quiet streets, but if it does not provide for alternative routes around hills, it is not suitable for all potential users. Accommodating a wider range of abilities and needs frequently does not require much time, effort, or cost. The solution may be as simple as providing signs pointing out an alternative route on existing streets with less of a gradient.

## ADVOCATES

Wonderful folks though they are, many cycling advocates have a blind spot when it comes to this facet of cycling. As a group, advocates are generally experienced cyclists in comparatively good physical shape, often male. So considering the needs of people who may be none of these things may be a bit of a stretch. "Vehicular

cycling" proponents — those who claim that cyclists should have the same rights, responsibilities, and treatment as drivers of cars — seem rarely to consider this aspect of advocacy.

Transportation planners' designs for bike infrastructure typically represent bicycle use with a symbol of a single bicycle with no encumbrances. These representations can make a bike path seem spacious, even generous; they can lead noncyclists to wonder why so much space has been set aside for those on bikes. However, after construction, some of these facilities barely accommodate real-world users.

# WAYS FORWARD

There is a great need to be met and a great opportunity for increasing exercise, a sense of community, and vitality among a significant portion of our population. Despite the promises of disability rights legislation and constitutional statements guaranteeing equal access, that promise has often not been fulfilled on the pavement, where it matters.

So what needs to be done? Advocacy groups and governments at all levels have to become conscious and attentive to all-abilities cycling and ways of accommodating it. Cities need to inventory and correct the barriers that restrict nonconventional bikes (as well as wheelchairs) from passage, such as the twisted barriers often used to exclude motor vehicles from footpaths and bikeways.

The images used by advocates, planners, and engineers must be expanded to include a much broader representation of people who ride bikes. Some advocates may see this requirement as adding just another complication to the struggle to get basic bike lanes and paths. Perhaps, but it is much cheaper and more effective to design facilities correctly at the start than to construct add-ons and retrofits later.

Improved bikeway design offers great potential benefits for people who cannot realistically cycle among cars. Those benefits will be realized only when we open our minds and include in our efforts the full range of potential users of the paths and routes that we all want to see expanded. And this is not just an exercise in altruism. In the long term the beneficiaries of our efforts are not "them" — they are us.

**RON RICHINGS** first biked, then biked to school, and later biked to work and for play. He moved and worked in the big city but didn't bike. He did sail, though. Eventually he biked to work and for play again. Now he promotes bike fun and posts bike advocacy information.

## Chapter Twenty-Four

# E-bikes Offer an Extra Push

## Sarah Ripplinger

*Riding* a bike is a great way to get around cities, but too often people go for the steering wheel instead of the handlebars. The reasons might be intimidating hills, long distances, muscle pain, physical disability, or a disinclination to build up a sweat. With the introduction of the electric-assist bicycle (e-bike), however, more people can bicycle for transportation than ever before.

E-bike technology is similar to electric-car technology in that a battery powers a motor that propels the vehicle forward. However, the rider usually still pedals the bike. Rechargeable batteries (the most promising being lithium-ion) provide enough energy to assist a rider for 15–20 miles (24–32 kilometers), depending on the type of motor, the terrain, and the amount of assistance the rider needs. For some riders, a boost every so often is enough; for others, the entire ride might be assisted.

The similarity of e-bikes to other engine-powered vehicles has caused some controversy regarding how to regulate and restrict their design and use. While a clear distinction can often be made between electric bikes and motorcycles, mopeds, or electric scooters, there are gray areas. For example, the electric bicycle scooter also comes with pedals that can be used to propel the vehicle forward. However, the build and bulk of the bicycle scooter are not conducive to pedaling, so the pedals are more for show than for practical use. These vehicles can also become a source of frustration and concern on a bikeway, as they take up more room than a normal bike and can intimidate cyclists sharing the road or path.

Some e-bikes have throttles — similar to those found on motorcycles — that a rider can engage without pedaling. Most models are pedal-assists, also called pedelecs, and require the rider to pedal in order to engage the motor. Some of these models also have throttles, but many states and provinces mandate that unlicensed bikes require the rider to pedal in order to engage the motor, keeping the e-bike well within the realm of the self-propelled vehicle.

To comply with speed restrictions on unlicensed, electrically powered vehicles, many e-bikes on the market today come equipped with limiters that cap their speed at 20 miles per hour (32 kilometers per hour) on flat ground. The output of the motor usually ranges from 250 to 750 watts. The speed cap, however, has not been enough to satisfy some critics, who believe any bike with a motor should be licensed and barred from bike lanes and paths.

Some of the most vociferous objections to e-bikes come from environmentalists who argue that e-bikes require more energy to manufacture than nonelectric bikes: batteries, electrical wires, and digital controllers are needed in addition to the materials used for the bicycle itself. Moreover, batteries need to be properly disposed of to avoid leaching harmful contaminants into landfills. And the electricity needed to charge the bikes often comes from fossil fuels, hydroelectric dams, and nuclear power plants.

Justin Lemire-Elmore, of the electric-bike component design and retail company Grin Technologies, attempts to nip these objections in the bud. In his 2004 paper "The Energy Cost of Electric and Human-Powered Bicycles," he argues that the increased efficiency of e-bikes reduces the energy needed to fuel bike riders, thus cutting down on the number of calories required to travel a given distance. Lemire-Elmore sells e-bike converter kits that enable the purchaser to transform a nonmotorized bike into an e-bike. He also participates in the online e-bike enthusiast forum www.endless-sphere.com.

The fact that people can travel farther using less energy means that more riders may opt to ride instead of drive or use a combination of biking and other means of transportation. E-bikes open doors for parents who tow children using trailers and trail-a-bikes and for people who want to carry all of their groceries home on a bike but need a bit of assistance to manage their loads. And better e-bike technology is helping to make cycling a more viable transportation option. The Clever Cycles Stokemonkey electric assist for Xtracycle bikes, for example, is designed specifically to help riders navigate hills and carry big loads. The weight of e-bikes has also been reduced dramatically over the years, increasing their attractiveness. Some models, such as the folding electric FMT bike, weigh less than 22.1 pounds (10 kilograms).

## On Bicycles

Improved technology, higher gas prices, and aging populations are some of the reasons why electric bikes are growing in popularity, particularly in cities with more bike commuters. Although electric bikes are often at least twice as expensive as other city bikes, e-bike sales in the Netherlands — where approximately 40 percent of all traffic movement is by bike — increased by 45 percent in 2009. More money was spent on e-bikes in the Dutch market than on city bikes in 2009 — about 140,000 e-bikes were sold. Japan experienced a 41.7 percent jump in the number of e-bikes sold in 2009, and China, by far the largest producer and distributor of e-bikes (accounting for 98 percent of sales worldwide), produced 22 million that year.

Sales of e-bikes in Europe and Asia could signal future growth in North America. While sales are still marginal in the United States — around 250,000 e-bikes were sold in 2010, up from 150,000 in 2009 — this market is expected to grow to more than 1 million sales per year by 2016, according to the market analyst organization Pike Research. Interbike, the largest bicycle trade show in North America, featured several different e-bike models in 2010, from folding bikes to city and mountain bikes with electric assists. Some companies offer trailers with a battery inside that cyclists can use to transform any bike into an electric-assist vehicle.

E-bikes are also becoming popular outside the mainstream market of individual riders. Many e-bike manufacturers are taking note of a demand from businesses interested in using bikes to transport and deliver goods. Companies such as the California Pizza Kitchen in San Francisco, California, benefit from the lower cost and increased efficiency that come with using e-bikes for delivering goods. The associated image of corporate social responsibility and sustainability is a selling point for many consumers and investors.

E-bikes empower riders of all stripes to use bikes for most of their transportation needs. People with sore knees or disabilities that once put biking out of reach can now hop onto the saddle. Riders can continue to travel the same distances as they grow older without putting too much stress on their bodies. And in hilly places, such as San Francisco and Vancouver, Canada, a little help can go a long way.

Cycling with an extra boost is an attractive option for many commuters. Improvements to e-bike technology and a rising need for practical alternatives to the personal automobile are just a couple of reasons why sales figures for e-bikes will likely continue to grow. From this standpoint, the future of e-cycling in North America looks bright.

**SARAH RIPPLINGER** is the editor of *Momentum* magazine. She never guessed how much fun riding an electric bike would be until she tried pedaling one up a hill in Vancouver, BC.

# Chapter Twenty-Five

# Shopping by Bike
## Racks, Baskets, Panniers, and More

## Denise Wrathall

*Every* enthusiast has a "big fish" story. For urban cyclists, it's sometimes about the weirdest or biggest thing we've carried by bike: furniture, pets, toilet augers. Before you bungee your new armchair to your bike, here are a few basics to get you started.

Shopping by bike is the hippest way to shop, hands down. We shop by bike because it's faster than walking. We shop as we commute. It's easier to carry things by bike than on the bus. We exercise as we shop. It costs nothing. It reduces our carbon footprint. Parking is right at the door. It's easy to make several stops. It soothes our environmental conscience.

Why, then, do so many shy away from shopping by bike? Stowing and hauling all that stuff can be a bit intimidating. And yet there are many options. Here we look at all the ways to shop using a conventional bicycle. Cargo bicycles are also a great way to shop by bike — see chapter 18.

# PACKS

Without special accessories, you can shop with a backpack. It's great for small loads, and several packs on the market are designed specifically for cyclists. A pack makes it easy to carry your purchases off the bike, and many have a strap or pocket to stow your helmet. The only downside is that cycling with a backpack isn't as comfortable. Your back gets sweaty, and the load shifts around as you ride. Still, a backpack is a great starting option, because you might not need to buy anything new to start shopping by bike.

# MESSENGER BAGS

Messenger bags are a popular and stylish option specifically designed for cycling. They usually come with both a shoulder strap and an anti-sway strap that prevents the bag from sliding around to the front of the rider — an important safety feature. For small purchases, a shoulder bag will also work, as long as the strap isn't so long that you could sit on it by accident after standing up to pedal. Messenger bags are best for lighter loads, since the weight is carried mostly on one shoulder, and this can be hard on your body.

For heavier purchases, consider letting the bike carry the load for you.

# RACKS

If you are willing to make a few changes to your bike, a cargo rack is a good place to start. Racks are available for front and rear wheels from any bike shop and can be lightweight or heavy-duty. All sorts of purchases can be strapped to the flat space on the top of a rack, and the weight that a rack adds to your bike is negligible compared to the cargo it can carry.

## Low Riders

One type of front rack is the low rider, which only lets you carry panniers. Nothing can be carried on top of the rack. With this design, weight is carried lower on the bike — a definite advantage for steering with heavy loads.

### Straps or bungees?

Everyone has a preference for strapping things to a rack. Bungee cords, straps with buckles, and plain old rope will all work. Just make sure there are no ends dangling to get caught in the wheels.

### What if your bike has front suspension?

Don't worry—racks and low riders are available for bikes with front suspension forks, and the prices have come down dramatically. Be aware, though, that once you attach a front rack, you'll have to remove your front skewer every time you need to take your wheel off.

# BASKETS

Rigid bike baskets come in many shapes and sizes. There are folding baskets, front baskets, rear baskets, and split baskets. They can be made of wicker, wood, metal, or synthetic materials. They're ideal for shopping. Some are even sized so that you can slip standard grocery bags inside them—no fuss, no muss! Baskets are convenient to use, and many versions can be attached securely to the bike, so that you can leave them on the bike with little fear of theft. I love my folding side basket — it allows me to spontaneously stop and pick something up, even if I didn't bring a pannier. Baskets are less likely to squish the veggies, and, properly packed, they will keep bottles upright.

Homemade bike baskets can be fashioned from milk crates or a wide variety of commercially available baskets. Strap these onto the rack with zap straps (zip ties), toe-clip straps, or bungees — just be sure they're well secured to your bike before you load it up and take it for a ride.

## On Bicycles

### Panniers

Panniers — bags with special clips for mounting to the side of a cargo rack — are a popular choice for bike shoppers. They keep the weight low on the bike, can be used in both front and back, and come in a wide variety of designs to suit your needs. The only trouble is that some panniers, when fully loaded, can be awkward to carry around by hand. Look for panniers that come with a shoulder strap or backpack harness. A great DIY option is to make your own panniers entirely — surf the web for instructions and ideas.

# WEIGHT

It's best to balance the weight on your bike, with equal weight on each side and at least some over each wheel. For a long time, the conventional wisdom was that you should carry most of the weight in the back, but many riders now prefer to have the heavy load on the front. This is because the front wheel is stronger than the rear wheel; the front part of the frame is less likely to break; many bikes are more stable and steer better with weight on the front rather than the back; and you can keep a better eye on your load. Either way, give yourself extra time to get used to the load the first time you cycle with extra weight, because your bike will handle differently. You can be caught off guard by the frame flexing with a heavy load on the back, especially when walking and parking, but it also takes more strength to steer when the weight is up front. If you are carrying a heavy load on the back, putting a bit of the load up front can greatly improve bike handling. A handlebar bag is often enough.

Side-to-side weight balance matters too, even with moderate

loads. I often ignore this fact and carry only one heavy rear pannier. But I nearly lost control of my bike on a corner when I carried a balanced load one day, because I was so used to compensating for the imbalance. My rack is also gradually being bent out of shape from being loaded on one side. Not recommended.

## TRAILERS

Panniers and baskets can hold a lot of groceries, but if you really want to haul all your household needs on a bike, you may end up wanting a trailer. Bike trailers have either one or two wheels. One-wheeled trailers like those made by BOB are narrow enough to navigate small spaces and trails, and they lean with the bike, making them less likely to tip over on corners, However one-wheelers offer less cargo space, and they need to be loaded symmetrically so as not to tip.  Two-wheeled trailers, though wider and less nimble, have much greater cargo capacity and stability during loading and unloading.

Trailers typically have a fairly low center of gravity and are stable on the road. Models that attach to the bike's rear axle affect the steering less than those that attach to the seatpost, especially when cornering. Trailers that clamp onto the bike's chainstay also have a low center of gravity but are positioned close to the rear wheel's spokes, which poses more of a hazard if the hitch releases accidentally.

Shopping trailers come with a variety of options. Some have removable bags or boxes, and others leave it up to you to attach a container. You can also use a child-carrying trailer for your groceries, possibly with your child on board as well! Some models of trailer also convert to a handcart, so you can bring them with you while shopping rather than locking them up. If you do need to lock the trailer, bring a second lock — it's hard to lock up both a cart and a bike with just one.

You can also make your own trailer. Search the web for designs and instructions, or check out the options for build-your-own trailer kits.

Although you can feel the extra weight, cycling with a trailer isn't as difficult as it looks — and it gives you a lot of hauling power! Mostly you'll find that you need to stay in a lower gear and take corners a smidge wider. Wheeling the bike and trailer around for parking takes the most getting used to — you can't just pick your bike up or drag it sideways, and it won't fit through doorways or pull over curbs as easily.

## IMPROMPTU CARGO-HAULING STRATEGIES

Even if you buy every piece of gear I've mentioned so far, you'll still occasionally find yourself carrying something you haven't planned for. Don't even consider cycling with plastic bags hanging from your handlebars. Swinging bags are dangerous: they make it harder to steer and balance, and they can hit your feet as you pedal or get caught in your spokes. If you have to carry them, it's better to walk your bike.

A good alternative is to strap the plastic bags to your rack. Tie the bag tightly shut and place a strap or bungee over it, but between items in the bag, so that it won't slip off. You can even carry produce this way without bruising it, although it's best for lightweight items. It helps if you've got panniers on the rack to support items that would otherwise dangle over the edges. To attach a cardboard box directly and securely to your rack, dent the edges of the box where the straps will go to keep the straps from slipping.

Take time to consider the details of your cargo system. You'll enjoy shopping by bike more when it's safe and comfortable. Any time you're attaching multiple accessories to your bike, think about how they are all going to work together. Where will you store the lock? How can you attach both a front light and a basket to the handlebars? Will the milk crate interfere with the rear light? With a bit of planning and ingenuity, you can work around any issues, and you'll find that shopping is just another of the fun things you can do with your bike. Happy hauling!

**DENISE WRATHALL** is a Vancouver commuter cyclist. She has carried pets, food processors, camping gear, and tons of groceries on her bike.

## Chapter Twenty-Six

# Riding in the Rain

## Amy Walker

*If there's* one great place to enjoy bad weather, it's on the seat of a bicycle. With a canopy of painted clouds, percussive splashing from car tires, and lights reflecting on wet streets, the watery world of rainy-day biking can be beautiful. When you're bundled up properly against the cold and rain, it feels like being 5 years old, full of wonder and out on a field trip.

For years, I was a fair-weather cyclist and would take the bus on rainy days. The few times a shower surprised me, I ended up at my destination a soggy, miserable mess, my pants soaked and heavy, a stripe of mud running up my rear.

When finally, after sixteen years of commuting, I bought raingear for about $300, it was the biggest and best investment I had ever made in cycling. Overnight, I had an alternative to standing in the rain waiting for and packing myself onto crowded, steaming buses. I gained more freedom. I saved money and time.

And I discovered something truly wonderful: a way to boost my energy and enjoy the rain.

At first you might feel hesitant or even fearful about riding in the rain. It can seem like a hassle, uncomfortable, or hazardous. But with a bit of preparation, the resistance fades, and you discover freedom and mobility.

In the workaday world, wet or cold weather doesn't hold a lot of appeal. But consider the outdoor sports you'd happily suit up for: skiing, hiking, hunting, fishing, or boating. With a positive mind-set, riding in the rain is exhilarating and refreshing; it feels like a little athletic adventure en route to the office. No commuter looks more hardcore than the rainy-day bicyclist (except perhaps the rainy-day unicyclist), but our secret is that it's actually fun to play outside, splashing through puddles.

What do you need to ride in the rain? You've got options. If you don't like one, there are other choices available.

Imagine that you ride your bike to work in bright sunshine, but by 5 PM it's pouring. You can still make it home without getting soaked by cutting armholes out of a garbage bag. Cover your shoes with plastic produce bags cinched up with rubber bands. Cost: a few pennies. Style factor: zero.

If you don't regularly ride in the rain but want to be prepared for the occasional surprise shower, a cycling rain poncho packs small in your bag and offers a simple, easy solution for keeping dry for short rides. Cycling ponchos extend over the handlebars and rear of the bike. They should have a waist tie, a hood, and elastic straps to keep the poncho attached to your hands. Cost: $25–50. Style factor: Fancy-free and easy.

Raingear made from polyvinyl (PVC) is waterproof, but it is not made for physical activity. Usually you find cheap raingear made of this stuff at surplus and bargain stores. These materials are not breathable, and the garments are usually not well articulated for the body's position and movement on a bike. Skip this for something more cycling appropriate.

You can often find "water-resistant" jackets made from coated fabrics like nylon or polyester. These will keep you dry in a light shower, but they're not waterproof, which is what you need for cycling, and they're not very breathable. I recommend saving your pennies to get the good stuff.

Cycling-specific, waterproof jackets and pants can be found at outdoor retailers like REI in the United States and MEC in Canada and at well-stocked independent bike shops. Well-engineered cycling raingear may seem expensive at first, but for a regular commuter, when you add up the money saved in gas, parking, or bus fare, it quickly pays for itself. When you shop, look for these features:

→ Breathable membrane materials (such as Gore-Tex and eVent). Since we make our own weather, this will prevent soaking from inside the jacket.

→ Taped seams: special waterproof seals on all the sewn joints where water might seep in.

→ Pit zips and venting: these let in a breeze when the weather is warmer.

→ Cuffs: better raingear has adjustable cuffs so you can let in air when it is warm and close them snug in colder weather. Cheaper jackets have elastic cuffs.

→ Elongated tail: protects your butt from wind and water as you lean forward over the handlebars.

→ Sealing zippers: just like taped seams, these will prevent water seepage.

→ Articulated elbows and knees: extra fabric here allows freedom of movement.

If you're looking for raingear that passes for regular clothing (alert: fashion designers, this is a great business opportunity!), check out Portland-based Showers Pass. When asked whether their stylish raingear helps people ride their bikes more often, Showers Pass co-president Ed Dalton said, "People tell us: 'I really want to ride, but I can't find the right clothes to ride my bike and feel normal. I don't need all this super-bright, super-technical-looking stuff that screams, "BIKE!" I need an everyday product that has those technologies in it, but I can go to lunch or go to dinner and wear the same jacket and it's a completely functional piece on or off the bike.' That's what we hear a lot." The company designs beautifully engineered gear, and their Portland jackets for men and women fit easily into professional or casual settings. Following the success of these models, Showers Pass will release further sophisticated rainwear designs in 2012.

There is a high environmental cost associated with synthetic materials — particularly those used in waterproof clothing. If you prefer your clothing to have a minimal environmental impact, try wool or waxed cotton. Wool is insulating in hot or cold weather, wicks moisture, is antimicrobial and antibacterial, does not retain body odors, and can be very comfortable against the skin. Nan Eastep of B. Spoke Tailor says: "Just get wet in your wool. We're

mammals and we should be wearing wool. It's just the right thing to wear in almost every circumstance." Waxed cotton is a waterproof and biodegradable British classic developed for sailors and adopted by sport fishers and duck hunters. Crafty types may want to try making waxed-cotton rainwear by impregnating a cotton jacket with paraffin-based wax. Check out waxed cotton from brands like B. Spoke Tailor (bspoketailor.com) and Barbour.

Keeping extremities comfortable is important. Cold, wet hands and feet will quickly bring you misery. Because your hands are out in front of you, they get cold and wet quickly and need adequate protection. Many cycling gloves are not truly waterproof, so ask lots of questions when selecting gloves. In cold weather you may want to layer gloves inside mitts. Half-finger gloves with a convertible mitt cover, a.k.a "glomitts," made of wool work surprisingly well. Lobster gloves are another good option that keeps the index finger free to operate brakes and shifters. To keep your feet dry and warm on longer rides, use waterproof booties that fasten closed over your shoes. Ears are very sensitive to wind, so wearing a thin

toque, headband, or earwarmers is essential. Wearing a waterproof helmet cover can look ridiculous, but some rainy-day riders swear by them.

Keep belongings dry by placing them in a sturdy plastic bag with a sealed top inside your pannier, or shell out for waterproof panniers. Ortlieb makes a variety of great ones, and their brand is pretty well synonymous with waterproof.

Your bike also needs preparation for the rain. Install fenders to protect you from water spray and protect your bike from road grime. Some people prefer disc brakes for riding in the rain as they are responsive and precise, and they eliminate wear on the the wheel rims. Grit and road grime will act like sandpaper on your drivetrain and wheel rims (if you have caliper or cantilever brakes), so it's a good habit to clean off the grime frequently, and keep your chain clean and lubed. Try to park your bike under cover; if you can't, use a seat cover, hotel shower cap, or plastic bag to cover the saddle.

The biggest hazard of riding in the rain is reduced visibility. Buy the brightest lights you can afford, and turn them on even in the daytime if it's dark and stormy. This helps car drivers to see you and allows you to ride with confidence. Reflective vests, while rarely glamorous, also help you to be seen in the rain.

Cyclists who wear glasses may find it difficult to see if their glasses get wet and fogged up. Some scooter helmets include a face shield and are light enough to wear on a bicycle. My friend Terry devised a great homemade rain visor by attaching a piece of flexible, clear plastic to his bike helmet with self-adhesive Velcro.

Once you've made your commute through the rain, you're going to change out of that wet gear, and you'll need a place to hang it. Consider carrying a towel or keeping one at work: you can dry yourself off and then roll your wet clothes in it to squeeze out moisture before hanging everything up. Finding a place to dry out raingear is vital, because it's no fun to put on wet gear to ride back home. A truly bike-friendly workplace will provide a drying area for wet raingear. This is something worth working with your employer to achieve, as it makes a huge difference for the bike riders on staff. Gloves and raingear forgotten in a pannier can get smelly, so make sure to keep your gear clean and dried for when you need it, and you'll be a happy rider on rainy days.

# PART THREE

# Community
### and Culture

## Chapter Twenty-Seven

# Bicycle Space

## Mykle Hansen

*People* can't sit still. Ever since the first prehumans fell out of trees, we've craved locomotion: to hunt, to gather, to explore and expand, to avoid and pursue one another. Undoubtedly we're built to wander, with long, muscular legs to hold us upright, strong backs to carry supplies, and hairless bodies for efficient cooling during urgent sprints and day-long hikes. And, being clever tool users, we humans have extended our range with such inventions as the shoe, the backpack, the sled, the wheel, the cart, the saddle, the bit, the boat, the sail, the balloon, the car, the airplane, and the rocket. In fact, when you consider the mind-boggling number of profound or ridiculous inventions that we've come up with just to bring "over there" closer to "over here," it seems the history of remarkable and ingenious ways to travel is human history itself.

Although our unique relationship with travel — both our skill and our romantic obsession with it — has served us brilliantly as a species, it now seems poised to become our fatal flaw: our hunger for fuel to move millions of objects in millions of directions for millions of reasons threatens to choke our planet. Ironically, we've gotten far too good at travel. We've reduced it to a desk job: a set of buttons and knobs arranged around a padded seat. Locomotion has become, for many, a chore to delegate instead of a joyful act. Our spirit of adventure has been stifled by a widely held belief that there's no more frontier, no more undiscovered landscape on this planet. The age of exploration has passed, we're told: welcome to the age of commuting.

But the charms of locomotion can still be known; one only needs the right equipment. Out of all our inventions for travel I prefer the bicycle, unique for its exquisite enhancement of the things our bodies already do so well. Like a hammer or a telescope, the bicycle gives you superpowers. Given a halfway-decent bike and a halfway decent road, there is no more efficient way for the sandwich you ate at lunchtime to propel you across the earth.

Consider, also, the mental effects of bicycling. Riding along, processing a moving landscape and finding your place in it, stimulates the visual cortex and activates the entire mind. Bicycling wakes you up and puts you in the world, in public space, on the roads and in the fields. On a bicycle you can quickly survey the reality of a neighborhood or a village. Your mind and body integrate the forces of wind, momentum, gravity, and balance as you seek the ideal route from point to point. Bicycling heightens your awareness of things others are blind to — that's why it's so great for sightseeing. You intuit the intentions behind pathways and roads and begin to understand (and question) city planning. It enhances your perception of scenic beauty, and of ugliness too, and danger — of all the inviting or frightening personality that a path can have.

This altered state of perception is intoxicating in itself, but it also has a way of stimulating and enhancing this human craving to explore, discover, and map places. When I'm in a strange area on a bike, searching the way to cross an insurmountable freeway or ascend an inconvenient cliff, the moment I adore is when I detect a shortcut: a footpath next to a Dead End sign, a narrow alley shunned by cars, an empty strip along the expressway, or a newly paved stretch of suburban slope. Aha! What is this? Where does it go? Let's find out!

Whenever I arrive in a foreign land, no matter how far I've come or how tired I might be, my first priority is not to rest but to get on a bike and start exploring; bicycling is my favorite way of seeing. And as I've biked around the cities of the world, I've learned that the view from a bike saddle — combined with an attitude of "be here now," rather than of "get there soon" — is a view into a parallel dimension of space, an inner urban frontier that I call Bicycle Space.

If a critical mass of cyclists undertake this process in the same area, they can't help but meet, ask directions, compare notes, and confirm to one another that their shared mental map describes a new place, superimposed on a known place but with a separate, bicycle-flavored set of entries and exits, rest stops, vistas, treacherous turns, secret passageways, and sacred points of interest.

This is Bicycle Space. When enough bicyclists perceive a stretch of Bicycle Space together, it becomes public, a social space. Seeing the road as others can't, bicyclists have found new uses for parts of cities and countryside that others only pass through. Dressed for outdoors, they've rediscovered the art of the picnic. Banding together in packs, they've invented the rolling party. Young people now look to bicycling as a fashion scene, a way to see and be seen.

And in cities around the world, bicyclists are adopting blighted stretches of bike routes, improving and enlarging them through political advocacy and direct action. Buoyed by our care and concern, Bicycle Space is stretching and widening, asserting itself, coming alive everywhere.

Our wild rush into Bicycle Space comes not a moment too soon, because humanity has just about run out of every other kind of space. And while outer space still beckons (I hear there's great single track on Mars), Bicycle Space is here today, within our reach. Individually or as nations, we can trade Car Space for Bicycle Space at a favorable rate, and thereby free up more space for everyone. It's a bargain: good for you, good for the planet. But the fundamental allure of Bicycle Space is that it's new, exciting, waiting to be explored. Human beings need a frontier, now more than ever. Without one, we'll drive in circles until we run out of everything.

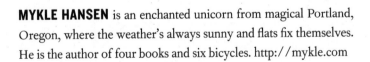

**MYKLE HANSEN** is an enchanted unicorn from magical Portland, Oregon, where the weather's always sunny and flats fix themselves. He is the author of four books and six bicycles. http://mykle.com

*Chapter Twenty-Eight*

# Sharing Biking through Culture

Amy Walker

**Culture** is the mirror that helps us to understand ourselves through art, language, entertainment, and conversation, and it is as vital as food, water, and air to life as we know it. Our ideals and interests are intrinsic to culture, and though culture sometimes brings clarity and understanding, at its best it often provokes further questions. Culture is something we do when we've covered the bases of survival: when we have extra time on our hands, our imaginations start wandering.

Bike culture can be any form of expression that portrays bicycling, including video, writing, music, TV, photography, painting, or performance. Nineteenth-century posters depicting scantily clad female cyclists; H. G. Wells's 1896 comic novel *The Wheels of Chance*; the movies *BMX Bandits* and *Breaking Away*; events like Critical Mass, the World Naked Bike Ride, and Portland's Pedalpalooza; products like R.E.Load messenger bags; Bilenky, Vanilla, and Ahearne handmade bikes; Filmed by Bike and the Bicycle Film

Festival; magazines like *Momentum*, *Urban Velo*, and *Bicycle Times*; Jemaine Clement and Bret McKenzie of *Flight of the Conchords* singing "Too Many Mother 'uckers" while riding their bikes — all of these and more are bike culture.

It helps to clarify what we mean when we are discussing *bike culture*. In the United States, Canada, and other places where transportation bikers constitute only about 1 percent of the population, biking is still perceived as mainly a sport or recreational activity. *Bike culture* can refer to road or track racing, mountain biking, BMX, or riding a bike for fitness and recreation, and many people assume that is what is meant. There are plenty of wonderful overlaps between the cultures of recreational and transportation biking, but they're not necessarily the same thing. Here I refer to bike culture in the context of transportation and lifestyle.

Because more people ride for recreation than for transport in the United States and Canada, the bike industry still makes most of its money from recreational equipment — though that pattern is slowly shifting. Many expressions of bike culture attempt to familiarize more people with everyday cycling and challenge the commonly held perception that cycling for transportation is something only a tiny minority can achieve. If our legislators were forward-thinking enough to accommodate cycling as part of the transportation mix, we would not rely so heavily on culture as a force for political and social change. But here in North America, governments are usually not particularly farsighted or proactive. So we rely on activists and advocates and cultural mavericks to educate and inform the public about cycling as well as to entertain it. When more people see bicycles as a part of the everyday landscape, changes to infrastructure, industry, policy, and law become easier to make. When cycling is more widely adopted, it will help solve health problems such as obesity, cut carbon emissions, create economic opportunity and financial savings, open up more urban space, and contribute to the effectiveness and happiness of our lives.

I love movies and TV shows with characters who just happen to bike for transportation, because they're a stealthy expression of bike culture. They seep into our consciousness without making the cycling message obvious. Biking isn't a big part of the plot, it's just something these people happen to do. It's even better when the characters are relatively normal people — or, even better, sexy leading men.

For example, David O. Russell's philosophical comedy *I Heart Huckabees* follows two clients of the Existential Detective Agency, run by the married couple Vivian and Bernard Jaffe (Lily Tomlin and Dustin Hoffman). The story revolves around the detectives, their two clients, and employees of the big-box "everything store," Huckabees. Russell weaves biking into the story in a relatively subtle way. Granted, Tommy Corn (Mark Wahlberg) is having an existential crisis linked to his antipetroleum politics, and Albert Markovski (Jason Schwartzman) is an environmentalist, but there is so much else going on in the film that the fact that they get around on bikes doesn't take center stage and is never really discussed. In one scene, Markovski and Corn easily weave their bikes through bumper-to-bumper traffic, past a frustrated Huckabees marketing man, Brad Stand (Jude Law), sitting in his car. The biking scenes are just a bonus in this smart and hilarious play on the angst and antidotes of modern life, but their presence is priceless, and I'm always looking to see more like them.

Much as he mocks it, the blogger Bike Snob NYC makes

fabulous bike culture, poking fun at all aspects of cycling, spreading the word, and familiarizing people with the biking vernacular — even as his savage wit makes earnest folks wince. Through his satirical Bike Snob persona, he skewers hipsters, messengers, roadies, the bike industry, wrong-way cyclists (salmon), those selling used bikes on Craigslist, smug bike advocates, and everyone else who happens to come anywhere near a bicycle. Starting out as an anonymous blogger, the Bike Snob quickly earned a large and faithful following. After three years of mystery, intrigue, and thumbing his nose at cycling's elite, he unmasked himself as the writer Eben Weiss, published a book, and now writes a regular column for *Bicycling* magazine. He has even begun making public appearances at bike expos, but if he continues doing that for long, it could undermine his sarcasm: it's hard to take the piss out of people one moment, then share a stage with them the next.

What about blogs and news stories that belittle biking, and advertisements that joke at the cyclist's expense? Is the anticycling backlash also bike culture? I'm not sure, but I think the answer is yes, because even anticycling expression provokes us, in its backhanded way, to think about cycling. It seems as though the backlash has been mounting lately. In my city of Vancouver, Canada, the pro-cycling mayor has taken flak from most of the major newspapers for his support of separated bike lanes in the downtown area. I interpret this kind of resistance to transportation cycling as misplaced fear and guilt, because it is apparent that the age of cheap gas and the highly subsidized automobile culture is coming to an end. What's so interesting about human expression is that even when we try to suppress or destroy something, we are often unwittingly sowing its seeds. By focusing attention on it, we enable its growth. So someone frustrated with cyclists and working that frustration into artwork, advertising, or writing is also fanning the cycling fire and dovetailing with the cycling advocates' plans.

So whose job is it to make bike culture now, and what's going to happen in the future? Well, these days, everyone makes culture. Ours is the age of the democratization of media. People share their daily lives and make culture through videos, photos, and blogs. The real heroes are people acting locally to make life better in simple, ordinary ways. In the old paradigm, we hear only the bad news: as the newspaper saying goes, "If it bleeds, it leads." But now we can tune into a million different, smaller channels, and make and share culture in a thousand ways. Who knows how long this amazing opportunity will exist? It is truly miraculous, and yet it has become accessible, even ordinary. As bicycling grows, perhaps it won't be such a distinct subculture; perhaps it will become a familiar part of our landscape. But I think we'll always have a special reverence for the bicycle. Bikes are a beautiful paradox: a tool and a toy, a job and a joy, fun and efficient at the same time. In the future I imagine, we'll see monuments built to the bike, where people will reflect on how a simple machine helped humanity to attain grace and balance.

# Chapter Twenty-Nine

# The Well-Tempered Cyclist

**Deb Greco**

*It used* to be true, what motorists have always suspected: when I get on my bike, a switch goes off in my brain, and consideration for anyone else ceases to exist. Each morning, amped on fresh air and adrenaline, I used to ride to work with a simple goal: to make it to work without stopping, or at least without putting a foot down. That's why I ran a red light and found myself in the middle of an intersection with a MUNI bus barreling toward me from the right. The bus came so close that I avoided a crash only by turning to ride with it, so intimately that I felt the kiss of steel along my right side. The bus driver slammed on his brakes, stuck his head out his side window, looked me right in the terrified eye, and yelled, "Asshole!" "Screw you!" I shouted back. "No, screw *you*!" he screamed, and stomped on the gas. The morning commuters on board lurched violently; those who managed to keep their footing glared at me malevolently. The other motorists at the intersection gave me the universal sign of disappointment: the baleful shake of the head. The bike traffic kept rolling, one bicyclist tossing me a sympathetic "MUNI drivers suck!" over his messenger bag. I laughed it off with relief and kept riding; just your average morning commute on Market Street.

In theory, I knew that running red lights was risky; in practice, I didn't care. Ever since I'd hopped on my first bike, I'd been blowing through traffic signs and signals. When I was a kid, it was all about going fast, but as I grew older, judgment began to play a role. Since I was traveling solely by my own pedal power, and the motorist opposite me was passively harnessing the power of an internal combustion engine, I reasoned that I deserved the right-of-way.

And then I met Martha. She's a midwesterner with much better manners than mine. She's also an avid bicyclist, so it wasn't long before we were biking together around the city. To my horror, Martha honored all red lights; but even worse, she stopped — actually stopped — at every single stop sign. Good grief! Waiting beside her with my feet on the ground felt like six kinds of wrong. We'd slowly crank back into motion only to stop again at the very next stop sign, one block away. That's for MUNI bus drivers, I thought to myself, not freewheeling bicyclists. There was plenty of time to think about these things as we rode slowly across town in awkward fits and starts.

It turns out that good manners and bicycling are not mutually exclusive. With Martha at my side, I began to perceive how my former, bad-tempered bicycling behavior created all kinds of ill will on our city's streets. I watched fellow bicyclists fly through red lights and cut off traffic, leaving drivers frustrated and unhappy about sharing the road with us. I saw messengers and fixie hipsters slaloming through rush-hour traffic, and I saw the fury — and fear — they left in their wake. I used to observe this dance with a kind of rebel glee, caring only about maintaining my own momentum. But somehow slowing down opened my eyes and awakened my compassion for the other people on the road.

These shifts in perspective happened gradually over weeks of riding with Martha, but one experience crystallized everything and made me aware of how much my riding style had changed. I was riding down Valencia Street on a summer day, with a long bike lane ahead. I was flying through an intersection with the green light when I saw that a MUNI bus just ahead of me was getting ready to pull back into traffic. I slowed to see if he was going to check his rearview mirror first, which he did. Spotting me, he gave me the go-ahead with a wave of his hand out his side window. Instead I stopped behind his rear wheel, giving him the go-ahead with a wave and a smile. With the flash of a return smile in his rearview mirror, he pulled out in front of me.

That MUNI bus and I leapfrogged all the way down Valencia that busy Saturday, passing each other a dozen times in as many blocks. We navigated around bus stops and intersections, erratic motorists in search of elusive parking, and jaywalking pedestrians. Usually sharing the road with a MUNI bus feels competitive or threatening, if not downright dangerous. But that day the bus driver and I developed a rapport and mutual respect. Just as he was kind enough to offer me the right-of-way, I had given it to him. In exchange, he looked out for me all the way down the road. Together we changed the whole car-bike dichotomy, and I'll never forget how good it felt to share the road with generosity, respect, and a smile.

This experience turned out to be the gateway to all kinds of other consciousness-changing experiences on the road, even when I wasn't on my bike. One day I was walking in my neighborhood on an active section of the Wiggle, a route that offers a way around some of San Francisco's steepest hills and is therefore much used and loved by the city's bicyclists. I stepped off the curb at an intersection to cross the street and was almost hit by a cavalcade of bicyclists coming along at a good clip, none of them inclined to stop, or even slow down, at the stop sign. As a bicyclist, I understood their way of thinking. They had fixed my position on the pavement and were flowing perfectly reasonably around me. As a pedestrian who could feel the wind in my face from each one passing me, it was unsettling. I quickly stepped back onto the curb to let them pass, and they whizzed by without any indication that they had even noticed my giving them the right-of-way. They simply took it as if they were entitled to it. I was uncomfortably reminded of how entitled I used to feel as a virtuous bicyclist in a sea of cars.

Back on my bike, I adopted a strict full-stop policy for pedestrians. Again and again I stopped and waited as other bicyclists flew past me, careened around the pedestrians, ignored the motorists, and pissed off the lot of us equally. Until recently, I too had considered it rebellious and romantic to flout the rules of the road. Slowing down showed me that it was really just selfish and stupid. Weren't those the very same qualities I had so long despised in car drivers? And that's when it hit me: we're all the same. We're all acting selfish, and we all want to go first! This irritating thought has been lodged in my brain ever since. And because we can't all go first, I try each day to remember to stop, slow down, and wave somebody else through ahead of me. Who knows? Maybe that person will give someone else the wave-through. Maybe not. But at least I have the satisfaction of knowing I've given respect on the road instead of merely demanding it. And one other thing I've noticed: I get a lot more smiles than I used to on my way to work.

**DEB GRECO** is a book geek who thinks writing is the most fun you can have after reading. She loves composting, gardening, and riding her bike around San Francisco.

*Chapter Thirty*

# Travels with a Bicycle

## Shawn Granton

*I have* an insatiable urge to travel. When I owned a car, my time off was filled with road trips. When I stopped driving, I discovered the romance of train travel. And when I moved to Portland a decade ago, I was bitten by the bicycling bug. For me, bicycling was the perfect way to explore the urban environment; you can move faster and cover more ground than on foot, and you're not confined to the set schedules and routes of public transit.

At first, when I left Portland to travel, I was perfectly content to leave the bike at home, put on a sturdy pair of boots, and pore over transit maps each time I arrived in a new town. Soon, though, I longed to explore these new places the same way I explored the City of Roses — on two wheels. But I was intimidated by logistics: how could I bring a bike with me? Should I rent or borrow a bike instead? How would I figure out how to get around?

After traveling several times with my bike to new cities, most of my worries have disappeared. With some forethought, all the hurdles can be overcome. Let me walk you, er, roll you through the process!

## BRINGING A BIKE VERSUS RENTING OR BORROWING

The biggest hurdle to bringing a bicycle is...bringing the bicycle. Bringing your own bike means you're riding your own trusty steed rather than an unfamiliar, unproven machine. I feel more comfortable exploring an unfamiliar place on a bike I know: it's one less thing to worry about. You'll usually need to box a bike and pay extra for shipping. Just the thought of this may make you consider renting a bike instead. However, renting or borrowing has its pitfalls. Most rental-bike fleets stock generic "hybrid comfort" bikes that somehow are supposed to fit riders of all sizes. These bikes are generally geared toward casual riders who want to roll along a flat waterfront for an hour or two, not someone who wants to ride all day across town.

And renting a bike can be expensive. In Portland, the average price for a daily rental is $30–40; for a week, it's $80–100. In comparison, bringing your bike on Amtrak will cost you $5–20 one way. Bringing a bike costs about the same as one day of rental!

Packing a bike into the boxes provided by rail services (VIA in Canada or Amtrak in the United States) is not as hard as you might think. Simply remove the pedals, loosen and turn the handlebars, and roll the bike into the box! Make sure you check the schedule, though; not all trains carry checked baggage, and both the departing and arriving station must offer checked baggage service. And while any Amtrak or VIA station that offers checked baggage services should have bike boxes in stock, sometimes they don't. It's wise to call ahead. Some trains, like the Cascade service operating in the Pacific Northwest, offer roll-on service, with no disassembly required.

If you're flying, bringing a bike may be trickier. Airlines have recently started charging a lot more for carrying oversized baggage like bikes, so check carriers for pricing and restrictions. They generally require bikes to be packed in smaller boxes than those supplied by Amtrak or VIA Rail, so more disassembly is required. A clever way to get around the whole boxing jazz is to bring a folding bike. Many airlines, and Amtrak, consider a folding bike to be a regular piece of luggage, so extra costs can be avoided.

# PREPARING TO RIDE IN A NEW CITY

One of the biggest hang-ups for those who want to ride in a new city is "What routes should I take?" Even if you know the town, the routes you choose on a bike are usually different from the ones you'd travel on foot or in a car, or the ones that most guidebooks suggest. The easiest way to sort them all out is to get yourself a bicycle map.

I prefer to get bike maps before I even arrive in a town. Sure, you can find a bike shop and pick up a map there, but this can involve extra time, and not all bike shops are stocked with such basic necessities. It's better to have the map mailed to you ahead of time if you can. Most major cities have some sort of bike map available. Check the city's website: usually bike information is listed under the department of transportation or a related bureau. Sometimes you have to print out a map that appears on the screen; sometimes the site has a handy link for requesting a print version. If you can't find any evidence of a bike map, or if there doesn't appear to be a print version, email the city's department of transportation or public-works department. In the United States, the county government may be the one that makes bike maps.

Once you get a map, locate the places you want to go and plot your routes. But stay flexible: a map is a good starting point, but nothing beats good firsthand advice. I usually hit up a bike shop or two and ask their advice about routes to take and routes to avoid because of hills, traffic, or other drawbacks.

Search the Internet for bicycle-specific information about a particular town. Some cities have good websites for bike news and information, like BikePortland.org; others may have a really active message board, like Minneapolis's MplsBikeLove.com. These are great resources if you are a bike geek and want to glean information on bike shops, infrastructure, happenings, and good places to ride.

## WHILE YOU'RE THERE

Unless you have limited time or a tight itinerary, the best way to explore a new city by bike is to go with the flow. Start your day with a couple of goals in mind, but be open to changing your route to follow a sweet bike path along the river or check out a neighborhood that looks cool. It's tempting to try to pack in too much (and I usually do), but if you can't see it all, save some spots for the next time you're in town.

Feel out the traffic. Some places, like college towns, may have low-traffic streets, designated bike routes, and a higher number of cyclists, so that drivers tend to be more courteous and accepting of two-wheeled traffic. These places invite a casual, relaxed pace. (But don't get too comfy and let your guard down!) In larger, less bike-friendly cities, a more aggressive approach may be appropriate, especially if you end up traveling on busy streets. If a street is too busy for your liking, there's no shame in getting on the sidewalk and walking (or riding very cautiously) until you find a better route.

## A FEW HIGHLIGHTS OF MY TRAVELS

### San Francisco

The city that birthed Critical Mass is fun to bike around. The key is to grab one of the city's handy bike maps, for sale in bicycle shops, which have the grade (steepness) of every single street noted, so you can plan a route that avoids the steepest of the hills.

## Los Angeles

It's a lot easier to get around by bike than you might think. It just takes a bit longer. And riding a bike gives you a chance to explore the less traveled neighborhoods.

## Madison, Wisconsin

Bike paths seem to lead everywhere you want to go. And that is to a lake, of course!

## Minneapolis

Also chockablock with bike paths, plus lots of interesting neighborhoods and bike culture out the wazoo. And more lakes.

## Chicago

The traffic can be intimidating, but there are scads of bike routes and fun settings of postindustrial decay. And it's flat.

## Victoria, Canada

The central city is compact and navigable, and rail trails lead you right from downtown to the edge of wilderness!

## Tucson, Arizona

There aren't many places in the world where you can ride from downtown to a national park in about a hour, checking out saguaro cactus on the way.

# FEEL LIKE A LOCAL

Riding a bicycle has changed my city explorations and in turn my views of cities. For starters, it has given me much more range. Back when I used transit and walking as my means of exploration, I stuck mostly to the central city and known "cool" neighborhoods. With a bike I can still hit up all those places, but then I can ramble farther. If I find a bike path that looks inviting, I can simply take it without worrying how far I can walk before having to turn around or wondering where I can catch a bus back. So I explore further, rolling down bike trails in places like Seattle, Madison, and Minneapolis.

Traveling by bike lets me see cities in a new and interesting light, in a way that some people might feel is crazy. Instead of renting a car in Los Angeles, I explored it by bicycle. The naysayers claim that L.A.'s too full of traffic, pollution, and danger to bike around, but I didn't feel it was that bad. Maybe that was because most people in L.A. are trapped in traffic in their metal boxes, but I could simply ride around the traffic jams.

And I get to feel like a local. Some people don't mind being tourists, but I've never liked the feeling; and nothing cries "Tourist!" more than poring over a guidebook or map on the subway. On a bike, I've been asked for directions more often than I've asked for them!

## On Bicycles

We will always travel, but we need to learn to explore places in a less harmful way. Besides having obvious environmental implications, cars isolate you from the world you're passing through. With a bicycle, there are no barriers. It's liberating to be able to interact more with people and your surroundings. And it's fun! If you take your time and follow your curiosity, biking is a great way to travel and get off the beaten path.

**SHAWN GRANTON** is a bicycle rider, sometime artist, and citizen of Portland, Oregon. He conducts bicycle and walking tours under the banner of the Urban Adventure League. He is also a contributor to *Momentum* magazine.

## Chapter Thirty-One

# Women and the Benefits of Biking

### Elly Blue

*Let me tell you what I think of bicycling. I think it has done more to emancipate women than anything else in the world. It gives women a feeling of freedom and self-reliance. I stand and rejoice every time I see a woman ride by on a wheel...the picture of free, untrammeled womanhood.*

**— SUSAN B. ANTHONY, 1896**

*The* safety bicycle became a craze in North America shortly after the 1888 invention of inflatable tires. It was an affordable personal vehicle, fast and freeing to ride. Unlike its predecessor, the high-wheel or penny-farthing, it didn't place the rider high in the air, under constant threat of pitching forward when the front wheel hit a rock. And this newer, safer machine could be used by a rider in a skirt. It provided an unexpected boon to women, who were ready to seize new freedoms, both in personal mobility and in clothing.

The 1890s saw what we now call the first wave of modern feminism. The suffrage movement was in full swing; the dress-reform movement, after simmering for decades, was well on its way to bringing a women's version of trousers to the mainstream; and the restrictive role to which women had been relegated for most of the Victorian period was being vigorously challenged.

The bicycle burst onto this scene with a roar. Its impact was scandalous, immediate, and pervasive. Photographs from the era show women in bicycling costumes with their stockinged legs showing to the knee. Discomfited cartoonists poked back at new fashion trends like athletic bloomers, showing women lounging with splayed legs at country clubs, smoking, and wearing men's suits, with bicycles by their sides. One cartoon shows a woman in her bicycle costume, talking with a lady friend:

**GERTRUDE:** My dear Jessie, what on earth is that bicycle suit for?
**JESSIE:** Why to wear, of course.
**GERTRUDE:** But you haven't got a bicycle.
**JESSIE:** But I've got a sewing machine!

Clearly, women were seizing these simultaneous advances in technology and the social order to improve their everyday lives. And the forces of social change, just like the trousered women scorching through Central Park astride their bicycles, could not be stopped.

Long skirts posed no barrier to climbing onto a safety bicycle and riding it anywhere, but women adopted knickerbockers or bloomers (named after Amelia Bloomer's failed fashion trend from forty years previously) — essentially loose, knee-length trousers — for athletic purposes, and inevitably they began to cross over into everyday dress. Corsets were completely incompatible with bicycling, as the wearer could neither breathe nor bend. The corset's days were numbered anyway — it had grown controversial even as it grew more popular and more tightly laced — but bicycling, which requires both breathing and bending, beat it into a hastier retreat.

The impact of cycling today is not the same as it was one hundred years ago. With personal cars now offering the freedom and flexibility that the bicycle initially promised, the bicycle has become a tool for mobility for those who cannot or choose not to drive — a population that is not clearly delineated by gender.

Nowadays the bicycle is more noted for its democratic qualities of widespread availability and affordability. In communities built and zoned with private car ownership in mind, the bicycle is often cheaper, more flexible, and more fun than alternatives. During the golden years of the automobile bicycling acquired a social stigma. As a consequence of car-centric infrastructure, it was seen as inferior to the automobile, something people resorted to if they were too young or too poor to drive.

Bicycling is becoming increasingly popular as the personal and societal costs of driving increase. The bicycle offers the opportunity for personal mobility, fitness, a sense of community, happiness, and freedom from stress. It is simple to repair. It offers its rider a way of directly reducing many of the world's woes.

On Bicycles

But, like many advantages, the benefits offered by the bicycle are not as readily available to women as to men. By all accounts, fewer than one-third of bicycle trips in the United States are made by women. The constraints that are keeping North American women off bicycles are not the corsets and culture of the 1890s, but they are in some ways more rigid, as they are built into the landscape.

Because our cities and suburbs are set up with driving in mind, homes, shopping, workplaces, and other destinations are far apart. For most women, more than for men, getting to and from work often involves stopping at a grocery store and running errands, with a child in tow for all or part of the trip — and nobody is waiting with dinner ready when they get home. Doing it all on a bicycle can seem daunting or impossible.

In the United States, men enjoy nearly 40 percent more leisure time than women; women's earnings, meanwhile, are only 76.5 percent of men's. Even in households where both a male and a female partner work full-time, child care and unpaid labor like running errands, cooking, and cleaning tend to fall to the woman. Policies that restrict paternity leave reinforce women's role as the primary caregiver for children. A mother's routine, with its trips to soccer practice, school, the store, and other, often far-flung destinations, often restricts transportation choices to one: the car.

In bicycle-friendly locations, roughly equal numbers of women and men ride bikes. In the Netherlands, where 27 percent of trips are made by bicycle, 55 percent of riders are women. In Germany, 49 percent of riders are women. In 2009, Minneapolis, Minnesota, was named the most bicycle-friendly city in the United

States; in 2010 it was also found to have the highest percentage of women riders, at 45 percent.

What measures would persuade — or enable — American women to bicycle more? A study in 2008, described in *Scientific American*, found that women in Portland, Oregon, were far more likely than men to use residential, traffic-calmed streets and even bike lanes rather than taking major roads — even if they had to go out of their way to do so.[1] The article referred to women as an "indicator species" of the bicycle-friendliness of a community. If you want more people riding bikes, these findings suggest, build bikeways that women want to ride on.

Solving this problem is complicated, of course. Bike infrastructure tends to be built only where planners perceive demand for it (just as bikes suitable for everyday riding aren't built and sold where there's nobody lusting to trade their car in for one). But when people choose not to ride to work because the only possible route is along a busy highway and they don't know anybody else who does it, it's easy for politicians to conclude that there's no demand for better bikeways.

The one constant factor that seems to exist in every bike-friendly community is a social movement. And those movements are shaped by the people they are made up of. Just as the bicycle provided a major boost for the women's liberation movement,

the contemporary movement for greater equality for women can do much to level the transportation playing field, freeing women from their cars and providing a better bicycling environment for everyone.

**ELLY BLUE** lives in Portland, Oregon, where she writes about bicycling, publishes a zine, co-organizes a women's bicycling business alliance, and is the co-owner of PDXbyBike.com.

1 See "How to Get More Bicyclists on the Road," *Scientific American*, October 16, 2009, www.scientificamerican.com/article.cfm?id=getting-more-bicyclists-on-the-road.

## Chapter Thirty-Two

# Biking with Kids

## Chris Keam

**North** America's resurgent cycling culture is maturing. Many early adopters of the bike lifestyle are beginning a new stage in their lives. In making the transition from youthful independence to being adults with dependents, they face a challenge their parents probably never considered: raising bike-friendly kids. It's a challenge that goes beyond simply getting kids on bikes.

To accommodate cycling kids means rethinking the way we design our neighborhoods, with safer streets and recreational amenities located closer to where children live. It means a new emphasis on function over fashion for manufacturers of children's bicycles. It certainly means that schools, employers, and businesses need to rethink the way they operate — for example, by providing more bike racks on the school grounds, lockers and showers in the workplace, and space for bike trailers at the mall parking lot. Most of all, it means leading by example.

When they cycle together, many parents and children develop a connection that cannot exist in an automobile. Cycling together is a shared experience, unlike a car trip, with its inherent power differential between driver and passenger. Nothing builds a child's self-esteem quite like trust and responsibility. Letting your kids ride for transportation means giving them both. And the benefits aren't all on the child's side.

For parents, cycling with their children opens up a range of possibilities that don't exist inside a car. It can be something as simple as a quick stop to enjoy the antics of a cheeky squirrel or mischievous crow, or the feeling of pride in a child who is pedaling hard on a tandem or trail-a-bike to make it a little easier to climb a hill. Or it might be something farther reaching, such as the awareness of creating a new future for everyone, setting an example of self-reliance and commitment that inspires others.

Most of all, though, it's the chance to share feelings that most people have forgotten. A bicycle can bring out the kid in a grown-up — and give a kid a chance to show resilience and strength. When those things happen, everybody wins.

But how do we make them happen? "One of the things we're finding is we need to teach kids and parents together," said Wendy Kallins, program director for Safe Routes to Schools, based in Marin County, California. Formed in 2003, the group works to encourage the development of kid- and bike-friendly infrastructure along road systems near schools. "One of the biggest impediments to getting kids on bikes is getting parents on bikes," added Kallins. "For parents who are not cyclists, everything seems dangerous."

Some of these fears are valid. Riders under the age of 16

accounted for 13 percent of all U.S. cycling fatalities in 2008, according to the Insurance Institute for Highway Safety, with kids between the ages of 13 and 15 cited as being particularly at risk. However, one mother thinks we need to give kids more freedom and trust their ability to make sensible choices. "What I always wonder," said Lenore Skenazy, author of *Free-Range Kids*, "is, do parents think their kids are so much less competent than they were?"

In some situations, cycling for transportation is obviously unsafe for kids, such as in exurbs where freeways and major roads are the only links between homes, schools, parks, and stores. When children can't use bikes for getting around, however, Skenazy believes, kids and parents both lose. "Why wouldn't you want your kid to gain some independence, have some fun, get some exercise,

and get themselves to school? As someone once wrote to me, there's not a prize for the most exhausted parent!"

It wasn't always this way. In 1969, 48 percent of American kids walked or cycled to school. By 2009, that number had dropped to 13 percent, where it stabilized. Thankfully, education, cycling clubs, and kids themselves are proving a powerful combination, removing fears and creating a new generation of pedal pushers. Determined to do their part for the planet, plenty of kids see cycling as a fun way to pitch in. Bike-friendly teachers and cycling advocacy groups are eager to support them, with clubs and bike-skills training. In addition, gridlocked transportation networks, skyrocketing rates of childhood obesity, and climate change are further convincing the public and policy makers that getting kids on bikes is an important step toward creating sustainable and healthy communities.

Still, the very design of our towns and cities can be a gigantic roadblock for kids who want to meet their transportation needs. Richard Gilbert is a Toronto transportation analyst working on developing child-friendly land-use and transport-planning guidelines for cities across North America. One of his key recommendations is to create kid-friendly routes to pools, libraries, parks, and schools so that youngsters can get places on their own. Too often, kids can't go anywhere without the help of Mom's (or Dad's) Taxi.

Wide adoption of Gilbert's guidelines will require big policy and funding changes. In the meantime, he has practical advice for parents who want to ensure bike trips are a manageable distance for children. "Kids can bike far, if they want to," said Richard. "A kilometer for each year of age is an easy recreational ride, but halve that or less for a functional ride (where something, like school, has to be done at the other end). With training, an 8-year-old can have good traffic sense and skills. Without training, parents might well worry about a 12-year-old."

Many groups recognize the need to accommodate and encourage young cyclists. Kidical Mass, described as a legal, safe, and fun ride for kids, is now bringing young families together for group cycling adventures in twelve cities in the United States and Canada. Pécs, Hungary, launched the first European version in 2009. Trips for Kids began in Marin County, California, in the late 1980s. The nonprofit organization takes at-risk kids out of the city for mountain biking trips. More than sixty thousand kids have participated, and the organization now has over sixty chapters in the United States and Canada, as well as a chapter in Israel.

In Oakland, California, Tyrone "Baybe Champ" Stevenson spawned a new cycling subculture of kids who co-opt the big wheels and flashy rims of scraper cars for their customized bikes. The scraper movement began as a program that gave young people an alternative to drugs and gangs, encouraged them to do well in school, and taught them how to deck out their bikes. It's now taking root as far afield as Germany.

Stephanie Gray coordinates the After School Bikes program at eleven schools in Vancouver, Canada. She says most of the kids come for fun, especially at the elementary level. Others are attracted to the earn-a-bike program, which helps kids without bikes build bikes of their own.

With the older participants, social and economic factors come into play. "Some of the high school students are motivated by the environmental reasons, as well as the freedom, and the fact that cycling is cheaper than a car," said Gray. "I had one parent say: 'You're not going to take those kids riding on the road?' Well, yeah, that's the point. After a couple of months, you see a huge difference with their skills and safety level on the road, so hopefully we are able to continue the dialogue and say: 'Look, watch your kids. They are actually now very capable and confident cyclists riding on the road.'"

The number of girls participating (in all aspects of the club) is another hopeful sign for Gray. "We have some schools where there are more girls than boys. The changes are also more extreme with the girls. Generally, they are more timid in the beginning, especially around the repair and mechanics side of things, but they make huge strides. I had one girl tell me it was her goal in life to prove that girls can do everything that boys can do!"

"If there was more education out there,...it would help so many people," said David Pulsipher, who rides in Culver City, California, with his toddler, George. A planner by trade and cycling dad by nature, Pulsipher's experiences inspired him to start a blog called *Kids, Bikes, Dads*. "With today's economy, it seems like every family is looking for ways to save money and spend more time together. The bicycle is a double whammy in that regard."

Traffic smarts are a form of literacy. Just as we understand the value of requiring kids to learn to read and write, we must realize that navigating transportation networks is another crucial skill in the modern age — and just as deserving of public funding. If governments are going to ask individuals of all ages to do their part when it comes to reducing our reliance on car travel, those who control the public purse strings must also shoulder their portion of the burden.

To get kids on bikes, we need to find the fortitude to spend money on kid-friendly road networks and comprehensive traffic-safety education from an early age, and the courage to stand up for those who can't cast a vote yet. When it comes to cycling, despite the lip service paid by so many politicians regarding principles of sustainability, too few are willing to find answers to a very simple question: What about the children?

**CHRIS KEAM** has been delivering words by bike since his days as a rural paperboy. He began combining cycling and writing again in the mid-1990s, covering racing, travel, and industry news. With public interest in active transportation reborn, much of Chris's cycling coverage now chronicles the cultural and personal effects of the shift to cycling-friendly cities.

## Chapter Thirty-Three

# Collective Bike Shops
## Amy Walker

**Collective** bike shops are colorful community centers dedicated to repairing and reviving used bicycles in the service of education, equality, and peace. These vibrant, volunteer-run spaces are not driven by profit motives, so what keeps them going? According to Camille Metcalfe at the Bike Dump, a collective in Winnipeg, Canada, "It's a space that facilitates cooperation and learning — and friends! A nonthreatening environment which leads to good community building and an encouraging space for people to explore what may have been intimidating otherwise."

Bikes are the focal point of these thriving social hubs. They are seen as tools for individual empowerment, environmental responsibility, community self-sufficiency, and learning. Collective bike shops share many of the following organizational characteristics:

→ Nonprofit
→ Run or staffed by volunteers

- → Nonhierarchical
- → Run by consensus decision making

Their typical activities, in addition to fee-based repair services, include the following:

- → Accepting donations of bikes and bike parts for reuse
- → Recycling and reusing bikes and bike parts
- → Providing free or low-cost services to the community
- → Teaching people how to fix bikes
- → Offering earn-a-bike programs for youth
- → Offering programs or shop times exclusively for certain groups, such as women and transgendered people
- → Shipping bikes to underprivileged communities in other countries

While staff and volunteers operate by collective principles in their shops, they also have ties to other community organizations. The Bike Collective Network (www.bikecollectives.org) is a resource for grassroots bike-shop organizers. The wiki page lists about 300 organizations worldwide (250 in the United States and Canada) and includes a bike-collective starter kit. This is an evolving resource that includes advice on philosophical, structural, and legal considerations, fund-raising, staffing, and suggested activities.

In 1984, the Boston bicycle mechanic and activist Carl Kurz launched Bikes Not Bombs by bringing two refurbished bikes to Nicaragua as a peaceful protest against aggressive American foreign policy. As it expanded into a program sending thousands of bikes to people in less affluent countries like South Africa, Ghana, and Guatemala, the organization also branched out into community education, including earn-a-bike programs. The shop became a model for the community bike-shop movement that took off in the 1990s. Today, Bikes Not Bombs continues to operate according to principles of equitable and sustainable use of resources, seeing equitable community engagement as a path to peace and social justice. The collective's work had a ripple effect that inspired people to form hundreds of nonprofit, community-based bike collectives worldwide.

One of those community bike shops, founded in 1992 and incorporated as a nonprofit in 1999, is Our Community Bikes (OCB) in Vancouver, Canada. Step into the usually busy shop at seventeenth and Main, you'll see a diverse collection of people, some sifting through large plastic bins full of bicycle parts, some working on bikes at the four repair stands in the rear workshop area, and maybe one or two standing, looking slightly bewildered, in the front of the store. The space is decorated with bicycle pieces, parts, and frames, funky posters, art, and a large message board beside the front door. The clients are mostly young transportation bikers with a do-it-yourself ethic, though the shop also serves people of a broad range of ages and ethnicities, including families.

When I spoke to Jesse Cooper, a senior staff member who has worked at OCB for eight years, he was sewing a screen-printed banner onto a 3' × 4' tool roll that volunteers and staff would use for testing and fixing bikes at one of many public events OCB attends throughout the spring and summer.

## On Bicycles

Although it has often struggled to stay open, OCB feels like a special scene, a sort of alternative community center. But what is it like to be an insider? According to Cooper, there's a family feeling among collective members, and staff have a great deal of autonomy in their work. "It is almost liberating to be able to accomplish work that you enjoy doing — if you like wrenching on bikes and fixing things and working with your community, talking and networking with people. It's very social. There's always conversation happening, apart from instruction or shop business. It's very political, because we're all opinionated, and we're all artists and musicians as well. It's very entertaining. It's great to be in an environment where you have the freedom to speak. You don't have to worry about a boss, and you don't have to worry about not having the support you need from your peers."

Part of this feeling of support and solidarity comes from sharing common goals. At OCB, these include education and alleviating poverty, creating a safe space where everyone is welcome, reducing attitudes of entitlement and materialism, and keeping people aware of what kind of impact they have in their community, as well as municipally and globally.

Work at a community shop can have deeper rewards when patrons offer feedback about the ways that having a bicycle has affected their lives. "Say you have someone who's in a severe state of depression and they're cloistered at home all the time.... We get amazing feedback from care workers, like, 'This person never would have been interested in being physically active without their bicycle. They started to motivate themselves, and then they started doing other things and going to class.'" Says Cooper, "And I'm thinking to myself, 'All because of a bicycle?' and they say, 'Yes, all because of a bicycle. We've seen these clients for years, and the bicycle was the catalyst for them being the master of their own destiny on a piece of transportation.'"

The Bike! Bike! conference is an annual gathering of community bicycle projects from across the United States and Canada, attended by more than one hundred representatives from approximately sixty community bike-repair organizations. Workshops, taught by participants, cover the range of issues that affect life in the bike shop, such as combating racism, gender inclusiveness, storage problems, facilitation, grant writing, and consensus decision making. Evening festivities include group bike rides, video screenings, and dance parties. Volunteers prepare vegetarian food, and entrance is by donation. The conference is held in a different city each year, hosted by a local organization. Bike! Bike! has visited New Orleans, Tucson, Milwaukee, Pittsburgh, San Francisco, Minneapolis, Toronto, and, in 2011, San Marcos, Texas.

For some reason, many Los Angeles bike collectives seem to have a connection to cooking. There's the Bicycle Kitchen or Bici Cocina, the Bike Oven, and also Bikerowave. For a suggested donation of around $7, volunteers who run these shops teach local people how to build or fix their own bikes.  In these shops, music plays as people learn mechanical skills and cooperation while they teach each other to build bikes for commuting, racing, polo, doing tricks, or just having fun and making friends. In these cauldrons of bike culture, people also cook up interesting events like Midnight Ridazz, a gigantic nighttime group ride. A look at the website Midnightridazz.com shows that there's a social bike ride almost every night of the year in L.A. (including milkshake rides, Taco Tuesdays, and plenty of other rides that end with food!). Could this robust bike culture be due to the large number of community bike shops in that city?

Bike collectives are about as humble as the bicycle. They are simple, purposeful, equitable, and effective. Sharing a workshop, like sharing a meal, brings people together in a positive way — and community bike shops have a recipe that is both good for you and delicious!

# Chapter Thirty-Four

# Earn-a-Bike Programs
## Lessons from Chicago's West Town Bikes

## John Greenfield

*Across* North America, dozens of nonprofit community bicycle shops are using earn-a-bike programs to teach mechanics, road safety, and life skills to underserved youth.

"It broadens their perspectives and teaches them the world is accessible," says Alex Wilson, founder and director of Chicago's West Town Bikes and a self-declared "bike freeek" (his spelling). "They learn you can take an old bike, fix it up, and use it for transportation. Meanwhile, they're learning job skills and responsibility."

There are approximately eighty earn-a-bike programs in the United States and about twenty in Canada. In a typical class, staff or volunteers teach students how to fix up old bikes, often abandoned cycles donated by building managers or other nonprofit organizations. The kids learn to take apart, clean, reassemble, and adjust the different systems of the bikes, including the drivetrain, wheels, bearings, brakes; they also learn maintenance skills like fixing flats.

Most programs also include bike-safety instruction, rides, and field trips. "We make a point of taking kids on rides to schools, colleges, and workplaces," says Wilson. "Being able to discover your city by bike is a pretty fantastic thing." After completing an earn-a-bike course, usually a month or two long, students get the satisfaction of keeping the bikes they have fixed up themselves.

Wilson founded West Town Bikes in 2004 in Chicago's Humboldt Park community, a low-income, mostly Latino and African American neighborhood on the city's West Side, where drugs, violence, and gangs are major issues. The shop is located on the Paseo Boricua (Puerto Rican Promenade) business strip, defined on both ends by 59-foot-tall arches shaped like Puerto Rican flags.

At the front of West Town's space is Ciclo Urbano (Urban Bike), a retail store offering refurbished rides, basic commuter gear, and repairs, with service available in Spanish and English. In back is the workshop and classroom, with multiple work stands and sets of tools.

West Town runs many programs for young people as well as mechanics classes and "Tinker Town" open-shop sessions for adults. Most of the youth programs are taught off-site at schools and community centers. In 2009 they served about 750 young people; in 2010 they served over a thousand in more than twenty-five programs; and in 2011 they plan to expand even more.

"The kids are learning communication, teamwork, and the value of being dependable," says the program manager, Liz Clarkson. "Being held accountable for your work does wonders. Introducing a structured environment around an unconventional activity that involves using your hands really brings out the best in kids who've had problems succeeding in school."

Because West Town has now been operating for the better part of a decade, it's possible to track the effect its programs have had on young adults who grew up with them. Reymel Matos, 21, got involved as a young teen through BickerBikes, an earn-a-bike program sponsored by Bickerdike Redevelopment Corporation, an affordable-housing provider. His favorite aspect of the program was the travel. "We did miles and miles of biking all over town," he says.

The next year Matos served as an assistant, and then he was hired to help teach a program at a neighborhood middle school. "I didn't see it as work," he says. "I was like, 'Getting paid to ride my bike around the city? Where do I sign up?'" Nowadays he works at a hip-hop music and clothing store and attends Wright College with plans to study business.

"If I didn't get involved with West Town, I'd have a lot less appreciation for how easy it is to get around by bike," Matos says. "And I learned that with a little effort you can go anywhere and make anything happen."

Damian Lee, 21, was a teen when he first interned with an earn-a-bike program at a South Side elementary school. "The students were tough kids, dealing with more stuff than you or I could fathom," he says. "They'd say, 'There's this gang — they want me.' Some of them were neglected by their parents. It was shocking, but it made me more compassionate."

In his second year with the program, he became a full-fledged instructor, and he currently studies biology at the University of Chicago, has a job delivering sandwiches by bike, and volunteers at a science museum and at a community center for lesbian, gay, bisexual, and transgendered youth. "Without West Town I would still be driving a car, and I'd be worried about things in life that you really shouldn't be worried about at my age," he says. "I love riding bikes. You are 100 percent connected to nature, and your bicycle expresses your individuality."

Before LaPorchia Birts, 22, interned with West Town as a teenager, she hadn't ridden a bike since she was a little girl. "I never saw myself working on bicycles, but once I started doing it I got really into it. I know how to change a flat, fix brakes, replace a bottom bracket — just about everything."

Nowadays Birts is studying criminal justice at Truman College. She's looking for a job to support her three daughters, and in the future she hopes to become a youth corrections officer. "West Town opened up a lot of doors for me," she says. "Before this I wanted to do fashion design, but now I want to help keep kids from getting into trouble and to fight childhood obesity. I wouldn't trade it for any experience in the world."

Isodoro "Izzy" Topete, 22, was a teen at Humboldt Park's Clemente High School when he joined a bike class run by West Town for After School Matters, a Chicago nonprofit organization. He soon helped teach an adult build-a-bike class at West Town and then taught after-school youth programs and adult classes solo for several years. His favorite aspect was working with the children. "Kids from lower-income neighborhoods were always open to hanging out and learning something different," he says.

His mechanic's skills have directly benefited his family. His brother Arturo, 25, has muscular dystrophy and can't ride a regular bike. "I built him a hybrid tricycle with a motor," Topete says. "Now he can do most warm-weather West Town and Critical Mass rides."

After high school, Topete studied chemistry at Wright College and Northeastern University and had earned his master's degree by the time he was 22. "I worked my butt off," he says. Currently he manages bike-parking corrals for summer festivals, and he eventually hopes to teach high school. "West Town bikes gave me a good foundation to 'independ-icize' myself," Topete says.

"All of these young people have real stories of how West Town Bikes and bicycling have changed their lives," Wilson says. "Bikes can't necessarily address issues of housing, child care, and employment. But I believe that having been involved with bicycling and West Town has had a real positive effect in their lives and the decisions they've made. I have high hopes for the young people who have been involved at West Town Bikes and believe that it has made a better world for all of them."

**JOHN GREENFIELD** is a Chicago-based freelance writer specializing in bicycling, walking, and transit issues. His writing has appeared in *Momentum*, *Bicycling*, *Urban Velo Dirt Rag*, *Kickstand*, and numerous Windy City publications.

## Chapter Thirty-Five

# Ciclovia
## A Celebration of Car-Free Streets

### Jeff Mapes

*When* I cycled between the traffic cones strung across Portland's North Shaver Street, I felt a moment of delicious disorientation. The light motor vehicle traffic of a Sunday morning had vanished, and the road in front of me was suddenly filled with cyclists, walkers, and skaters.

But what really struck me were the kids. They were everywhere, riding in trailers or on a tandem with Mom or Dad. Or they were pedaling furiously on their miniature bikes and trikes, or dashing back and forth across the street on foot. Was there any young family in the city that hadn't taken to the streets on this summer morning?

That's how it seemed at Portland's first Sunday Parkways event in the summer of 2008. An estimated fifteen thousand people made their way to a six-mile loop of streets through one of the city's pleasant but otherwise unremarkable neighborhoods.

## On Bicycles

What was the attraction? Well, the loop passed four parks where local bands played and an assortment of vendors and non-profit groups had set up booths. But the real draw was nothing fancier than residential streets temporarily free of vehicle traffic. They turned into an instant park that attracted thousands of people with the sheer novelty of being able to walk or pedal down an ordinary street without having to worry about cars.

Linda Ginenthal, the City of Portland official who organized the event, was amazed at the size of the crowd attracted by this one simple notion. "We wanted to have people play in the streets together," she said.

And so they did. From that one gathering in 2008, Sunday Parkways has now grown to five events a year, each held in a different neighborhood. It's a big part of Portland's summer social calendar, and one clearly welcomed by parents looking for some cheap and healthy fun with their children.

The idea of the Ciclovia (essentially a car-free street party) originated in Bogotá, Colombia. Although Portland was one of the first cities to import it, the concept has taken North America by storm. By 2010, more than forty cities in the United States and Canada — and one entire state, Kentucky — had launched their own car-free-street events. And it's a movement that shows no sign of abating. In late 2010, Los Angeles — the symbolic home of North America's auto culture — hosted a "CicLAvia" through the heart of the city that allowed Angelenos to experience their wide boulevards at walking and biking speeds. Between 50,000 and 100,000 people took the city up on the offer, according to media accounts.

Bike advocates, who have been the prime movers of Ciclovia events in North America, see them as a way to get more people to experience the joy of cycling and to plant the idea that they could do the same even on an ordinary day. The public-health community sees it as an easy way to encourage people to engage in physical activity. Civic activists talk about the Ciclovia as a way to build community and bring different ethnic groups and neighborhoods together. And for politicians, it brings the festive atmosphere and plaudits of a ribbon cutting for a grand public-works project — without the expense of actually building anything.

Bogotá's Ciclovia has long been talked about in the bicycling and "livable-streets" community, particularly since Bogotá's former mayor Enrique Peñalosa hit the international lecture circuit to talk about how he brought recreation to the masses when he ran the city from 1998 to 2001. On Peñalosa's watch — and that of his brother, Gil Peñalosa, who was Bogotá's parks commissioner — the Ciclovia was expanded to cover more than seventy miles in the huge, sprawling city. For the Peñalosas, it was part of a drive to provide recreation and transport to the masses instead of catering primarily to the car-owning elite.

Bogotá's weekly Ciclovia inspired similar events in several other cities in Latin America. But it was a 2007 video — not quite ten minutes long — from the videographer Clarence Eckerson that really launched the Ciclovia in North America.

Eckerson works for Streetfilms, one of the projects launched by the New York hedge fund millionaire Mark Gorton, who has become one of the most prominent backers of the livable-streets movement. Eckerson's video is inspirational, showing everyone from grandmas to tots enjoying Bogotá's car-free streets and the mass aerobics sessions offered in the city parks. Gil Peñalosa, who accompanied Eckerson when he made the video, describes it as being "like a big party that everybody attends, the rich, the poor, the old, the young — everybody."

Given Bogotá's hard-to-shake reputation as one of the world's most violent cities, the social cohesion of the Ciclovia is no minor accomplishment. The event attracts a mind-boggling 1.5 million residents. For many, this one event gives them the minimum weekly exercise that health experts say they need.

Eckerson's video — which has had at least a quarter-million views on the Internet — had an impact. Requests for more information poured into Streetfilms, and pretty soon Eckerson found himself documenting Ciclovias in places like Portland, San Francisco, and his own city, New York. "Politicians really started getting on board," said Eckerson. "They realized how many people loved it, and they saw this as being maybe something people will remember when they go into the voting booth."

The events are not without their difficulties. Portland's Ginenthal said cities need to mobilize a large corps of volunteers, find community acceptance for the route, and pay the overtime costs for police (who are needed to control traffic at major intersections along the route). Some cities have held one or two Ciclovias but have not found the funding to make it a regular event.

Portland estimated that its five Sunday Parkways cost about $360,000 in 2010, with private sponsors picking up just over half of the tab. Kaiser Permanente, a national health-care provider, was the chief sponsor, kicking in $100,000. (In fact, hospitals and other health organizations often like to attach their names to Ciclovias. In New York City, the major sponsor is the grocery chain Whole Foods, suggesting that the event definitely appeals to affluent urbanites.)

Mike Lydon, an urban planner and a coauthor of the *Smart Growth Manual* who frequently writes about cycling issues, helped bring the Ciclovia to Miami and has studied the movement around North America. Because it's relatively easy for a city to implement, it can serve multiple goals, he said. In Miami, it helped bring people back to an often-neglected part of downtown. In Kentucky, the focus has been on encouraging physical activity in a state that has one of the highest rates of child obesity in the country. And in many cities, bike advocates see it as a way to get political leaders to start talking about the harder work of creating a permanent bicycling network.

"It introduces people to the idea, again, that they can ride their bike," said Lydon. And it introduces political leaders to the idea that they can give their residents an intimate view of their city they don't usually get.

Here's my favorite example of the latter. In Lexington, Kentucky, officials gave people a chance to bike, walk, and skate on a newly built runway at the local airport. "Communities like Lexington have begun looking for new and more frequent opportunities to use existing infrastructure throughout the year to promote healthy and active lifestyles," said one city councilman, Jay McChord, in a press release announcing the event.

Comfortable though I am riding in everyday traffic, I never want to miss one of Portland's Sunday Parkways. It's like a block party spread out over several miles. I never fail to see friends from all areas of my life. Once a half-dozen of us decided to walk one of the parkways that looped through downtown and the trendy Pearl District. In some ways, it was more fun than cycling. It was easier to talk, and we didn't have to deliberate over whether to stop at a particular booth or park. And there was a certain rush to walking down the middle of the street without having to look out for cars.

Whether I'm on a bike or on foot, I still find myself seeing new things along streets I have been down dozens of times before, whether it's the way trees form a canopy over a street or simply an interesting architectural detail on a house.

The one time I rode in New York City's Summer Streets, I gaped at the dramatic concrete canyons of Fifth Avenue as I casually rode down the middle of the street. It was almost like seeing the city for the first time.

That experience of finding joy and wonder in our everyday streets — whether it's Fifth Avenue or an unheralded neighborhood street in a small Kentucky town — is certainly a big part of what has led to the rapid growth of the Ciclovia in North America. The next question is whether the Ciclovia will change the way people use public space on every other day of the year.

**JEFF MAPES** is a writer and blogger for *The Oregonian* in Portland who has covered politics for more than three decades. He is also the author of *Pedaling Revolution: How Cyclists Are Changing American Cities*. His last transportation purchase was an eighty-pound cargo bike.

# Chapter Thirty-Six

# Bike Party
## Dan Goldwater

*It's* New Year's Eve, 2010, and I'm riding around downtown San Francisco with fifty friends. Clear skies are holding. On most nights the streets are for transport, but tonight the boundary is pushed as seas of people flow to and from parties. The excitement spills out onto the pavement. Everywhere we go, people cheer and dance as we roll by. We encourage them out of their shells. Come out! Party in the street with us! Eventually we make our way to the waterfront, where thousands sit bundled up, solemnly waiting for the fireworks. As we roll up, there's a wave of smiles. We park our bikes on the boardwalk, crank up our trailer-mounted sound system with some Afro-Cuban All Stars, and the salsa dancing breaks out. It doesn't stop until an hour later with the first "Kaboom!" from the fireworks erupting overhead.

I hope you are thinking, why can't this happen where I live? It can. And not just on New Year's — it can happen any time you want it to.

## On Bicycles

Across America, our pavement is usually just used for going places or parking. This is an unfortunate result of our isolating, car-centric culture. In a car, each person is boxed away. Rolling together by bike, we share a common social space, not just with other riders but with everyone on the street.

Bike Party is a group ride that takes advantage of this common social space. Using music and dancing, it engages everyone on the street in a positive energy. Bike Party started in San Jose in 2008 and spread to Oakland and San Francisco in 2010. Bike Party is a mobile celebration — it's for riders of all types and skill levels, using planned routes to explore the city. Participants often dress in costume, according to the theme of the month, and they bring mobile sound systems so you can ride behind the one playing your favorite tunes. Bike Party brings together riders and nonriders by making the ride fun and safe, with stops to dance and socialize.

Bike Party has become tremendously popular, not just among avid cyclists but among occasional riders who don't always think of themselves as cyclists. On Friday nights, we often pass entire families cheering on their front lawn as the party rolls by. Bike Party gives people a new and compelling reason to hop on a bike. It is empowering and transformative, too: after participating a few times, new riders have the skills and confidence to bike around town anytime, and many do.

Bike Party's success is not accidental. Growing to more than three thousand riders each month is a result of innovations in both organizing and technology. Many of these were learned from or inspired by other bike events, but Bike Party puts them all together.

Whatever city or town you live in, I'd like to help you make your own Bike Party.

## HOW WE RIDE

Bike Party has some simple ride rules to help set a positive tone. Different Bike Party rides adjust their rules slightly depending on their local customs. All participants are encouraged to remind others of these rules. Riders who ignore these rules and act negatively toward others on the street are asked to leave.

- Stay in the right lane (avoid blocking traffic when possible).
- Leave no trace.
- Stop at red lights.
- Ride predictably and in control.
- Roll past conflict.
- Ride prepared.
- Tell people it's a Bike Party!
- Communicate the rules to other riders.

## ORGANIZING

A few organizing steps are needed to create a ride that is more than just an in-crowd event for you and your experienced cyclist friends. Bike Party is designed to welcome novice cyclists and to grow by attracting people who might never have considered participating in a bike-based event. It takes a little planning to do this well.

- Get three or four friends to help organize. This will be enough to manage a ride of 250 people or so.

→ Set the ride for Friday night or Saturday night, starting around 8 PM.

→ Plan a ten- to fifteen-mile route around your town, with two or three stops for partying.

→ Pick a party theme — something that's easy to pull off on a bike.

→ Set up a website (we use Wordpress.com), email list (we use Google Groups), a Facebook group, and maybe a Twitter feed. For a small ride, just one of these channels will probably be enough.

→ During a ride, we communicate using Twitter or group texting (using a service like Textmarks.com). We text riders to warn them of any snafu, and we get the word out to latecomers when we arrive at party spots.

→ Print some ride flyers. Post them around town, and "spoke card" all the bikes at public-transit stops, college campuses, etc. We printed up five thousand 3" × 4" cards at Uprinting.com for about $100.

→ Post the route a few days before the ride. If people know where they're going, they won't need to run red lights to keep up with the leaders, and riders can easily join up for just the first half or second half of the ride.

→ Make a turn-by-turn sheet of directions for the route. These are usually the easiest kinds of directions for riders to follow without having to stop.

# SOUND

Music really gets the party going; it instantly engages the people you pass on the street, making this a party for everyone. Mobile sound systems are much better than they used to be: lighter, louder, less expensive, and easy to put together. At Instructables.com/member/dan, I have instructions for putting together several different sizes of sound systems, from rear-rack size to trailer size.

When choosing music, think about the people on the street around you. I recommend danceable beats — if you see people jamming with the tune, you know it's working! Angry, yelling music will not get you many smiles.

# ROUTE PLANNING

Planning a route for fifty or more riders, including novices, is a lot different from planning one for yourself. The leaders need to be 100 percent sure about where they're going. Always plan and test your route beforehand.

We usually do two test rides. On the first, we explore different routes to see what works best. We always find things like road construction or problem intersections that make us change things around. On the second, all the organizers ride the finalized route together; it helps everyone remember the route.

→ The ride is a great way to learn about and explore your city. If you are just starting out and want to grow your ride, start at a well-known, central location. Plan different routes and party spots each time. As your ride grows, you can start at different locations.

→ Minimize left turns on busy streets; make them where the road has a left-turn lane.

→ When you need to cross a busy road, do it at a light. Crossings at stop signs are a challenge with a big group.

→ Minimize hills. Learn to get around your city while avoiding the hills.

→ Plazas, large parking lots, and city parks are all good party stops.

→ Pass near public-transit stops a couple of times during the ride in case someone has an unfixable mechanical problem. On your route sheet, indicate where public-transit connections can be made.

## MARKING

You may find it helpful to have badges, sashes, or some other creative way to identify ride volunteers. Moderate-sized groups will often get broken into clumps because of traffic, and it helps keep everyone on track when they can easily identify someone nearby who knows the correct route.

## THE LAW

Bike Party encourages all participants to follow the law. Be aware of your local traffic laws and noise ordinances. Sadly, you may encounter law-enforcement officers who are unfamiliar with bicycle-related traffic laws or may simply be suspicious of your motives. It helps to have a printed "ride rules" sheet for this circumstance.

Over time, these officers will see that your ride is a positive social event for the community.

# ON THE RIDE

## At the Start

Ride leaders should show up at the start of the ride about thirty minutes early.

Assign four to six people to be "turn guides." Give each one a copy of the turn-by-turn directions. You can assign them to specific turns if you want, or let people manage the turns they get to first (see below).

Announce the ride rules before you start.

Make sure people know where the ride will end and places along the ride where they can connect with public transport.

## During the Ride

Organizers take the following positions:

- → 1–2 leaders
- → 1–2 mechanics at the rear with tool kits
- → 4–8 turn guides

Instructions for turn guides:

- → Start at the front of the ride.
- → At the first turn, stop and stand near the turn.
- → Point out the turn to all the riders as they pass you.
- → Wait until the last rider passes.
- → Then bust your ass up to the front and do it again!

→ While busting up to the front, help keep people in the right lane, watch for anyone having trouble, and say hi to your new friends!

With two to four turn guides, you'll be able to station someone at every turn. At busy intersections, the turn guide can temporarily block opposing traffic to let riders cross, but we try to avoid doing this.

Instructions for leaders:

→ The leader must keep a slow pace. Experienced riders naturally go too fast for novices. I use a speedometer (or a 100-pound sound trailer) to keep my speed down to 10–12 mph.

→ If people ride off in front of you, don't worry about it. Some people just like to do that, and nothing you can do will make them stop. If you wear some visual identification, it will help those behind you to find the right person to follow.

Mechanics stay at the rear and make sure nobody gets left behind.

Plan party stops lasting ten to thirty minutes. When people get to the stop, let them know how long you'll be staying.

Bike Party resources:

→ SJBikeParty.org
→ SFBikeParty.org
→ EastBayBikeParty.org

**DAN GOLDWATER** operates MonkeyLectric, where he develops revolutionary bike-lighting products. He also writes a DIY column for *Momentum* magazine and cofounded Instructables.com.

# PART FOUR

## Getting Serious

## Chapter Thirty-Seven

# Bike-Friendly Workplaces
## Bonnie Fenton

*I used* to pretend I was Superman, twice a day. I didn't leap tall buildings or save people or anything. But I changed my clothes in small spaces, and the Superman image always came to mind. I cycled to work, and my workplace had no changing facilities. So morning and evening I did my Superman routine, using a toilet stall for my phone booth. Most mornings, I would step into my stall in shorts and a T-shirt, pannier in hand, and emerge in a skirt and top. My commute wasn't long enough to make sweat an issue, but still, the process wasn't very dignified, and there was always the risk of dipping a sleeve in the toilet.

At that job, I ran downstairs on breaks and at lunchtime to make sure my bike was still safely parked in the rack on the street. I knew I liked riding my bike, that my health benefited, that I had a fuller pocketbook, and that cycling was "green," but it didn't occur to me that my employer was benefiting or that he should do anything to support my transportation choices. That was a long time ago, though, and many people — employers and employees alike — see a cycling-friendly workplace as much more important today.

Some companies look at their support of sustainable commuting as a perk they can offer their employees. Others regard it as a demonstration of green corporate citizenship. But there is — or at least there certainly could be — an element of self-interest as well. It's possible to be a generous employer and a good corporate citizen while still maintaining a focus on the bottom line.

In San Francisco, for example, where parking is notoriously scarce, some employers have found a parking "cash-out" effective in allocating scarce parking and managing demand. Employees can choose to forgo the use of a company parking space and receive the taxable cash value instead. Cashing out has proved effective because it doesn't coerce anyone into giving up his or her car or company-provided parking, but it rewards those who do. With the construction cost of a parking stall in a city garage priced at more than $30,000, employers can realize significant savings.

In order to be fair to non–car drivers and to support sustainable transportation, other employers offer different incentives to their employees to cycle. San Francisco–based BabyCenter.com, for example, gives every employee a $70 per month transportation subsidy. Employees can choose to put it toward parking (which costs almost $200 a month in nearby lots) or public transit, or they can pocket the cash and cycle or walk to work.

As early as 1989, the chemical company Ciba-Geigy Switzerland was taking this initiative a step farther: they entirely avoided having to build a new parking garage by encouraging their employees to cycle to work. Any worker willing to give up a parking space was given a new bicycle. Two hundred thirty employees chose this option, which was far less costly for the company than building a new parking structure, as well as healthier for the employees.

New York City took steps to address a long-standing problem for bike commuters by enacting the Bicycle Access to Office Buildings Law in December 2009. The law requires that cyclists be given the opportunity to securely park their bicycles in or close to their workplaces, in effect forcing employers to make workplaces more bike-friendly.

Governments can promote bike commuting and bike-friendly workplaces with tax incentives. In the United Kingdom, for example, the government's Green Transport Plan enables workers to obtain a new bike and related equipment at approximately half the retail price. Under the plan, the employer registers for the scheme, pays for the bike, gear, and safety equipment, and then in effect leases it to the employee. At the end of the lease period (typically twelve to eighteen months), the employee can buy the bike and equipment outright at a discounted cost.

While tax breaks and bike storage improve attitudes toward commuter cycling, they are not enough to actually encourage biking to work. What does a truly cycling-friendly workplace look like?

At Pottinger Gaherty Environmental Consultants (PGL) in Vancouver, Canada, many of the employees cycle to work. PGL has a secure bike-storage room in the building and a shower room for employees. Employees are also eligible for an allowance of $40 a month to apply to fitness, bike purchase or maintenance, or public transit. The company also participates in local Bike to Work Week activities.

PGL supports sustainable commuting in other ways, too. It chose to locate its offices downtown rather than in a less expensive suburban business park so that employees could use public transit. And while junior employees in many comparable companies are required to have their own cars to do fieldwork, PGL avoids this requirement by participating in a local car-sharing organization. Employees have access to vehicles when they need them, but they don't need to have their own, and there are no company cars standing around idle — also a cost saving for the company. The results? PGL has low employee turnover (another source of savings), and people enjoy working there.

While relocating an office may not be practical in the short term, employers can take steps to make their current premises friendlier to bike commuters. The San Francisco Bicycle Coalition provides an online handbook called *The Employer's Commuting Guide* that describes a step-by-step process for making a worksite bike-friendly. Taking this idea a step farther, goDCgo in Washington established a program called "Bike Brand Your Biz," which advises local employers on how to make their workplaces more welcoming to pedal-powered commuters.

More and more employers are jumping on the biking bandwagon. In 2010, the furniture giant IKEA announced that it was giving every one of its 14,200 U.S. employees a new bike for Christmas. Why a bike? "Because," it says, "when it comes to sustainable transport, a bicycle is a great option." Why announce it to the world? Presumably the company believed an association with bikes would reflect well on it.

There are prizes to be won for being bike-friendly these days.

The League of American Bicyclists, one of the leading cycling organizations in the United States, has established a program to honor employers' efforts to promote cycling and to provide technical assistance and information to help them become even better. Businesses are rated bronze, silver, gold, or platinum (cleverly building in goals for improvement for all who fall short of platinum) for their support of bike commuting. While the rating process is rigorous, the green accolades are apparently worth the effort to many businesses: applications increased by 45 percent in 2010 over 2009. If the trend continues, it will no longer be necessary to feel like a superhero to ride a bike to work.

If you're curious about how commuter-friendly your employer is, go to the Best Workplaces for Commuters website at www.bestworkplaces.org/join/online-application/ and fill out their questionnaire.

If you're an employer who'd like to make your workplace more bike-friendly, here are some suggestions from some commuter cyclists on what to offer:

→ a welcoming attitude in the workplace
→ a secure, accessible, dry place to park
→ changing, shower, and storage facilities
→ direct, safe, convenient, and attractive bike routes to work
→ information on routes and location of facilities

**BONNIE FENTON** rode and wrote in Vancouver, Canada, for many years before moving to Germany in 2008 — where she does pretty much the same. Some things aren't meant to change.

# Chapter Thirty-Eight

# Bikes Work
## The Development and Impact of Small Bicycle Businesses

**Sarah Mirk**

*Yes,* bikes are fun to ride. And you can decorate them, and they're great for the environment. But they're not just good clean fun: nationally and internationally, they're big business. And in cities where solid bike infrastructure and a vibrant bike culture have led to increased ridership, bikes offer a unique opportunity for small entrepreneurs to tap into a hearty niche market and start a business for relatively low capital cost.

In Portland, Oregon, bikes work. Not only do they save Portland money on health care and long-term transportation spending, but they also make money for the city and business owners.

## THE BICYCLE ECONOMY

A rough count these days turns up about 157 bike businesses in Portland. That includes 56 dealers and repair shops, 33 artisan bike builders, 15 bike-apparel manufacturers, 10 businesses that deliver food or goods exclusively by bike, and 8 bicycle cultural institutions, including a film festival, publishing company, and temple. These businesses have contributed to Portland's economy through creating jobs and promoting tourism by building Portland's brand.

A 2008 study by the consulting company Alta Planning and Design found that bike industries create $90 million annually in economic activity for Portland (up from $63 million in 2006) and provide 1,150 local jobs. About 60 percent of the bike businesses in Portland are regular bike shops — places that rent, repair, or sell bikes. Frame building, component manufacturing, and apparel make up another 20 percent. Events and races, numbering about four thousand annually, make up another 11 percent of the industry (Oregon boasts the nation's largest cyclocross event series). Bike-based professional services like messengers, nonprofit bike organizations, and coaching round out the total. In recent years, Alta reports, new bike businesses have been primarily small and locally owned.

Of course, making money has required spending some. Portland's expanding bike infrastructure and culture are the main factors contributing to the current boom in the bicycle economy. Thanks to city-government investment in a long-range plan to promote biking, between 1991 and 2010 Portland's network of bikeways tripled in size to about 325 miles, and ridership has grown from about 2,500 daily bike riders in 1991 to 17,500 in 2010.

## HOW BIKES MAKE JOBS

Interviews with small bike business owners in Portland reveal a handful of traits that distinguish successful bike enterprises:

- → Create a customer base by tapping into existing grassroots bike culture.
- → Take advantage of existing bike infrastructure and local public government or nonprofit support (such as public contracts and subsidized loans).
- → Offer a high-quality product or service. Just being bikey isn't enough.

Ayleen Crotty likely knows more than anyone in Portland's bike scene about the intersection of bike culture, concrete bike infrastructure, and small business. Crotty founded a long list of Portland's most hilarious and long-running grassroots bike events, like the Midnight Mystery Ride (where riders meet up once a month and pedal through the night to an undisclosed location) and Filmed by Bike, a raucous film festival. Six years after she became involved in Portland's bike scene, Crotty joined the two-member company Good Sport Promotion and now organizes paid rides very similar to the free, chaotic, and questionably legal ones that helped build (and continue to color) Portland's vibrant bike culture. For $40 per person, the Night Ride, for example, offers an organized version of the more anarchic Midnight Mystery Ride, complete with proper permits, first aid, mechanics, and karaoke contest. The rides attract around 1,400 people.

In 2010, Good Sport Promotion hosted fourteen events in Oregon and Washington with a total of 150,000 participants. The capital cost of the events is very low because Good Sport uses volunteers, who are easy to recruit because many people in Portland are happy to support a bike event (and score a free ticket). The seven full-time employees of Good Sport are helped by a whopping

*Downtown delivery by cargo bike is fast, cheap, and a marketing magnet.*

two to three thousand volunteers annually. The rides bolster Portland's image as a bike-friendly city and attract racers and casual riders from around the state and country.

The company received a major boost when the City of Portland contracted with Good Sport to host a series of summer events called Sunday Parkways, when several miles of streets are closed to cars, and residents are encouraged to get out and walk or bike around the neighborhood. The city is willing to invest in Sunday Parkways events because they promote the kind of healthy lifestyle and sustainable habits that Portland is hoping to make its hallmark. They also boost Portland's reputation as a green, livable city: videos of happy families biking through Portland neighborhoods and news stories about the event show up in the national media. And that kind of public, local government support for biking can have big benefits for the industry.

The great advantage of starting a bike business — in many places across North America — is that it has a built-in and currently growing market. "If we were just to create a random event, I don't think we'd get as many people to turn out at all," says Crotty. "Just being about bikes isn't enough to be successful, but it's a good start."

Although the niche appeal of biking may be lost over time, Crotty thinks her business is in good shape because it has diversified to host events for all sorts of cyclists, from athletic road bikers to fun-loving baby boomers who are wobbly on wheels. "We're multidisciplinary," says Crotty.

"It could flatten out, for sure. There's only so many hat makers you can have," adds Crotty, speaking from behind her booth at BikeCraft, an annual bike-themed craft fair in Portland that attracts several dozen vendors (including, indeed, several cycling hat makers). "I think biking will reach a point where it's not a big deal. We won't have bike-craft fairs because all craft fairs will have biking things."

The success of Good Sport hinges on Portland's solidly developed bike infrastructure. The increasing safety of biking in the city attracts new, nontraditional riders (like women and seniors) who buy tickets to Good Sport's events. And because the city government is amenable to supporting bike events, the company can easily secure permits, road closures, and police support for its larger events (albeit for a hefty fee).

Another, somewhat different Portland bike business is Soup-Cycle. This company, which delivers soup by bike, was started in 2008 by partners Jed Lazar and Shauna Lambert. The pair cook up giant pots of soup in a commercial kitchen and deliver the organic concoctions to weekly Soupscribers around the city, at home or at work. Like Good Sport Promotion, SoupCycle created a customer base for a completely new service by tapping into the network of Portland's bike culture. And like Good Sport Promotion, it has grown swiftly for relatively low capital cost.

Lazar estimates the start-up cost of SoupCycle at $20,000. In two and a half years, the team has grown to four 30-hour-a-week employees (plus Lazar and Lambert), who have made over 22,000 deliveries to 411 Soupscribers.

Lazar and Lambert are regular cyclists, but their decision to use bikes for delivery was based on dollars and cents rather than personal preference. "We did a cost-benefit analysis of using bikes versus electric cars versus regular cars. Bikes came out ahead because of the brandability, the low start-up cost, and the low maintenance cost," said Lazar. "Riders use their own bikes for deliveries, and the lower cost of maintenance makes up for the increased labor costs in that it takes longer to deliver." Part of the start-up cost was covered by a small business loan from the locally based nonprofit Mercy Corps.

SoupCycle has been able to gain free exposure and advertising through bike-positive and food-culture media that see bike delivery as a quirk worth reporting on. The company has found many of its customers by handing out free samples at bike events (like Bike-Craft and Sunday Parkways), where there's a ready-made market interested in their product. "We would not be reaching our customers without bikes," says Lazar.

But while the bike is what gets many customers to sign up, it's the quality of the soup that keeps them paying. All the soups are organic, available in a vegetarian version, and (I'll vouch personally) delicious.

Portland's several hundred miles of bike lanes make the business possible. The bulky 200-pound trailers towed by soup delivery riders would block traffic in a city with less infrastructure. In Portland, the Soupcyclers stick mostly to bike lanes, which makes confrontations or backed-up traffic a rarity.

## SEEING GREEN

The prominence of bike businesses in Portland contributes to the city's image as a sustainable, bike-friendly city, and that reputation translates into serious tourism dollars. The *New York Times* devoted the front page of its April 2, 2009, travel section to visiting Portland by bike, splashing color photos of Portland bike commuters above an article reveling in the joy of touring the city by bike. *National Geographic* and *Travel and Leisure* both ranked Portland as a top U.S. destination in 2010, noting its green status and bike culture, and it was *Bicycling* magazine's top American biking city from

1996 to 2009 (though we were beat out in 2010 by Minneapolis — the ruffians).

Bike events run by local small businesses, like Good Sport's numerous theme rides and the several racing series and tours run in Portland, give cyclists around the state a reason to visit Portland, while the city's reputation as a hub of bike planning, business, and culture brings tourists from around the nation and the world.

Tourists lured to Portland by this good publicity can get around the city on two wheels with the help of more small bike businesses. Numerous boutique hotels in town offer free bikes for their guests, and those who stay elsewhere can get a tour from one of two bike-tour agencies in Portland or rent a bike at one of a dozen shops.

The experiences of Crotty, Lazar, and thousands of entrepreneurs and workers like them have created the major bike industry in Portland, not only contributing millions to its economy but also shaping its image.

For the people involved in the bike industry, part of the payoff is incorporating their passion for biking into a paying gig that helps share that passion with other people. As Crotty says, "I think we definitely work harder and do a better job because it does involve bikes, which means we're always working on projects we care about."

**SARAH MIRK** is a journalist based in Portland, Oregon. She writes about bikes, history, cities, and crazy people.

## Chapter Thirty-Nine

# Bike Businesses and the Bike-Craft Boom

## Amy Walker

*While* North Americans' renewed fascination with bicycling obviously increases the demand for bikes, accessories, and bike infrastructure, it has also inspired a raft of peripheral products: all kinds of books (heh!), magazines, art, objects, and clothing to express the wild, passionate love that many people feel for biking. And that presents a basketful of big and small business opportunities.

Through my work at *Momentum* magazine, I spent several years getting familiar with biking options and the bike industry. I met and spoke with people who biked and people who wished they could bike more, and I participated in bike trade and consumer shows. One of the things I noticed is that many people who work in the bike industry are different from a significant group of their potential customers, the large numbers of people who want to bike for transport. Many in the industry seem to have entered it through competitive cycling. The bike industry is still dominated by competition-oriented male cyclists, and that makeup is reflected in the culture of the industry as well as in its products, which tend to be overwhelmingly sporty. I'm not trying to knock competition cycling, or men. But in the current renaissance of biking in North America, as a way for ordinary people to get from A to B, the bike-industry types are a shining illustration of an old business chestnut: "You are not your customer."

Biking as a primary means of transportation is not yet a mainstream activity, but it already represents a sizable market. According to the 2008 U.S. Census American Community Survey, 0.55 percent of Americans used a bicycle as their primary means of getting to work. But because that figure represents a very conservative assessment — based on the mode of travel people used most days and over the longest distances — I'll take the liberty of rounding it

up and saying approximately 1 percent of the U.S. population bikes for transportation some of the time. That works out to about 3.1 million regular transportation cyclists in the United States. If we can extrapolate further, imagine that for every person who is biking to work now, there are at least two people considering or even actively planning to start biking to work. So let's bump that potential market up to 9 million people. I still think that's a very conservative estimate, but if you're talking about business (and especially if you're talking to the bank), it's helpful to have numbers.

We desperately need more bike shops that are accessible to people who are just learning about bikes, and we need manufacturers who are willing to get out of their own bubbles and be open-minded about who their potential customers are, what they need, and what they want in a bike. Transportation-oriented bike shops like Clever Cycles in Portland meet this need, but shops like this are still too few and far between. It would be a mistake for bigger bike manufacturers and distributors to assume that their future customer base is going to have the same needs and tastes as the customers they have courted in recent decades for performance road and mountain biking (young adult to middle-aged, predominantly white males). In fact, the transportation cycling demographic is much larger and more diverse (consisting of people of many ethnicities, women, children, and senior citizens) with a correspondingly wide variety of needs.

I'm curious about what would happen if bicycle manufacturers took some cues from the auto industry. Because transportation bikers buy bikes as vehicles, they're prepared to spend more — but it's up to the manufacturer to provide value for money. Creating complete vehicles is the first step. You don't see cars being sold without lights and windshield wipers; by the same reasoning, comfortable city bikes with built-in lights, fenders, chain guards, and luggage racks should become standard. It's also important to connect with the aspirations of the bike-mobile public. I can see it now: a TV commercial with a slick aesthetic, shot in sophisticated silvery hues, the rider deftly navigating city streets, the voiceover purring: "Alert, aware, responsive. You know each curve, each stone, and painted line on this road, as you travel at the speed of . . . integrity."

Bikes are about self-expression as well as practicality. To feed their bike lust, many people find vintage bikes and refurbish them because the old steel bikes have the classic style they're looking for. A few bike shops, like Manifesto Cycles in Oakland (www .wearemanifesto.com), are recycling and rebuilding beautiful old bikes to meet this demand.

Likewise, many handmade bicycle builders offer the possibility of interesting aesthetic choices of frame style and color — a lot more varied than what you'll find on bike-store racks. Several events celebrate handmade bikes. The Oregon Manifest is a biennial bicycle design-and-build competition launched in 2009. The 2011 event challenges thirty-four professional builder teams and six student teams to create the "ultimate utility bicycle." In seven years, attendance at the North American Handmade Bicycle Show (NAHBS) has grown tenfold, and the diversity of designs exhibited has grown vastly. The market for handmade bikes is flourishing: builders often have customer wait lists of several years, and there are hundreds of people learning the craft of bike building as apprentices and at schools like Oregon's United Bicycle Institute (www.bikeschool.com). The innovation and experimentation happening in this part of the bike world are inspiring. And you can often enjoy them for not much more than the price of a high-end factory-made bike.

The growth in hand-built bicycles is part of a craft-revival trend in North America. People are learning traditional fabrication skills and taking the initiative to make things themselves. The popularity of magazines like *Make* (www.makezine.com) and its Maker Faires and do-it-yourself websites like Instructables (www.instructables.com) attest to this trend. The maker movement is fueled by desires for self-sufficiency and economic sustainability and by the feeling of accomplishment and connection many people experience by making things with their heads, hearts, and hands.

By a wonderful twist, the computer age enables more individuals to make a living as craftspeople. The web connects artisans to wider audiences, and websites like Etsy (www.etsy.com) provide an accessible marketplace for online selling as well as an informative and supportive community for crafters.

The commuter cycling market is a great fit with independent craftspeople. People who take up cycling are often looking at the global picture: they want to reduce their environmental impact and shop ethically and sustainably, and they are interested in high-quality goods that will last a long time. These customers have needs that the traditional bike industry is not meeting, not only for bikes but also for well-designed bike accessories, such as racks, baskets, saddle covers, bells, panniers, and bags. Companies producing great short-run and handcrafted items include Cetma (Eugene, Oregon), Queen Bee (Portland), Fabric Horse (Philadelphia), and R.E.Load Bags (Philadelphia and Seattle). In bike clothing, B. Spoke Tailor (Oakland), Swrve (Los Angeles), and Outlier (New York City) are leading the way with stylish pants, skirts, raingear, hats, socks, leg warmers, arm warmers, and gloves. Because prices for bike-specific gear are already high, craftspeople and small business owners can enter the market and still be competitive.

Many customers also value knowing who made the things they buy. There's peace of mind in knowing that your goods were not made in a sweatshop. And buying locally or from a small company makes it possible to contact the maker to locate extra parts, have repairs done, or just ask questions.

Many people have found themselves without work or needing to switch careers because of the recession. One place to look for new jobs is in the smart-growth sector, which includes planning for and building cycling infrastructure within livable communities.

## On Bicycles

Shifting our economy to one that is more sustainable requires creative vision, expert management, and muscle. As part of a green economy, you might consider creating a bicycle-related business or investing in a bicycle-related cottage industry.

Because it is not yet commonplace to bike for transportation in North America, we are not accustomed to fitting bikes into the places where we live, work, and play. This means we still encounter lots of problems in making bikes fit into our lives. As designers and entrepreneurs know, problems offer the greatest opportunities. All kinds of great solutions are just waiting to be discovered that will enhance or improve on existing designs for bikes, accessories, clothing, and ways to accommodate bicycles in our lives. If you've ever considered making biking a part of making your living, there's never been a better time than now.

## Chapter Forty

# The Individuation of the Cyclist

## Working with the Law to Attain Perfect Consciousness

### David Hay

*I am* a bike lawyer. Many people do not know what that is, so I start by telling people what I am not. I am not someone who represents damaged bikes; I represent people damaged on bikes. That is, I act for cyclists injured as a result of the negligence of others, usually drivers of cars. I started this work in the late 1980s in Vancouver, Canada, and I have seen a lot in my time.

I like to draw a parallel between the development of cycling in North America and the development of the psyche of the average human being. When I started practicing law, cycling in the Western Hemisphere's car culture seemed to be in its infancy. From the legal perspective, cyclists were treated like children — that is, poorly. Drivers regarded them as a nuisance. In the minds of other road users, cyclists had no place on the streets. A cyclist who was injured probably "had it coming" in one way or another. Even when the motorist was obviously at fault in a crash, the view persisted that the cyclist would not have been injured had he or she not been on the road in the first place. Cyclists were better not seen, and certainly not heard.

But the child slowly grew. Soon a number of environmentally inspired advocacy groups began holding clandestine meetings in basements (usually in public offices) to plot the "revolution." I participated in many of these meetings and steered the development of a few groups myself. These groups realized it was essential to get more people on bikes to free them from the slavish addiction to motor vehicle travel, particularly in the inner cities.

At first no one listened. But eventually, as it became clear the child would not relent, organizations with money and influence began to pay attention. I would say cycling was then at the preschool stage of its development. Governments throughout North America began to act to provide the growing cycling population with a future. Traffic legislation was amended in many jurisdictions to stipulate that cyclists had the same rights and obligations as motorists. A collective decision was made to no longer treat cyclists like babies.

The legislative change put differing perspectives on transportation into stark relief. Motorists (through their insurers and lawyers) cited a whole new regimen of obligations that should fall on cyclists. Cyclists cited their new rights under the legislation. Many fights between the parents and children ensued in these preteen years as we entered an era of somewhat disgruntled coexistence.

But the cyclist continued to grow. Advocacy groups hob-nobbed with politicians and people of influence, while ridership mushroomed. Civil disobedience was inevitable: one expression of it was Critical Mass, an anarchical group ride no doubt inspired by the memory of Woodstock, which in some cities resulted in whole streets being shut down and vehicular traffic being completely disrupted. There seemed to be nothing the parent could do in the face of this act of teenage rebellion.

The teenage cycling world worked hard at its self-realization. Legal victories were won, with appellate courts deciding that cyclists injured in collisions with cars were not liable for failing to anticipate the presence of motorists, because cyclists were the more vulnerable of the two parties. The political landscape also changed. Cyclists won all sorts of victories at the local-government level. Engineers and urban planners with fresh outlooks created bike lanes and exerted their local powers to define maps and pathways. The moral victory was not lost on anyone.

Unfortunately, as the cyclist developed, so did the business of lawyers like me. This was perhaps inevitable, given the increasing number of cyclists on the road and the persistence of an unhappy and often tense set of motorists. At times, disagreements turned violent. I once obtained a judgment against an enraged motorist who beat up a cyclist in a well-publicized road-rage case. He even refused to pay the judgment until I threatened to sell his home. These skirmishes were exceptional but always served as a reminder of the anger that characterized the teenage years.

The maturation of the cyclist is not yet complete. Whether we will ever attain the respected status of cyclists in many European cities remains unknown. But, increasingly, we want our cities to be more livable. For that change to occur, the rules need to change at all levels. One example is mandatory helmet laws, which represent a serious impediment to bike-share programs and have been recently abolished in many larger and older jurisdictions.

No matter how popular and widespread cycling becomes, it will always need the support of government and legal institutions. One of the goals of the law is harm reduction: that was the purpose of the original amendments creating equal rights and obligations. The view that cyclists are inferior must be discredited. The view that an injured cyclist seeking compensation is opportunistic must be abandoned. On all sides, generalizations must be renounced, and forgiveness offered. I once had a deposition in a case arising out of a bike accident in which my cyclist client, a 50-year-old window washer, was rendered a high-level quadriplegic. The young driver responsible entered the boardroom, saw my client in his wheelchair, and burst into tears. My client asked for a moment alone with him and consoled him until he stopped crying, fifteen minutes later. Momentary inattention is human. Collisions are inevitable when cyclists share the road with automobiles. Understanding this and working together on ways to reduce the risks ought to be our purpose, fueled by mutual respect and a desire for peaceful coexistence.

## The Individuation of the Cyclist

Much clarification of traffic laws is needed to assure fair treatment for cyclists. When can a cyclist pass on the right? What is the nature of a cyclist's right-of-way while riding in a bike lane? Do motorists have a higher duty of care on designated bike routes? Should mandatory helmet laws be modified to accommodate inner-city bike-share systems? Should the laws be modified to allow cyclists to ride side by side? Should there be a reverse onus of proof, so that drivers who collide with cyclists would have to prove they were not negligent? Some jurisdictions have recognized a reverse onus as a way of leveling a playing field rendered uneven by trauma-induced memory loss. Seems fair, no?

All of these questions have hitherto been left to the courts. But in choosing to bring a case to court, cyclists typically must assume considerable financial risk in attempting to establish what ought to have been admitted in the first instance. Our elected representatives need to take the lead.

Cycling throughout the world is growing up strong, thanks to the efforts of many unsung cycling heroes. The next ten years, however, are critical for its development. Governments need to make progressive changes in laws and infrastructure that acknowledge the needs and status of cyclists. Police investigations of accidents involving cyclists need to be conducted responsibly and with zeal; police officers need to be trained in bike-accident reconstruction. Motorists need to acknowledge that the world has changed and that the old models of behavior around cyclists are inappropriate. After all, in a democratic society, people generally follow the rules, provided they are clearly codified and enforced.

*On Bicycles*

It is often said that there are three stages of human psychic development: perfect unconsciousness, imperfect consciousness, and perfect consciousness. As cyclists, we can achieve perfect consciousness, but only if our legal system embraces the cyclist and provides a legal framework for the ride. How about a Universal Declaration of Cyclists' Rights as a common goal?

And one day, in a perfect world, I will retire.

**DAVID HAY** is a partner at Richards Buell Sutton LLP. A trusted ally of the cycling community, he has litigated cyclists' injury claims over the past twenty-three years. He has offered education in the law of negligence to individuals, insurers, cycling societies, advocates, the media, and government.

## Chapter Forty-One

# A History of Bike Advocacy

## Jeff Mapes

*By* the late 1980s, people who wanted to make cycling a main-stream transportation choice in North America were in a tough spot. Local bike advocacy groups in cities across the United States and Canada were largely moribund as cheap oil fueled another rapid spurt of suburbanization, and the roads became clogged with SUVs and minivans that resembled mobile living rooms.

Politicians and transportation agencies were focused on build-ing massive highways, and traffic engineers gave little thought to the idea that anyone astride a bicycle had much to contribute to mobility. Perhaps most grimly, it was no longer common to see children riding their bikes to school. The fear of abduction or as-sault, the increasing ferocity of auto traffic on the streets, and the decline of the neighborhood school all accelerated the decline of this childhood rite.

So it was perhaps fitting that the surviving cycling advocacy groups — chiefly the Bicycle Federation of America and the Rails-to-Trails Conservancy — helped form a new lobby group in Washington, DC, that was informally known as the "losers' coalition." More formally known as the Surface Transportation Policy Project, this coalition represented the dispossessed of the American transportation scene. The public-transit agencies, which always came in a distant second to the road builders in securing federal funding, were joined by architects, city planners, environmentalists, and urbanists — as well as mayors and other urban politicians tired of the stranglehold that state departments of transportation held on federal money for roads.

Their goal was to hijack the legislation Congress passed every four or five years setting the nation's transportation priorities. And, to the amazement of a lot of people, including the highway lobby, they succeeded. With the crucial help of Senator Daniel Patrick Moynihan (D-NY), the reformers pushed through the Intermodal Surface Transportation Efficiency Act of 1991, known as ISTEA and pronounced "ice tea."

For the first time, the federal government diverted funds from gasoline taxes to projects that promoted biking and walking as transportation modes. While it still accounted for only a tiny percentage of federal spending on transportation, ISTEA and its successors provided billions of dollars for bike lanes, off-street paths, and other projects that began the process of remaking American cities with cyclists and walkers in mind.

It was, in many ways, the lubrication that turned the wheels of a modern bike advocacy movement that has become a force to be reckoned with in many U.S. and Canadian cities.

The federal money helped inspire the bike industry — with the chief of Trek Bicycle, John Burke, playing a leading role — to step up its lobbying and support local advocacy groups. One of the key moments for advocacy came in 1996, when about twenty activists from a dozen local groups met at the Thunderhead Ranch in Wyoming to network and plot strategy. Out of that meeting came a group now known as the Alliance for Biking and Walking, which has 160 member groups scattered across North America.

Cycling also gained powerful new support from the public-health establishment as obesity became a growing concern in the 1990s. The U.S. surgeon general warned in 1996 that Americans were simply not getting enough exercise, in large part because of the sedentary nature of the modern workplace and the long hours spent in automobiles to get to increasingly far-flung jobs, schools, and stores. The report recommended that policy makers figure out how to integrate cycling and walking into people's daily lives, and it cited polling showing that Americans were open to the idea of cycling to work and other destinations if it was safe and convenient.

The powerful Robert Wood Johnson Foundation, the folks who helped bring you smoke-free workplaces and restaurants, started funding "active living" projects aimed at figuring out how to spur biking and walking. Bill Wilkinson, a pioneering bike advocate who for many years headed the Bicycle Federation of America (later renamed the National Center for Bicycling and Walking), was ecstatic to find such a powerful ally. "The best thing that has happened to bicycling advocacy in thirty years," he told me in

2007, "is having the public-health community come in with concerns about obesity and starting to do research that says the nature of the built environment has dramatic health impacts."

Growing concern about global warming also focused new attention on cycling and other transportation alternatives, as did the rising price of oil. A new generation of urban transportation leaders realized that focusing solely on pumping as many cars as possible through their streets was not a sustainable long-term strategy. This thinking is perhaps best exemplified by New York City's transportation director, Janette Sadik-Kahn, who has accelerated the city's construction of bikeways and carved out new urban plazas for pedestrians at the expense of motorists. Most notably, she closed several blocks of Broadway to vehicle traffic, including Times Square.

But perhaps most important to the success of the bike movement, cycling gained cachet among a new generation growing up in an age when driving was less a ticket to freedom than an expensive hassle. Bike advocates increasingly understood they were marketing a lifestyle as much as a transportation option.

"We work hard to build the idea that biking is sexy and fun," said Andy Thornley, program director at the San Francisco Bicycle Coalition. "You know, put something hot between your legs, get a bike." The San Francisco group for several years sponsored a "Love on Wheels" fund-raiser at a local bar that featured a dating-game format and promoted cycling as a "natural Viagra."

They knew they were on to something when bicycles started

appearing in mainstream advertising. In 2007, for example, Ford ran a commercial showing a father driving his adolescent daughter to a movie in their SUV. She hesitantly asks to be let out a few blocks away from the theater, explaining that people in that "part of town are riding bikes and have hybrids and stuff." Dad assures her that they are actually in a hybrid, which seems to satisfy the daughter.

You could debate the ad's message, but it certainly showed that the world's best marketers were starting to realize that biking was a sign of urban cool — and that they were in a battle for the hearts and wallets of a generation that didn't find it odd to see someone hop on a bike to go a mile to the store for a six-pack.

The collapse of the financial markets in 2008 and the resulting deep recession threw a curveball at the bike movement. In many cases, governments were less willing to put money into bicycling improvements, which many voters didn't see as an essential service. Still, the Obama administration strongly supported cycling, with Transportation Secretary Raymond LaHood announcing he wanted to treat nonmotorized transportation as an equally valid alternative. In fact, LaHood famously stood on a table at the National Bicycle Summit in 2010 in Washington, DC, and pronounced his support for the "livable community" movement. "People want walking paths, biking paths, and opportunities for families to really do the things they do best — which is to hang together and have fun," he said to raucous applause.

By the start of 2011, control of the U.S. House of Representatives had shifted to the Republicans, many of whom opposed federal support for such "frills" as bike paths. The new chair of the

House Committee on Transportation and Infrastructure, Florida Republican John Mica, said he wanted to allow states to shift federal money for bicycling and pedestrian projects to road projects if they so desired. Bicycle lobbyists hunkered down for another storm, prepared to fight to protect their gains.

But out on the street, bicycling was more visible than ever. For young people struggling to launch a career in hard economic times, the urban bike boom was a welcome marriage of style and necessity.

The bike movement has become well enough established now that it's hard to see cycling ever again retreating to the far fringes of society. The League of American Bicyclists now lists more than 150 communities that have earned its "bicycle-friendly" designation. Those with the league's top rating of platinum include Davis, California; Portland, Oregon; and Boulder, Colorado, all famous for their bikeway systems. In Canada, Montreal and Vancouver are often ranked with the world's best bike cities.

But the LAB's list also includes less glamorous cities, such as Dayton, Ohio, and Sioux Falls, South Dakota. Bikes Belong, the bike industry's lobbying arm, awards small grants to communities to help spur bikeway construction. As you scroll through their list of recipients, it's easy to see how broad the interest has become in cycling. For example, one $2,250 grant announced in November 2010 to the city of Conway, South Carolina (population roughly sixteen thousand), will help provide "new bicycle-safe drainage grates and a redesigned trail crossing at U.S. Highway 378," which the city sees as "an important part of its goal to create a bike route around the city and ultimately connect to the East Coast Greenway."

It sounds like small stuff, until you realize that bike advocates are doing the same things throughout North America: literally re-making the streetscape, one intersection and one block at a time.

**JEFF MAPES** is a writer and blogger for *The Oregonian* in Portland who has covered politics for more than three decades. He is also the author of *Pedaling Revolution: How Cyclists are Changing American Cities*. His last transportation purchase was an eighty-pound cargo bike.

*Chapter Forty-Two*

# From Vision to Victory
*Grassroots Bicycle Advocacy*

## Kristen Steele

*Never doubt that a small group of concerned citizens can change the world. Indeed, it's the only thing that ever has.*

## — MARGARET MEAD

*In* 1999, the South Carolina Department of Transportation (DOT) decided to replace two aging bridges over the Cooper River connecting the city of Charleston to the town of Mount Pleasant. The original design didn't include accommodations for bicyclists. A small group of concerned citizens got organized. They attended dozens of community group meetings to share their vision for a bikeable bridge. They didn't have much money, but a coalition of local groups supported their cause.

They decided to target the mayors on either side of the bridge and the DOT commissioner. Pooling limited resources, they printed thousands of postcards addressed to the mayors asking them to ensure the new bridge was bikeable. Their tactic with the DOT was to publicly thank them for including bike accommodations in the new bridge design before the DOT had ever agreed to such a thing. They printed T-shirts and bumper stickers and took out a full-page ad in the local paper with the slogan "Can't Wait to Bike the New Bridge: Thanks SCDOT!" Because of this campaign to put pressure on the DOT, along with the thousands of postcards delivered to the mayors and a broad-based coalition of support, the final bridge design included a twelve-foot-wide bicycle and pedestrian path.

There is no shortage of challenges and opportunities for cycling advocacy. The Charleston story is just one example of how a small group of concerned citizens can make a big impact. If you're interested in making your community a better place to bike, you can make a difference. First, make a list of the obstacles and opportunities you see. What is in the way of a safe ride for you, or anyone, where you live? What is your vision for a bicycle-friendly neighborhood or town? You might find you come up with a dozen things you'd like to tackle. Which of these things will make the biggest impact on bicycling and safety? Try to narrow the choices down to a winnable issue.

While a complete network of off-road bicycle paths might be your big vision, don't bite off more than you can chew at first. Start with an issue that matches your capacity — perhaps a short trail that could be part of a bigger network later on, or bicycle access on a critical bridge. Try to pick an issue that many people care about, and at least a few people care passionately about. This is important because the more people you enlist to work on the campaign, the more political power you'll wield. If you're working with an established or new advocacy group, you should also think about the long-term impact of your campaign. How will it help your group grow so that you are stronger and prepared to take on an even bigger campaign the next time?

Once you've identified the problem you want to tackle, here are some tips for translating your vision to victory.

1. **DEFINE YOUR ISSUE.** What problem are you addressing? What is your proposed solution? Boiling these answers down to a concise and hopeful statement that can be recited in thirty seconds is a crucial first step.

2. **SET GOALS.** How will you know when your campaign is over and you can hold your victory celebration? Be clear about your end goal. You may also want to set short- and medium-term goals that will help achieve your ultimate goal.

3. **ASSESS RESOURCES.** Be realistic about the strengths and weaknesses of your team. What allies do you have who will support your issue? Who are your potential opponents? Do you have lots of connections but little money? Taking inventory of your assets will help you pick a winning strategy.

4. **STRATEGIZE.** Whose minds do you need to change to get the results you seek? Identify the decision makers: they are your primary targets. Next, think about people who can influence those decision makers: they are your secondary targets. Do you know any

of them? Develop a path for reaching your primary target.

5. **CRAFT YOUR MESSAGE.** Hone your elevator speech — the quick pitch for your issue that you can make in a short elevator ride with a decision maker. This will also come in handy when you're talking to the media. A clever and memorable slogan can also make a big impact and can be printed on postcards, bumper stickers, and signs.

6. **DEVELOP TACTICS.** This is the fun part. Many organizers will want to skip right to this step, but the other steps should come first to help you choose the right tactics. Tactics should address a primary or secondary target or public audience: they should help achieve your goals and be realistic given your resources. Tactics should unite your supporters and not alienate others. Also think about tactics that will attract media to your issue. Though not always the most appropriate choice, media attention can help you gain more supporters and catch the attention of your key targets.

7. **MANAGE RESOURCES.** Every campaign effort takes some resources: time, money, or both. What resources do you need to win your campaign? You might need money to buy signs or postcards, or a hundred people to show up for a rally. Be realistic about what resources are needed and how you will obtain them.

When you win what you set out to achieve, be sure to celebrate and thank everyone who helped. The reward for all your hard work is an awesome sense of accomplishment. You can take pride in being a spark that started a flame and transformed the landscape for cycling. And hopefully you'll also enjoy a smoother ride.

**KRISTEN STEELE** works for the Alliance for Biking and Walking. She has more than eleven years of experience working with nonprofits and seven years as a professional bicycle and pedestrian advocate.

# RESOURCES

These resources are published by the Alliance for Biking and Walking and are not publicly viewable online.

Alliance for Biking and Walking, *Campaign Checklist* (Washington, DC: Alliance for Biking and Walking, 2010).

———, *Winning Campaigns Workbook* (Washington, DC: Alliance for Biking and Walking, 2010).

# Chapter Forty-Three

# Safety in Numbers
## Elly Blue

*In Portland,* Oregon, riding a bicycle threatened to become a little less fun for a few months back in 2008. It was a gorgeous summer, fuel prices were hitting record highs, and the entire city seemed to have discovered cycling as a fashionable and economical form of transportation. Bicycle tourism was booming as well, and the streets, bike lanes, bridge paths, and sidewalks were full of new riders, not all of them exhibiting either experience or caution. People in cars didn't know how to handle the abrupt change in the traffic mix. You never could tell if the driver behind you was going to rev past with inches to spare or follow you nervously for blocks.

Gradually, people took a collective deep breath and figured out how to handle everyday encounters with the great bicycle hordes, and things got better. At some point I realized that riding around had actually begun to feel safer than it had before the bike boom.

Statistically speaking, I was right. As droves of people, from wobbly new riders to the law-abiding to the outright reckless, take to city streets on two wheels, we might expect the bicycle crash rate to go up; but instead, the opposite happens. Research has been consistently showing that the more people are out there riding bicycles, the safer bicycling becomes. As ridership goes up, crash rates stay flat or even decline. In Portland, the city's relatively sophisticated bicycle-count graphs show a blue line rising for traffic over the city's iconic central bridges, with a stark red line, representing fatal bike crashes, heading downward.[1]

Surely much of the ridership increase is due to cities' investments in bicycle-specific infrastructure. But the efficacy of that infrastructure in improving safety is often questioned. And there's one theory, based on a growing body of data, that suggests that a few painted lines on the road, bike racks, and bike-specific signals form only part of the safety equation, and maybe a smaller part than we tend to assume. Another phenomenon may be at work.

This phenomenon, dubbed "safety in numbers," was first identified in 2003, in an academic paper by the public-health researcher Peter Jacobsen.[2] After being asked by officials in Pasadena, California, if their city "was a dangerous place to bicycle," Jacobsen looked at crash data from various communities where bicycle ridership had fluctuated over time.

What he found surprised him: the number of crashes involving bikes correlated *inversely* with the number of riders in a community. As ridership increased, the rate of crashes decreased. This shift happened too abruptly, he decided, to be caused by slower-moving factors like infrastructure development and cultural change. Bicycling became safer, he concluded, at least in part because of the number of riders. Surprising as these figures are, their impact has been revolutionary.

The idea behind safety in numbers in transportation goes back to the 1940s, when researchers noticed that as the number of cars on the roads increased, the roads became safer. Jacobsen's 2003 publication brought the idea into vogue among a generation of urban planners and traffic engineers who are increasingly concerned with bicycle and pedestrian issues.

Bike safety is often considered in a vacuum. Helmets dominate the conversation, with visibility — lights and bright clothing — coming a close second. More sophisticated conversations get deep into infrastructure: which are best, regular lanes shared with cars, on-road painted bike lanes, or separated cycle tracks? And we discuss education for bicyclists in defensive riding and the rules of the road.

All of these are important efforts, but they neglect the cause of nearly all traffic crashes: cars. In his article, Jacobsen asks: "Whose behavior changes, the motorist's or that of the people walking and bicycling? It seems unlikely that people walking or bicycling obey traffic laws more or defer to motorists more in societies or time periods with greater walking and bicycling. Indeed it seems less likely. ...Adaptation in motorist behavior seems more plausible."[3] A serious bicycle crash almost always involves a collision between a cyclist and someone driving a car. There are many ways that drivers become involved in these crashes, but the most common are excessive speed, turning, and the myriad distractions that are common behind the wheel. When such behaviors lead to a crash with another car, the consequences are often no more than a dinged fender. When a bicycle is involved, the stakes are higher.

But the presence of bicycles can also, counterintuitively, reduce the potential for harm. When there are more bicyclists on the road, according to the safety-in-numbers theory, they have a curious traffic-calming effect. Drivers become more attentive, slow down, pass more cautiously, double-check their blind spots, and learn to expect the unexpected. They sense that the road has become a more dangerous place, and adjust their behavior accordingly — and the road becomes safer for everyone.

This reality is palpable every day as I ride across town. One of my regular routes is a ten-block stretch with one lane in each direction, moderate car traffic, and parking on each side. No shoulder, no bike lane. I used to think of this part of my commute as the gauntlet. But it's been a couple years at least since someone sped up to cut me off and turn right, and it's rare to hear a car horn behind me even when I take the lane at 15 mph.

The effect is visible among people riding bikes as well. Living here, it's easy to only notice the outliers, but every time I come home from a trip to another city it's hard to believe my eyes. Everywhere I go, Portlanders on bikes stop at lights, yield at stop signs, take the lane, signal their turns, stop to wave pedestrians across the street. It's not all 100 percent legal, but it's an emerging vernacular that seems to work for everyone. It's amazing to watch the ways people in cars, on bikes, and on foot learn from observing each other's behavior and collectively come up with creative ways to navigate the imperfect infrastructure that could create a much more deadly mix.

ELLY BLUE lives in Portland, Oregon, where she writes about bicycling, publishes a zine, co-organizes a women's bicycling business alliance, and is the co-owner of PDXbyBike.com.

1 Chart for Portland, http://bikeportland.org/wp-content/images/bridge_crashes_big.jpg; and for New York City: http://www.streetsblog.org/2009/06/05/safety-in-numbers-its-happening-in-nyc/.
2 Peter Jacobsen, "Safety in Numbers," *Injury Prevention* 9 (2003): 205–9. The original article is available for free download at safetrec.berkeley.edu/newsletter/Spring04/JacobsenPaper.pdf.
3 Ibid.

# Chapter Forty-Four

# Safe Routes to School
## Deb Hubsmith

*Many* adults remember bicycling or walking to school when they were kids. They can recall the house with the friendly dog, flowers blooming in the springtime, and which streets were the hardest to cross. The bicycle ride or walk to school gave them some healthy exercise and a sense of responsibility and freedom.

Today's kids aren't so lucky. According to the U.S. National Household Travel Survey, in 1969, 48 percent of children ages 5–14 usually walked or bicycled to school, as compared with only 13 percent in 2009. During the same period, according to the Centers for Disease Control and Prevention, the percentage of kids who were overweight or obese jumped from 8 percent to 48 percent.

And you don't have to be a traffic engineer to notice that morning rush-hour traffic now peaks in most communities when kids are arriving at schools. In fact, some traffic departments report that anywhere from 15 to 30 percent of morning traffic can be attributed to parents driving their children to school.

When you combine the crisis of childhood obesity with additional concerns related to traffic safety, personal safety, and greenhouse gas emissions, it's obvious that interventions are needed. Enter Safe Routes to School, a program that in the United States has been supported by almost a billion dollars in federal funds since 2005 and now serves more than eleven thousand schools, from kindergarten through eighth grade, in all fifty states.

The goal of Safe Routes to School is simple: to make it safe, easy, and fun for kids to walk and bicycle to school. By achieving this, we help to increase children's physical activity, improve safety, reduce traffic, and decrease greenhouse gas emissions, creating a healthier society with more livable communities that serve all residents.

The first official Safe Routes to School program was born in Odense, Denmark, in 1978. The area had the highest childhood pedestrian fatality rate in Europe, and parents demanded that safety be improved. They worked with the city and school district to improve routes and street crossings, and over ten years, pedestrian fatalities fell by 80 percent.

The concept of Safe Routes to School spread to other European countries and cities in the late 1970s and into the eighties, and from there around the world. The Netherlands began to require schoolchildren to demonstrate detailed knowledge about bicycle and pedestrian safety in order to graduate. Construction of separated bikeways has led to residents of many Dutch cities using bicycles for as many as 40 to 50 percent of all local trips. Australia started childhood bicycle and pedestrian safety programs, and Canada launched Active and Safe Routes to School in the 1990s.

## On Bicycles

In the mid-nineties Sustrans, a nonprofit organization in the United Kingdom, created a Safe Routes to School program funded by lottery dollars. These European successes, particularly the Sustrans program, inspired communities in the United States to follow suit.

Walk- and bike-to-school programs began sprouting up in the United States in 1997, including the first Walk to School Day in Chicago, a program in the Bronx to improve traffic safety, and promotional programs at schools in California. These programs got a boost in 1999, when legislation was introduced in California to redirect one-third of federal highway safety funding to Safe Routes to School infrastructure programs. Support for the bill came from many sectors, including parents, transportation planners, bicycle and pedestrian advocates, municipalities, and engineers. Starting in 2000, California began a grant program that provides approximately $24 million per year for sidewalks, pathways, bike lanes, and street crossings that improve safety on neighborhood routes to school. The program is still in effect.

Word of this California legislation spread quickly throughout the United States. Most important, it reached the ears of Congressman James L. Oberstar (D-MN), who was then the ranking member of the U.S. House of Representatives Transportation and Infrastructure Committee. He had recently heard a presentation by the Centers for Disease Control and Prevention on the rise in childhood obesity. As an avid bicyclist himself, he explained he wanted to do something big to "change the habits of an entire generation."

In 2000, Congressman Oberstar worked through the National Highway Traffic Safety Administration to establish two federal pilot programs for Safe Routes to School, one in Marin County, California, and one in Arlington, Massachusetts. For the 2000–2001 school year, each program was given a $50,000 contract to test a comprehensive approach to promote active travel to school, which has now become known as the "5Es": education, encouragement, engineering, enforcement, and evaluation.

As one of the people responsible for implementing the Marin County program, I knew that we had to make this pilot program a success. We obtained matching funds for the grant from the State of California's Department of Health Services, the Marin Community Foundation, and the *Marin Independent Journal*, and we got to work collaborating with engineers, school principals, law-enforcement agencies, and teams of parent volunteers at each of the nine schools involved in the pilot program. We assessed infrastructure improvements needed on the routes to schools, increased ticketing of speeders, ran contests and events to introduce walking and bicycling to new people, taught traffic safety in the schools, organized walking school buses and bike trains, and collected data in the spring and the fall. In the end, we saw an average 57 percent increase in walking and bicycling to participating schools during the 2000–2001 school year. The other pilot site, Arlington, Massachusetts, also had a successful program.

The bikes had left the rack. Almost overnight, communities, states, and advocates across the United States began seeking funds to develop Safe Routes to School programs in their own communities. With data from the federal pilot program in hand and childhood obesity still on the rise, Congressman Oberstar was empowered to call for funding for a federal Safe Routes to School program that would serve all fifty states and the District of Columbia. The organization America Bikes was formed to coordinate the lobbying efforts of bicycle organizations for the upcoming federal transportation bill, and passing a Safe Routes to School bill became a priority.

I traveled to Washington, DC, regularly to promote Safe Routes to School and worked closely with Congressman Oberstar's staff to draft language for the proposed bill. It called for the establishment of full-time Safe Routes to School coordinators in every state's department of transportation, federal funding for grant programs in every state for infrastructure and educational measures, the creation of a national clearinghouse for data collection and technical assistance, and a task force to make future recommendations to Congress. In 2003 Congressman Oberstar introduced the Pedestrian and Cycling Equity Act for the 21st Century. The measure gained bipartisan support, and ultimately the Safe Routes to School provisions from that bill were incorporated into the 2005 U.S. federal transportation bill.

Safe Routes to School is now well established and making a big difference in schools and communities. We're hearing that the program is indeed living up to Congressman Oberstar's vision of "changing the habits of an entire generation." Here are two examples:

→ In Longmont and Boulder, Colorado, Safe Routes to School grants of $270,000 helped fund encouragement and education programs at several elementary schools. Before the program began at one of the elementary schools, only about a dozen children were bicycling to school regularly. By the end of the school year, the program averaged sixty participants per day, a fivefold increase.

→ Hillrise Elementary School in Las Cruces, New Mexico, conducted a pilot program to document the environmental benefit of reducing car trips by encouraging more children to walk and bicycle to school. A survey showed a 7.3 percent reduction in trips to school made by parents, equivalent to thirty-eight fewer cars arriving at school each morning to drop children off. Assuming an average trip length of three-quarters of a mile each way, that is a reduction of 5,130 miles driven over the school year — which equates to a reduction of 2 tons of carbon dioxide and 283 pounds of other harmful pollutants. Just a few students walking and bicycling can make a huge difference in a community. The city was so impressed with the initial results that it is expanding Safe Routes to School across the entire school district.

And here's what some people are saying:

I have been doing Safe Routes to School for years. It is very important to me because it is good for the air, it saves oil, and it stops pollution. Whenever I walk to school in the morning I feel refreshed. I love walking. And I love riding on a bike to school!

— Guy, third grader, Las Cruces, New Mexico

The Safe Routes to School Program makes physical activity part of everyday life for many students, teaching them to engage in healthy behaviors that last a lifetime and reduce their risk of obesity and chronic diseases as adults.

— Carrie Fielder,
Mississippi State Department of Public Health

Since 2005, the Safe Routes to School National Partnership has been sharing best practices, initiating policy changes at national, state, and local levels, providing technical assistance, and working to ensure that the Safe Routes to School program and movement continue to grow and flourish in the United States. The National Partnership is a network that includes more than five hundred organizations, schools, and professional groups and is hosted by the nonprofit Bikes Belong Foundation.

But there are threats to these successful and popular programs. In November 2010, the congressional founder of Safe Routes to School, Jim Oberstar, lost his seat in a tough election. In the wake of the global economic recession and growing national debt, some leaders in the current House of Representatives are calling for federal transportation spending to return to funding only highways. These changes are being proposed in spite of the fact that spending on bicycling and walking accounts for less than 1.5 percent of all

federal transportation dollars, even though these modes of transportation represent 12 percent of all trips. In addition, 50 percent of trips in the U.S. are three miles or less in length, the perfect-length trip for bicycling or walking.

Despite these potential challenges, the Safe Routes to School National Partnership intends to continue its efforts with America Bikes, Bikes Belong, and other partner groups to emphasize the ways bicycling and walking can save money, improve safety, provide transportation choices, and benefit public health. Constituents are meeting with their congressional representatives to show how Safe Routes to School and bicycle programs benefit local residents and make good economic sense.

In the end, all politics is local, so we invite you to help. Please visit www.saferoutespartnership.org for more information and resources about how to get involved in efforts to promote Safe Routes to School wherever you live and to help this movement reach its full potential.

**DEB HUBSMITH** is the director of the Safe Routes to School National Partnership, a network of more than five hundred organizations. She rides her bicycle as a primary means of transportation.

## Chapter Forty-Five

# Designing Our Cities for Bikes
### Digging Up the Parking Lot

## Lori Kessler

*Joni* Mitchell was right: we paved paradise to put up a parking lot. The natural soil and vegetation of our cities are overlaid with asphalt carpets designed for smooth travel and storage for our motor vehicles. Travel by human-powered pedal, crank, and chain has a much smaller environmental footprint than the combustion engine.[1] But there are also other ecological benefits when we design our cities for pedestrians and cyclists and reduce our pavement.

First, consider rainfall. When rain hits natural soil, it percolates into the ground and recharges natural aquifers. As an aquifer reaches saturation, excess water trickles out, eventually finding its way into streams. But when rain hits asphalt instead, it flows in sheets over the surface until it is conveyed, through stormwater pipes, to streams, rivers, lakes, and oceans. Along the way, it is contaminated by pollutants like oil, fuel, combustion by-products, tire residue, and deicing salts. Stormwater runoff is sudden, with high, immediate volumes that cause massive erosion. The contaminants in the water harm living systems. When we pave less, the natural rainwater cycle is maintained, and fewer stormwater pipes and treatment facilities are needed.

Paving less also decreases the urban heat-island effect. Dark paving materials absorb and radiate solar heat, increasing local temperatures by more than 5 degrees Celsius.[2] This creates an un-balanced microclimate. In the summer, the increased radiated heat in paved urban areas places higher demands on the cooling systems for buildings and on energy supplies. Larger, more numerous, or higher-performance air-handling units must be designed into new buildings to respond to the higher demand.

Decreasing pavement increases the available space for plants. Vegetation provides natural cooling through shade and evapo-transpiration, mitigating the heat-island effect; it improves air quality and reduces greenhouse gases. More vegetation in urban areas supports greater biodiversity and habitat.

An additional benefit, both environmental and economical, is that bicycle-oriented communities are built with fewer construction materials, thus reducing the mining, production, and transportation of asphalt. Reduced underground or multistory parking also re-duces the need for and substantial expense of concrete, reinforcing steel, weatherproofing, artificial lighting, and mechanical ventila-tion systems. Designing cities more for bikes benefits people in the community in social, environmental, aesthetic, and economic ways.

Michigan's Mackinac Island is an entirely car-free community. With six hundred residents and a huge influx of seasonal visitors, the island is accessible by a pedestrian ferry. Modes of transportation include bicycle, horse-drawn carriage, and walking. Roller skates and Rollerblades are also allowed, except in the downtown area. Motor vehicles are banned from the island, with the exceptions of emergency and construction vehicles.

The island is a joy to experience. It is little wonder that the peak season can see as many as fifteen thousand visitors a day! Streets are lively and full of pedestrians, storefronts are quaint and inviting, public green space abounds, bike facilities are available, and not a single parking lot is in sight! An afternoon can be spent biking from store to ice-cream stand on a rented bike with a handlebar basket, or circling the island on the quiet, paved bike route, enjoying sandy beaches along the way.

Mackinac is not the only car-free island in North America. Tangier Island, in Virginia's Chesapeake Bay, is a community of similar size with foot and bicycle transportation only; California's Catalina Island has about thirty-seven hundred residents and is car-free, with the exception of motorized golf carts. Canada's Toronto Island, with about seven hundred residents, is car-free with the exception of City of Toronto service vehicles. Located in Lake Ontario, just offshore from the city center, Toronto Island actually consists of a chain of small islands connected to the mainland by ferry. Most bridges on the islands are for bicycles and pedestrians only.

Many large North American cities have city centers or streets restricted to pedestrians and cyclists. A few examples include Minneapolis, Minnesota; Boston, Massachusetts; Davis, California; Memphis, Tennessee; and Quebec City in Canada.

An interesting and successful example of a new "sustainable model district" is the Vauban neighborhood of Freiburg, Germany. Its population is about five thousand, with six hundred jobs; it is about 4 km from the town center in Freiburg. Transportation is mainly by foot or bicycle. The neighborhood is connected to the city center by tram; homes are laid out within easy walking distance of tram stops.

Vauban's street network favors pedestrian and bicycle use that "filters out" the car. Most streets are discontinuous for vehicles, but connecting bike paths permeate the neighborhood. An early survey showed that over 50 percent of households owned a car, but, due in part to the successful urban design for active transport, car ownership has declined over time: by 2009, over 70 percent of the households had chosen to live without a private car.

Cars take up space — valuable space, which in its natural state is fertile ground supporting healthy ecosystems. Drivers travel along paved roads to and from almost any place imaginable — and park there. In 2001, there were 520 million cars worldwide, 217 million of which were in Canada and the United States.[3] Parking a car requires an area of about 15 square meters (160 square feet).[4] A conservative minimum estimate of two parking spaces per vehicle (one at each end of a journey) yields 15.6 billion square meters of space devoted to parking. Providing maneuvering space between cars (in a highly efficient parking-lot layout) adds an additional 45 percent paved area, for a total of 22.62 billion square meters, or 22,620 square kilometers.[5] That's an area nearly the size of the state of New Hampshire.

Most municipal bylaws and building codes require a minimum

number of parking spaces in proportion to the maximum number of occupants for every building development: residential, commercial, and institutional. This requirement results in a staggering number of paved parking stalls. Not including operating costs (such as lighting and ventilation), the cost of building one underground parking space can be $30,000–$50,000. By comparison, ten to fifteen bicycles can fit into the space required by a single car. Transitioning from cars to bikes could substantially decrease construction costs for housing and other developments.

The transition to bicycles is promoted in Canada and the United States by the Leadership in Energy and Environmental Design (LEED) rating system.[6] The system recognizes healthy, high-performance buildings, with reduced environmental impacts ("green" buildings). Each environmental measure that is recognized by LEED and implemented in the building earns credits that improve the building's LEED rating. One of the LEED credits is titled "Alternative Transportation: Bicycle Storage and Changing Rooms." Its intent is to "reduce pollution and land development impacts from automobile use."[7]

To earn this credit, commercial buildings must provide bike storage and convenient changing and shower facilities for at least 5 percent of the building occupants, and at least one shower for every eight bicycling occupants. Residential buildings must provide covered bicycle-storage facilities for at least 15 percent of their occupants.

Bike- and pedestrian-friendly urban development can improve social as well as environmental health. The American-born Canadian author and urban activist Jane Jacobs devoted her career to promoting the benefits of creating dense, human-scaled neighborhoods, most famously in *The Death and Life of Great American Cities* (1961). Her advice to increase density, diversity, and dynamism — in the words of Douglas Martin, to create a "jumping, joyous urban jumble" — has influenced urban planners ever since.[8] She advised designing streets for a "fabric of intricate cross-use" among the users of a city neighborhood.[9]

Similarly, Christopher Alexander's *A Pattern Language: Towns, Buildings, Construction* sets out 253 patterns of human habitation that have been shown throughout the centuries to fulfill basic human needs. These include mixed-use neighborhoods and green spaces within walking distance: such patterns lend themselves to bicycle transport.

Because of energy constraints and increased demands for clean air and water, the next several generations in North America and around the world will see bicycle use become more common. The foresight of writers like Jacobs and Alexander and the examples set by existing car-free communities point the way for the redesign of our towns and the restoration of livable communities.

Hell isn't other people, as Jean-Paul Sartre suggested. Hell is other people's cars. Cars and major roads bring noise, danger, and isolation to our cities, whereas bicycles can provide a healthy and relaxing means of getting around that still allows for speedy transit and carrying loads.

As we design our cities more for bikes, we not only restore the natural environment; we create happier, healthier, more socially engaged communities. We restore paradise.

**LORI KESSLER** is a Vancouver architect, a performing B:C:Clette, and vice president of the Vancouver Area Cycling Coalition. Her architectural work includes sustainable design in public buildings and LEED consultation.

1 Such assessments take account of bikes' reduced fuel consumption, gasoline-production impacts, air and water pollution, and greenhouse effects. The Vancouver Area Cycling Coalition calculated the reduction of greenhouse gases produced during their semiannual Bike to Work Week in November 2010: with 2,302 active cycling participants traveling an estimated total of 178,311 km by bike, 37,067 fewer kilograms of greenhouse gases were released.

2 Asphalt, for example, has a solar reflectance index (SRI) of only 0.05 to 0.10 on a scale of 0 (standard black) to 100 (standard white). SRI is a measure of a material's ability to reject solar heat.

3 *LEED Green Building Reference Guide Version 2.0* (Washington, DC: US Green Building Council, 2001); *LEED Canada: NC Version 1.0 Reference Guide* (Ottawa, ON: Canada Green Building Council, 2004).

4 Victoria Transport Policy Institute, *Parking Solutions: A Comprehensive Menu of Solutions to Parking Problems*, February 2011, www.vtpi.org.

5 This calculation of paved parking area does not include roads, means of travel from one destination to another, or parking for oversized vehicles. In actuality, there are many times more than two parking spaces per vehicle; this calculation does not include these additional spaces.

6  Developed by the U.S. Green Building Council (Usgbc.org) and the Canada Green Building Council (Cagbc.org). Complying with LEED prerequisites and qualifying for a number of additional credits can earn a building LEED certification at one of four levels: certified, silver, gold, or platinum. LEED is the most widely accepted rating system for green buildings throughout North America. Many city, state, and provincial governments and even the federal government have mandated that new public buildings be LEED certified, often requiring a silver or gold rating. Certification is also mandated by many school districts, universities, and corporations and voluntarily achieved by many private building owners.

7  *LEED Green Building Reference Guide Version 1.0* (Washington, DC: US Green Building Council, 1998).

8  Douglas Martin, "Jane Jacobs, Urban Activist, Is Dead at 89," *New York Times*, April 25, 2006.

9  Jane Jacobs, *The Death and Life of Great American Cities* (New York: Random House, 1961), 243.

## Chapter Forty-Six

# Mixing Cycling with Other Transportation
## Go Farther, Faster, with Greater Flexibility

### Eric Doherty

*Cycling* is a great way to get around. But for some trips, cycling may take you only part of the way in safety and comfort. In such cases, it may make sense to use your bike along with another mode of transport. This is the basic idea behind multimodal transportation — using multiple transportation modes in the ways they serve you best.

The most common type of multimodal trip involving cycling is cycle-transit-walk: riding to a public-transit stop, parking your bike, riding transit until you're close to your destination, and then walking the last stretch. But there are dozens of possible combinations involving bikes, car and van pools, taxis, trains, long-distance buses, ferries, and private cars.

One of the more common and useful combinations is the one-way transit or carpool trip. I went to a university on top of a steep hill, Simon Fraser University near Vancouver, Canada. Rather than ride up the hill, I would put my bicycle on the bicycle rack on the front of a bus and ride the bus to the top. On the way back, I got the fun of riding downhill and the flexibility of shopping by bicycle on the way home. With this mode of commuting, people who don't want to arrive at work sweaty from a long ride can save their exercise for the trip home.

Public-transit systems that carry bikes allow cyclists to be flexible: if you get tired or it starts to rain, you can get most of the way home by public transit. You can also stay in the pub for another beer and still bring your bicycle home safely. They also offer a solution to a common barrier to cycling: bridges and tunnels that do not accommodate cyclists.

Including cycling on longer trips opens up numerous vacation possibilities. Cycling onto car ferries can sometimes get you to your destination more quickly (as well as more cheaply) than driving. Where I live, a three-hour wait for cars to get onto ferries is not uncommon, while cyclists usually roll right on. Most trains accommodate bicycles for a modest fee or for free — often without any disassembly or special packing. For example, Amtrak generally charges between $5 and $10 to reserve a space on the bike racks found on many of their trains. Flying or traveling by long-distance bus with a bicycle can be more complex, as fees and packing requirements vary.

Multimodal transportation lets cyclists travel farther and faster and integrate healthy exercise into their daily routines. It also allows many families to live with fewer cars, saving thousands of dollars every year. But multimodal travel can take some figuring out.

# MULTIMODAL CHALLENGES

If you're lucky, your commute includes a good bike route to public transit, a rack or space to carry your bike on board, and another good bicycle route to your final destination, which has secure bike parking. Usually, though, things are not so simple, and solving the problems requires some research and creative thinking.

Most public-transit systems now make some accommodation for bicycles, but if your bus only comes once an hour and the two spaces on the bus's bike rack are already full, you have a problem. It pays to be flexible, for example by being ready to lock your bike at the nearest suitable spot if you see that the rack on the front of the bus is already full as the bus approaches. Even if you have to walk at the other end, this can be much faster than waiting for the next bus.

Bike racks for cars make carrying bicycles easy. But bicycles also fit in the trunks of many taxis and cars; the front wheel may hang out the back, but it works as long as the trunk is secured with a good bungee cord.

Many rail systems have space for bicycles inside the cars, but often only at off-peak times. And often transit stations and bus stops don't have suitable storage for higher-quality bicycles, so leaving your bike there may not be a secure alternative. However, within a couple of blocks of most transit stations you can find a reasonably secure place to lock your bike: a parking meter outside the window of a busy coffee shop is far more secure than the bike rack hidden behind a post at a transit station. The grocery store across the street from my local SkyTrain rapid-transit stop has a rack that offers much better security than the racks at the station.

Some bikes are easier to carry along with you than others. The most flexible are small, folding bikes that can be put in a bag and carried on board almost any transit vehicle, or put in the trunk of a carpool car. If you're in the market for a folding bike, it pays to do some research ahead of time: some transit systems have very specific requirements about the maximum size of bike that can be carried on board. However, transit staff usually overlook a small folding bike in a bag as long as it does not inconvenience other passengers. Longer recumbent bicycles pose challenges, as many do not fit on racks designed for standard bicycles. Some agencies limit the length of bikes allowed on board. For example, Caltrain in the San Francisco Bay Area limits bike length to 80 inches (203 cm).

Very expensive bicycles can be a significant disadvantage for multimodal travel; with an ordinary bike, you can usually sit down and relax when your bicycle is on the front of a bus or in the bicycle area on a train, but you would probably want to stand and watch over a $4,000 racing bike.

Some multimodal commuters use two bicycles: one to get from home to public transit and the other to travel between the destination stop and the workplace. In low-crime areas, inexpensive bikes can be locked outside overnight, but secure bike lockers at transit stations are a more attractive option.

One of the most dramatic examples of multimodal cycling improvements comes from Bogotá, Colombia. Cycling in the city used to be dangerous and unpleasant, so almost nobody did it. But starting in 1998, the city government began building a network of bicycle routes at the same time that construction proceeded on the Transmilenio rapid-transit system. The transit stations were built with bike stations that hold hundreds of bikes, guarded by attendants. In only five years, the number of bicycle riders increased sixfold. Now many cities and transportation agencies are taking big steps to make multimodal cycling safe and convenient.

The multimodal future holds many possible developments.

One rapidly expanding addition to multimodal travel options is bike-sharing systems with automated docking stations near public-transit stops. With these systems, anyone with a subscription or a credit card can use a bike and return the bicycle to another docking station. Often the first thirty minutes of use are free. The first successful system opened in Lyon, France, in 2005. Only five years later there were more than two hundred, including systems in Montreal, Washington, DC, and Mexico City.

Card-access bicycle lockers and cages are now becoming common at transit stops, making secure bicycle parking more widely available to both regular commuters and occasional cyclists. Carrying bicycles on long-distance trains and buses is gradually becoming easier as racks are installed inside train cars and in luggage compartments of buses.

The future of multimodal travel is being created by the cycling community. You can help by writing to your transit agency or municipality about the changes you would like to see, or by joining a local cycling advocacy group.

If you want to try multimodal commuting, here are some tips:

Most transit agencies have good information for cyclists on the web, including how-to videos. If your transit agency does not have what you need, take a look at what other agencies have to offer. Metro Transit in the Minneapolis–St. Paul area has some good resources at www.metrotransit.org.

Watch how other cyclists use transit, and don't be afraid to ask. You may be surprised how simple tricks make life easier —

like carrying a bungee cord to secure your bike in a train car so you can sit down.

Unfortunately, some rail vehicles are designed so that bikes and wheelchairs compete for the same spaces. Be ready to move your bike quickly if a wheelchair user needs the space.

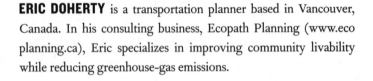

**ERIC DOHERTY** is a transportation planner based in Vancouver, Canada. In his consulting business, Ecopath Planning (www.eco planning.ca), Eric specializes in improving community livability while reducing greenhouse-gas emissions.

## Chapter Forty-Seven

# Thanks for (Bike) Sharing
## Greg Borzo

*Bike*-sharing programs offer free or inexpensive access to bicycles for temporary and one-way use, most often in urban areas and along transit corridors. They could be described as public libraries for bikes. Their goal is to reduce traffic congestion, noise, air pollution, and carbon emissions, all the while building community and promoting healthy, active lifestyles.

Bike sharing is most popular in Europe, where dozens of cities operate programs, large and small. Until recently, however, there was a conspicuous dearth of bike sharing in the United States. That began to change in 2008, after the successful, high-profile use of bike sharing during the two national political conventions in Denver and Minneapolis. These two temporary systems were so popular and functioned so well that both cities subsequently launched permanent bike-sharing programs.

Modest programs were then launched in Washington, DC, Chicago, and elsewhere. But when middle-of-the-road Des Moines,

Iowa, launched a public bike-share program with eighteen bikes in August 2010, it was clear that what was once a fringe concept had gone mainstream. That same summer, Miami Beach launched a program with 1,000 bikes, and the following cities announced programs: San Antonio, Texas, with 140 bikes spread over 14 locations; Boulder, Colorado, with 200 bikes and 25 docking stations; Broward County (which encompasses Orlando, Florida), with 75 bikes; and Boston, with 600 bikes at 61 docking stations. The contract to create Boston's system, dubbed Hubway, was signed in April 2011, and the system was set to launch the following summer. Now many other cities are considering the idea.

Some of these programs were inspired by BIXI in Montreal, North America's first large-scale bike-share program. Launched in 2009, the system provided more than a million rides in its first year and more than three million rides in 2010. It operates from April to November and sports 5,000 specially designed bikes and 400 docking stations concentrated in the city center.

## GOING REGIONAL

Regional programs represent the newest approach to bike sharing, not only in the United States but around the world. Geographically spread-out systems, typically more integrated with transit, have far more potential than the small, token operations that have been most common until recently. Furthermore, they offer economies of scale so that the cost of planning, marketing, and managing a system can be spread out over a larger number of bikes and kiosks.

In December 2010, the United States' first regional bike-sharing program was launched in Washington, DC, and neighboring

Arlington, Virginia. This regional program superseded Washington's modest Smartbike program, dating from 2008, with 1,100 new bikes and 110 new docking stations.

On the other side of the country, California is embracing regional bike sharing as well. In the pilot phase of a program on the San Francisco Peninsula, 1,000 bikes will be made available in 2011 to commuters and tourists in and around San Francisco, Redwood City, Palo Alto, Mountain View, and San Jose. These and other cities are located along the Caltrain corridor, a commuter rail line with more than thirty stops between San Francisco and Gilroy, about seventy miles to the south. Once the program is fully operational, 13,000 bikes are envisioned along this corridor.

The country's most ambitious regional bike-sharing program, however, is being developed in New York City with private funds. In November 2010, the city issued a request for proposals to build a regional bike-share program with 10,000 bikes that would commence operations in 2012. It reportedly envisions 30,000 shared bikes within a few years. Meanwhile, Beijing is reportedly considering a regional bike-share program with 50,000 bikes!

If successful, such regional programs would be more than just a few additional spokes in the bike-sharing wheel. Rather, they would raise the bar and lead to larger and more efficient, solid and sustainable programs.

Expansion raises the related questions of just how bike-share programs are used and what benefits they have. Experts say that until now bike sharing has not been a game changer: that is, it does not wean a city from a dependence on automobiles. Nor does it convince people to sell their automobiles and convert to an active-transportation lifestyle.

This view is confirmed by surveys that show that bike-share trips replace walking and public transit far more frequently than car trips. For example, a survey of users in London, Barcelona, Paris, and Lyon found that 55 to 85 percent of bike-share trips replaced walking and public transit, while only 6 to 10 percent replaced car trips. In the United States, where public transit is not as well developed as in Europe, bike sharing replaced slightly more car trips. In Minneapolis, for example, users reported that 20 percent of their bike-share trips replaced car trips.

The situation is analogous to changes in the media. Just as television did not eliminate radio and the Internet did not eliminate books, bike sharing will complement rather than replace other forms of transportation, experts say. Nevertheless, bike-share programs are important because they encourage multimodal transportation and offer a healthy, environmentally friendly alternative form of transportation. The very presence of bike sharing makes self-propulsion and active transportation to more visible alternatives, opening people's minds to new ways of thinking and seeing their world, whether they are local residents or tourists, avid cyclists or neophytes. Over time, this new mind set could generate gradual — and contagious — changes in society, energy consumption, and consumer habits, as well as transportation choices.

## THE HISTORY OF BIKE SHARING

One of the earliest forms of bike sharing was spawned in 1968 by Amsterdam's White Bikes program, which released fifty bicycles painted white into the city for free public use. Alas, the program failed quickly because of the small number of bikes, which were soon stolen or destroyed. Although community-minded programs like this, characterized by the unrestricted use of unsecured, non-descript bikes, were short-lived, they blazed the trail for the more elaborate programs that followed in their tire tracks.

The second generation of sharing schemes addressed the theft issue with customized parts that could not be used on other bikes, distinctive fleets of bikes, requiring financial deposits, and low-tech locking mechanisms. Nevertheless, theft, unreliability, and unavailability continued to be problems.

The current, third generation employs sophisticated information technology to track bikes, monitor usage, assure availability, hold deposits, and collect user fees. Smart cards or credit cards identify users and encourage responsible use of the bikes. Equipping bikes with GPS tracking devices deters theft and allows programs to inform users via the Internet precisely how many bikes — and docking slots — are available at each docking station at any given moment. Such technology also allows organizers to study usage patterns by time of day, season, holidays, and so on and to shuttle bikes around to meet predictable demand.

The first large-scale third-generation program was introduced in 2005 in Lyon, France. Vélo'V flooded the city with 2,000 bikes and quickly converted Lyon from a bike-neutral city into a strikingly bike-friendly one, taming traffic along the way. At the same time, it demonstrated the feasibility of comprehensive, well-planned, and fully supported bike sharing.

# SHARE AND SHARE ALIKE

Lyon's Vélo'V is a public-private partnership funded by the outdoor advertising company JCDecaux. In exchange for sponsoring the system, the agency sells advertising space on the bikes and docking stations as well as at other locations around town. Clear Channel is another advertising company that has developed bike-sharing programs using this sponsorship model, most notably in Barcelona, Spain; Rennes, France; Washington, DC; and Stockholm, Sweden. And London's bike share is sponsored by Barclays Bank.

The extremely robust Vélib' in Paris is also a public-private partnership with JCDecaux. Launched in 2007, it is the most widely watched and most frequently cited bike-sharing program in the world. Vélib' sports more than 20,600 bikes, available at more than 1,450 docking stations; that's one almost every three hundred meters (at least in central Paris). This essentially saturates Paris with bikes, with one mount per hundred Parisians. No wonder the system is so successful, averaging eighty thousand users a day.

One problem with this advertiser-supported model, however, is that advertising revenue varies depending on the state of the economy, so funding is uncertain. In addition, critics of this model maintain that transit companies or nonprofits do a better job than advertising companies of running what often amounts to public transit or a community service.

Most programs are public or public-private partnerships. Nevertheless, hundreds of private companies, institutions, and universities also run bike-sharing programs on a smaller scale. In Chicago, for example, the following entities are among those offering bike sharing to their employees, tenants, and students: the Field Museum, SRAM (a bicycle component maker), the Willis Tower (formerly the Sears Tower), Argonne National Laboratory, the University of Chicago, Saint Xavier University, and Loyola University. Such below-the-radar activity makes bike sharing more widespread than most people, even its adherents, realize.

Montreal's trendsetting BIXI system is operated by the city's parking authority, a semiautonomous city department, which allows good coordination with the transit systems. The city hopes to make BIXI financially self-sufficient, partly through licensing some of its patented components. For example, because its docking stations are portable, modular, and solar powered, they can be installed virtually anywhere, easily replaced for repairs, and placed into hibernation for the winter. An annual subscription costs CAN$78, while day users pay $5. The first half hour is free for all users; and the second half hour costs $1.50. This pricing model encourages short, quick trips.

In May 2011, Toronto launched a program with 1,000 bikes available at 80 downtown stations, spaced no more than 300 meters apart. In February 2010, Mexico City launched a program with 1,000 bikes distributed over 85 stations. Now that it has gotten off to a good start, a fleet of 6,000 bikes is envisioned.

## OPERATIONAL ISSUES

No matter how bike-sharing programs are supported, they all face similar operational questions pertaining to their business plan. These include the following:

→ whether to charge and, if so, how much

→ whether to set a rental time limit

→ whether to operate during the winter or inclement weather

→ whether to require users to subscribe or become members, a practice that typically rules out participation by tourists, a potentially large group of users

How such questions are answered depends on the program's overall goals. The program in Barcelona (launched in 2007 with 6,000 bikes) restricts rentals to two hours because one of its goals is to encourage multimodal transport. In Denver (2010, 425 bikes), where the system is managed by a nonprofit organization, members ride free for the first half hour. In Minneapolis (2010, 1,000 bikes) the system closes during the winter. The first experiment with bike sharing in Washington, DC, Smartbike (2008, 120 bikes) failed in part because it did not accommodate tourists, though many of its docking stations were located in tourist areas.

To succeed, programs must fit local customs and laws. For example, because Australia has a mandatory helmet law for cyclists, Melbourne Bike Share (2010, 600 bikes) decided to include helmet rentals four months after it launched to encourage increased usage. In London (2010, 6,000 bikes and 400 docking stations), the program is designed to support that city's aggressive campaign to limit traffic congestion in the central city.

The movement is picking up momentum. In fact, there are so many bike-sharing programs that it's getting difficult to keep count. And the programs are getting larger, better funded, and more likely to survive as they are increasingly better integrated into regional transportation plans and goals.

An award-winning journalist, **GREG BORZO** has been a writer and editor at *Modern Railroads*, *Traffic World*, the American Medical Association, the Field Museum, *Momentum*, and the University of Chicago. He's the author of *The Chicago "L"* and *Where to Bike Chicago*, which maps and describes seventy-two of Chicagoland's best rides.

# Chapter Forty-Eight

# Cycling Rights-of-Way

John Pucher

**Providing** safe and convenient rights-of-way is the most important step in making cycling possible for everyone. Cycling remains a marginal mode of transport in most North American cities because it is viewed as requiring special equipment and training, physical fitness, and the courage, agility, and willingness to battle with motor vehicles on the streets. Cycling is a mainstream mode of urban travel in northern Europe precisely because it does not require any of those things.

In spite of their affluence and high rates of car ownership, countries in northern Europe have achieved a high overall rate of cycling in their urban travel, ranging from almost 10 percent of trips in Belgium and Germany to about 20 percent in Denmark and 30 percent in the Netherlands. Women cycle as much as men, and all age groups make a considerable percentage of their daily trips by bike. That is quite a contrast to the situation in Canada and the

United States, where only about 1 percent of trips are by bike, and most cyclists are young men. Two important aims of cycling policies in North America should be to raise the overall proportion of trips made by bike while making cycling feasible, safe, and convenient for everyone who wants to ride.

## MAKING CYCLING SAFE AND CONVENIENT

The cornerstone of cycling infrastructure in northern European cities is the provision of separate cycling facilities along heavily traveled roads and at intersections, combined with extensive traffic calming of residential neighborhoods. Safe and stress-free cycling routes are especially important for less assertive and more physically vulnerable cyclists, including children. Separate facilities that connect practical points of origin and destinations also promote cycling for work, school, and shopping trips. That contrasts with the situation in Canada and the United States, where most separate cycling facilities are recreational and are placed in urban parks, along rivers and waterfronts, and in rural areas.

Having a safe and comfortable place to ride is the most obvious prerequisite for cycling. Cyclists vary in their preferences for cycling facilities: strong cyclists may opt for on-road bike lanes, while others prefer to share paths with walkers. These alternatives should be viewed not as mutually exclusive but rather as complementary, permitting as many choices as possible.

## BIKE PATHS AND LANES

From the mid-1970s to the mid-1990s, northern European countries greatly expanded their systems of separate cycling facilities, such as bike paths and cycle tracks, which are protected from motor vehicle traffic by physical barriers, not simply markings on the roadway. In Germany, for example, the bikeway network almost tripled in length, from 12,911 km in 1976 to 31,236 km in 1996. In the Netherlands, the bikeway network doubled in length, from 9,282 km in 1978 to 18,948 km in 1996. Data for individual cities suggest continued expansion, albeit at a slower rate. The main focus now appears to be on refining the design of cycle paths and lanes to improve safety.

In 2004, for example, Berlin (with 3.4 million inhabitants) had 1,140 km of separate bike paths and lanes. Amsterdam (735,000 inhabitants) and Copenhagen (504,000 inhabitants) each have roughly 400 km of completely separate bike paths and lanes. Even much smaller cities, however, have extensive cycling facilities. There are 320 km of bike paths and lanes in Münster, Germany (278,000 inhabitants), over 500 km in Odense, Denmark (185,000 inhabitants), and over 420 km in Groningen, the Netherlands (181,000).

These figures far outstrip those for most Canadian and American cities. In 2010, for example, the extent of bike paths and cycle tracks (physically separated from motor vehicle traffic) was 76 km per 100,000 residents in Copenhagen, 61 km in Amsterdam, and 33 km in Berlin. That compares to 14 km per 100,000 residents in Vancouver, Canada; 7 km in Toronto, 6 km in San Francisco, 3 km in New York City, and 2 km in Chicago. The exceptions are Portland, Oregon, and Minneapolis, Minnesota, which have the highest levels of cycling of any large American cities as well as the best provision of separate cycling facilities: 38 km per 100,000 residents in Minneapolis and 21 km in Portland.

The bicycling networks in most northern European cities include off-street shortcut connections that run between streets and traverse blocks, enabling cyclists to take the most direct route. The result is a truly complete, integrated system of bicycling routes that allows cyclists to cover almost any trip either on completely separate paths and lanes or on lightly traveled, traffic-calmed residential streets.

Not only has the network of separate cycling facilities greatly expanded since the 1970s, but their design, quality, and maintenance have continually improved to ensure safer, more convenient, and more attractive cycling. In addition, most cities have directional signs for cyclists, color-coded to correspond to different types of bike routes. Most cities also provide detailed maps of their cycling facilities.

Separate cycling facilities are designed to feel safe, comfortable, and convenient for cyclists of all ages and abilities. Virtually all studies of the effects of separate facilities confirm that most cyclists prefer them to on-road routes. Separate paths, in particular, are perceived as being much safer and more pleasant than cycling on the roadway, thus leading to significant growth in cycling volumes when such facilities are expanded.

## TRAFFIC CALMING

It is neither possible nor necessary to provide separate bike paths and lanes on lightly traveled residential streets. Instead, planners in northern European cities have engineered traffic calming on most streets in residential neighborhoods, reducing the legal speed to 30 kph (19 mph) and often restricting through traffic. In addition,

*A "complete street" is designed and operated to enable safe access for all users, including pedestrians, bicyclists, motorists, and public-transportation users of all ages and abilities.*

many cities — especially in the Netherlands — have effected alterations to the streets themselves, such as road narrowing, raised intersections and crosswalks, traffic circles, extra curves and zig-zags, speed humps, and artificial dead ends created by midblock street closures. Cycling is almost always allowed in both directions on all such streets, even when they are restricted to one-way travel for cars; such measures further enhance the flexibility of bike travel.

In addition, almost all northern European cities have created extensive car-free zones in their centers, mainly intended for pedestrian use but generally permitting cycling during off-peak hours. In some Dutch cities, these car-free zones specifically include cycling facilities, such as bike lanes and parking. In some cities, the combination of traffic calming of residential streets and prohibition of cars in city centers makes it almost impossible for cars to travel directly across the city. Such measures strongly discourage motor vehicle traffic in the city center, thus making it safer and more pleasant for people to walk and bike there.

Another kind of traffic calming is the "bicycle street," a narrow street on which cyclists are given absolute traffic priority. Cars are usually permitted to use the streets as well, but they are limited to 30 kph (or less) and must yield to cyclists.

Traffic-calmed residential neighborhoods, car-free city centers, and special bicycle streets greatly enhance these bicycling networks. Most important, they offer safer, less stressful cycling than streets filled with fast-moving motor vehicles. Since most bike trips start at home, traffic calming of neighborhood streets enables bike trips to start in a safe, pleasant environment.

All available evidence shows that traffic calming improves overall traffic safety. The benefits tend to be greatest for pedestrians, but serious cyclist injuries also fall sharply. Moreover, all studies of areas where such measures are implemented report large increases in rates of walking and cycling. There are, of course, many different kinds of traffic calming, and it is conceivable that certain measures (perhaps traffic circles or speed humps) might detract from cycling safety. Overall, however, both pedestrian and cyclist safety is enhanced by reducing speeds on secondary roads.

# INTERSECTION MODIFICATIONS

While bike paths and lanes help protect cyclists from exposure to many traffic dangers, they can pose safety problems at intersections, where most crashes occur. Dutch, Danish, and German planners have worked on redesigning intersections to facilitate safe cyclist crossings. The extent and specific design of intersection modifications vary, but they generally include most of the following:

- Special bike lanes leading up to the intersection, with stop lines for cyclists placed in front of those for waiting cars; these are called bike boxes or advance stop boxes in North America.
- Highly visible, distinctively colored bike-lane crossings.
- Turn restrictions for cars.
- Moving bike pathways away from their parallel streets when they approach intersections to help avoid collisions with right-turning cars.
- Advance green traffic signals for cyclists.
- Extra green signal phases for cyclists at intersections with heavy cycling volumes.
- Special cyclist-activated traffic lights.

→     Timing traffic lights to provide a "green wave" for cyclists instead of for car drivers, generally assuming a 14–22 kph bike speed.

## MAKING ALL ROADS MORE BIKEABLE

No major North American city even comes close to providing a complete and fully integrated system of separate cycling facilities or is likely to do so in the near future. Thus it is crucial that roads in general be made safer and more convenient for cycling. Necessary measures include proper design of drain grates, inclusion of wide outside lanes and shoulders, repair of potholes, and removal of debris on the roadway and shoulders. Roads should also offer clear signage of convenient bike routes and reminders to motorists to share the road with cyclists.

In short, roads should be designed for use by cyclists and not just by motorists. Except on certain high-speed, high-volume highways, cycling is both possible and legally permitted on the vast majority of roads in both Canada and the United States. The legal rights of cyclists to ride on roads must be clearly and convincingly conveyed to motorists and enforced by the police and courts.

The many social, environmental, and health benefits of cycling provide strong reasons for all of us (the public, politicians, and business owners) to support better cycling facilities, along with education, policy changes, and promotional measures supporting cycling. To make cycling in North America more than just a marginal mode of transportation, we must provide safe, well-designed cycling rights-of-way for everyone.

**JOHN PUCHER** is a professor at Rutgers University. His research examines differences in travel behavior, transport systems, and transport policies in Europe, Canada, and the United States, with a focus on policies to increase walking and cycling.

## Chapter Forty-Nine

# Bike Parking

## John Pucher

***Convenient*** and secure bike parking is important for encouraging cycling. Just as a car driver relies on being able to park at both ends of a trip, so does every cyclist.

## BIKE PARKING IN EUROPE

Most northern European cities offer extensive bike-parking options. Local governments and public-transport systems provide a large number of bike-parking facilities, and private developers and building owners are required by local ordinances to provide a specified minimum level of bike parking both within and adjacent to their buildings.

Aside from the large number of bicycle racks throughout these cities, the most visible and innovative aspect of bike-parking policy is the state-of-the-art parking facilities at train stations. Most main train stations offer a full range of bike parking. At the very least, long-distance train stations offer simple, unsheltered bike racks, but most stations offer some sort of sheltered or guarded parking as well.

Some cities offer more elaborate facilities. Immediately in front of the main train station in Münster, Germany, for example, there is a modern, attractive "bike station" (built in 1999) that offers secure parking for 3,300 bikes as well as bike repairs, accessories, washing, rentals, touring advice, and direct access to all train platforms. Since the bike station is usually full, Münster is now constructing a second one just behind the train station, with enough spaces for an additional 2,000 bikes. In 2012 Amsterdam will complete a new bike station in front of its main train station that provides sheltered parking for over 10,000 bikes and the same range of services as Münster's. As of 2011, there were 98 full-service bike stations in the Netherlands (with 84,660 parking spaces), 106 in Germany (31,846 spaces), and 28 in Switzerland (7,783 spaces).

Local and regional rail stations in Dutch, Danish, and German metropolitan areas also offer bike parking of one sort or another. In 2011, for example, there were 31,600 bike-and-ride parking spots at local and regional train stations in Berlin and 45,000 bike-and-ride parking spaces in Munich.

Many European city centers also offer special bike parking facilities. The city of Odense, Denmark, recently added 400 sheltered bike racks near its main shopping area as well as a state-of-the-art automatic, secure parking station. Groningen offers 36 major bike-parking facilities in its town center, including 7 guarded ones. In 2007, Münster added a secure, sheltered parking facility for 300 bikes adjacent to its main shopping district. Copenhagen has 3,700 bike-parking spaces in its center. Amsterdam has 15 guarded bicycle-parking facilities in its downtown area.

Because bike theft is a major problem, Dutch, Danish, and German cities focus on improving the security of bike parking. Some cities equip unattended bike-parking areas with bright lighting and video surveillance, but an increasing number of bike-parking lots have an attendant who guards the parked bikes and controls access to the secured parking area. Attended facilities are also being introduced at Dutch and Danish schools. The fee for guarded bike parking is modest but fully covers the costs of such facilities.

Overall, the supply of bike parking is much greater in large northern European cities than in large Canadian and American cities. For example, the number of bike-parking spaces per 100,000 residents in 2010 was 30,272 in Amsterdam and 6,960 in Copenhagen, compared to 1,286 in Toronto, 1,121 in Chicago, 802 in Montreal, 725 in Portland, and 466 in San Francisco. New York City lags woefully behind, with only 75. The extensive New York subway system provides no bike parking at all at its 467 stations. Similarly, there is no secure public bike parking of any kind in Manhattan, even at major train and bus terminals.

Fortunately, some cities in North America have been making great progress at expanding and improving bike parking. Toronto and Chicago have been the leaders.

## TORONTO

Toronto has long been the North American leader in bike parking. Its comprehensive program offers two levels of services to meet cyclists' needs. Short-term parking in 2010 included over 33,600 spaces on sidewalks, mainly in 16,000 iconic post-and-ring bike stands (accommodating two bikes per stand) but also in more traditional bike racks of various sorts. Long-term parking is provided by 152 bike lockers and by the city's first bike station, at Union Station in downtown Toronto, which offers spaces for 180 bikes. The city plans to add more post-and-ring bike stands on sidewalks as well as more bike lockers. There are also plans for secure bike-parking kiosks at subway stations and for a second, larger bike station near city hall.

The greater Toronto area has not been left out; it has benefited from the vastly expanded bike parking at the suburban rail stations of the Greater Toronto Transit Authority (GO Transit). Metrolinx, a regional transportation funding agency, provided $2.2 million for racks and bike lockers at stations throughout the region. GO Transit installed covered bike-storage areas to provide better security and protection from the weather, which can be severe during Toronto's winters.

The city of Toronto amended its zoning bylaw in 1993 to require all new residential and commercial buildings of more than 2,500 square meters to provide bike parking. The city has also developed a document for planners, developers, and property managers titled *Guidelines for the Design and Management of Bicycle Parking Facilities*. In particular, the guidelines provide recommendations for improving accessibility, shelter, and security from theft.

## CHICAGO

Between 1993 and 2008, the city of Chicago installed more than 12,000 bike racks on public property (on sidewalks and in schools, parks, and transit stations) — more than any other city in the United States. As the number of people cycling in Chicago increases, so does the popularity of bicycle parking. To meet the demand for new bike racks from the general public, politicians, and business owners, roughly 500 new bicycle racks are installed each year.

One of the city's most impressive accomplishments is the Cycle Center in Millennium Park. Easily accessed from the eighteen-mile Lakefront Trail and downtown Chicago, the facility provides secure, indoor parking for 300 bikes. Lockers, showers and towel service, bike rentals, bike repairs, and guided bicycling tours are also available.

Chicago's zoning ordinance now requires the provision of bike racks for short-term parking as part of all new commercial, office, multifamily residential, and institutional buildings; planned developments; and some commercial parking garages. All applications for building permits must report the number of bike parking spaces provided.

In order to integrate cycling with public transit, bike parking is available at 110 of the 124 Chicago Transit Authority (CTA) subway and elevated stations and at 50 of the 76 Metra suburban rail stations. Indoor or sheltered bike parking is available at 83 CTA stations, more than in any other transit system in North America. Indoor parking provides weather protection and greater security, as it is often within sight of station attendants and passengers. The current plan calls for more bike-parking facilities at both CTA and Metra stations, with a focus on providing sheltered parking facilities with brighter lighting and better security.

Just as northern European cities have a long history of providing bike parking, they have been at the forefront of advances in bike-parking design. More and more North American cities have been learning from these successes. Toronto and Chicago have surely been leaders in this area, but San Francisco, Vancouver, Ottawa, Seattle, and Portland also provide examples of innovative, forward-thinking provisions for bike parking. This trend is already spreading to more and more cities in North America. But full implementation will require

**On Bicycles**

concerted advocacy and political engagement at all government levels, and especially in local communities.

**JOHN PUCHER** is a professor at Rutgers University. His research examines differences in travel behavior, transport systems, and transport policies in Europe, Canada, and the United States, with a focus on policies to increase walking and cycling.

## Chapter Fifty

# Disappearing Car Traffic
*Making Space for People*

## Bonnie Fenton

*Transportation* engineers sometimes use water as a metaphor for traffic movement. If one channel is blocked, they say, the flow will all divert into the nearest path of least resistance. This intuitively logical analogy has helped to justify transportation decisions for half a century.

Over that same period, a tension has built up over the various potential uses of urban public space, and transportation space is particularly coveted. In many cities, we've just about reached capacity: there is very little "new" space left to exploit. In looking at the results of our efforts, we can see that we've dedicated the lion's share of our transportation space to the use of private cars.

Managing road space isn't just about the free flow of motor vehicles. It also entails improving the environment for people who live, work, or visit in a city. Cycling has been demonstrated to be one good way to improve the urban environment (and personal health and air quality at the same time), but people —

understandably — won't ride bikes if they feel the dangers outweigh the benefits.

One of the best ways to make cycling safer and more appealing is to separate bike traffic from car traffic. But if there's not enough space to go around, that option is a nonstarter.

But what if it could be demonstrated that improving cycling conditions actually improves conditions for all road users? Counterintuitive as it sounds, that case is slowly being made in cities around the world.

The traffic-as-water analogy has been used again and again to squelch efforts to improve our cities for cycling. As long as we believe that reducing capacity for cars will lead to a traffic "dam," the logical conclusion is that reallocating space from cars to cycling or walking will lead to dangerous "car floods" in our neighborhoods.

To see how we arrived at this impasse, it's useful to look at the history of traffic management and traffic modeling. Starting in the late 1950s, the dominant philosophy of transportation planning could be described as "predict and provide." When traffic levels approached capacity, capacity was simply increased. This attitude resulted in a rapid expansion of road capacity and produced scores of new highways.

Predictions of how much road space we need, and where, are made by engineers and traffic planners using computer traffic modeling. Trip-based traffic models are created based on information provided by residents of given geographic areas — known as "traffic analysis zones" — through surveys. The survey results tell modelers where people live, where they go, and what they do there. Modelers use this information to determine the number of trips taken and therefore the road capacity needed between any one traffic analysis zone (TAZ) and another. The model determines the path of least resistance from one TAZ to another and yields a calculation of how much road space is needed between any two points.

In trip-based traffic modeling, every "need" corresponds to a trip. Thus grocery shopping is counted as one trip, and a visit to the library is another, even if the library is next door to the supermarket and most people would combine the two trips into one. As a result, models may end up telling us we need to accommodate many more trips than are actually made. The only possible outcome of such predictions is an ever-increasing need for space. And almost inevitably, the newly provided space fills up even faster than predicted. On that basis, the suggestion of taking road space away from cars seems ludicrous to many. But the renowned urbanist Jane Jacobs notes that the traffic-as-water analogy has been used again and again to threaten anyone who dares to suggest a reallocation of road space, without ever demonstrating that it actually holds up. In her book *Dark Age Ahead*, she writes that "the water flow hypothesis to explain traffic flow had been discredited by the real world. But... reasons why it was wrong were not investigated."[1]

The Australian researcher Jeff Kenworthy offers an alternative to the water metaphor, claiming "traffic is a gas, not a liquid."[2] In other words, it disperses rather than flowing elsewhere. While Kenworthy's metaphor may be more descriptive of what we see on our roads, we need to remember that traffic is in reality neither a liquid nor a gas but rather a collection of individual vehicles, each driven by a human being who makes decisions based on individual needs and desires.

Indeed, the British researcher Phil Goodwin finds that assessments of potential road closures are often calculated using the assumption that all displaced traffic will divert to other streets. These calculations, of course, make it impossible for modeling to predict anything but displaced congestion. Thus traffic models give us an idea why the engineers who use them don't believe that traffic can disappear: it simply doesn't compute. Following this reasoning, proposed road closures are assessed by engineers using traffic models and rejected as impossible.

But research shows that just as new traffic lanes fill up as soon as they are built, lanes that are taken out of commission experience the opposite phenomenon. That's to say, when the road space is no longer available, some of the traffic simply disappears.

In a paper titled "Disappearing Traffic? The Story So Far," Goodwin and two colleagues report that reallocating road space from general traffic to improve conditions for pedestrians, cyclists, or transit doesn't have to cause traffic problems on neighboring streets.[3] Having examined over seventy case studies in eleven countries and consulted over two hundred transportation professionals, Cairns, Atkins, and Goodwin claim that predictions of gridlock are often unnecessarily alarmist, and that significant reductions in overall traffic levels can, and do, occur. In fact, they found that after a road-space reallocation, on average, 11 percent of vehicles couldn't be accounted for in the surrounding area. But until they began their work, no one had taken the time to figure out where traffic goes when it disappears. According to traditional transportation models, it all continues to travel from its origin TAZ to its destination TAZ; but clearly other factors are in play.

The researchers found that people make complex travel

choices that are difficult to account for using traditional traffic modeling. Traffic movements depend on the daily human drama of births and deaths, hirings and firings, new houses and new shoes, a need for milk and a need for exercise. Thousands of people make millions of large and small decisions on a daily basis, alone or in conjunction with colleagues, other members of their households, and the outside world. In other words, human movement is more complex than we've been acknowledging.

This complexity is made clear by license-plate surveys showing that, on two consecutive days, even while overall traffic levels remain similar, as many as 50 percent of cars on a major commuter route can be different.[4] This finding suggests that people are more flexible in their transportation decisions than we may have imagined. A reallocation of road space might simply tip the balance in decisions that are being made for other reasons. Rather than making an extra trip, for example, people stop at the grocery store on the way home from work.

The research on disappearing traffic is part of the theory behind the dramatic changes New York City's transportation commissioner, Janette Sadik-Kahn, began introducing when she took on that job in 2007. Since then, she has turned more than 3.5 miles (5 kilometers) of traffic lanes and parking on Broadway into bike lanes and pedestrian space and turned Times Square into a pedestrian plaza. The results have been significant drops in congestion and accident rates (for cars as well as bikes), faster taxi trips across the city, and space for thousands more pedestrians.

As part of the effort, the New York Department of Transportation plans to double its existing bicycle infrastructure in 2011 by installing 180 miles (300 kilometers) of permanent, separated bicycle lanes on major thoroughfares. And the results are coming in. The number of cyclists in New York and the distance they travel both increased by almost 30 percent from 2008 to 2009.

We've been building for the car for about half a century now, so it's understandable that old habits die hard. But the evidence is growing that traffic does indeed disappear, and that reallocating road space will lead not to commuter chaos but rather to better conditions for those on foot and on bikes. Research has established the theory of disappearing traffic. Now leading cities around the world are beginning to road-test it.

**BONNIE FENTON** rode and wrote in Vancouver, Canada, for many years before moving to Germany in 2008 — where she does pretty much the same. Some things aren't meant to change.

1 Jane Jacobs, *Dark Age Ahead* (Toronto: Vintage Canada, 2004), 74.

2 Jeff Kenworthy, "Disappearing Traffic: The Challenge of Reallocating Public Space," presentation for the Vancouver Area Cycling Coalition, Simon Fraser University, Vancouver, Canada, June 28, 2006.

3 S. Cairns, S. Atkins, and P. Goodwin, "Disappearing Traffic? The Story So Far," *Proceedings of the Institution of Civil Engineers: Municipal Engineer* 151, no. 1 (March 2002): 13–22.

4 Ibid., 19.

# *Index*

# About the Editor

Clancy Dennehy

*When* Amy Walker was sixteen, a major life puzzle piece fell into place when she started biking forty-five minutes each way to school. Cycling clicked. It offered fast transport, exercise, a clear environmental conscience, and rosy cheeks. She knew that if it worked well for her, it could work well for others too. In 2001 she cofounded *Momentum* magazine, and she contributed as a publisher, creative director, editor, writer, and photographer for ten years. She has studied graphic design, film, and furniture making, and she plans to continue using creative means to share the love of bicycling. If she could be granted only one wish, it would be for all humans to know that we are part of a beautiful and interconnected system — the Earth; that we all have important gifts to share and lessons to learn; and that we are all loved. She lives in Vancouver, Canada, where she enjoys biking in the rain. Visit her at www.onbicycles.com.